# The Influence of Family Blockholders on the Financial Behavior of Listed Family Firms

FABIO FRANZOI

Dissertation der Zeppelin Universität

Gutachter: Prof. Dr. Mark Mietzner

Prof. Dr. Dirk Schiereck

Prof. Dr. Denis Schweizer

Datum der Disputation: 14. Oktober 2022

# The Influence of Family Blockholders on the Financial Behavior of Listed Family Firms

# FINANCE, BANKING AND ACCOUNTING

Edited by Mark Mietzner

VOL. 3

Fabio Franzoi

# The Influence of Family Blockholders on the Financial Behavior of Listed Family Firms

PETER LANG

Lausanne · Berlin · Bruxelles · Chennai · New York · Oxford

**Bibliographic Information published by the Deutsche Nationalbibliothek**
The Deutsche Nationalbibliothek lists this publication in the Deutsche Nationalbibliografie; detailed bibliographic data is available online at http://dnb.d-nb.de.

**Library of Congress Cataloging-in-Publication Data**
A CIP catalog record for this book has been applied for at the Library of Congress.

ISSN 2698-637X
ISBN 978-3-631-90127-4 (Print)
E-ISBN 978-3-631-90259-2 (E-PDF)
E-ISBN 978-3-631-90260-8 (EPUB)
DOI 10.3726/b20854



Published by:
Peter Lang GmbH, Berlin, Deutschland

info@peterlang.com - www.peterlang.com

# Vorwort

Diese Dissertation ist das Ergebnis einer in der Tat langen akademischen Reise, an deren Ende ich ohne die folgenden Menschen nicht angekommen wäre. Ihnen gilt mein tiefer Dank.

Mein mit weitem Abstand größter akademischer Dank gilt meinem Doktorvater Prof. Dr. Mark Mietzner. Er war es, der mich seit dem Bachelorstudium zur empirischen Forschung motiviert und später zum Start dieser Dissertation und diesem Themenfeld motiviert hat. Ich danke ihm für seine Nachsicht, sein Mentoring, die gemeinsamen Gespräche auch abseits der Promotion und vor allem seine gesamte investierte Zeit. Er hat mich mit seinem Optimismus über jede akademische Tiefebene getragen und mich bei diesem Projekt mehr unterstützt hat, als man es sich von seinem Doktorvater wünschen könnte.

Mein Dank gilt auch meinem Zweitgutachter Prof. Dr. Dirk Schiereck, der mit seinem gesamten Lehrstuhl beispielhaft für den gemeinsamen akademischen Austausch an einer Universität steht und dessen Doktorandenkolloquien stets eine große Freude waren. Ferner danke ich Prof. Dr. Denis Schweizer, dass er als Drittgutachter zur Verfügung steht.

Es waren Dr. Ursula Koners, Prof. Dr. Reinhard Prügl, Prof. Dr. Hermut Kormann und Hon. Prof. Dr. Andreas Wiedemann und das gesamte Team des Friedrichshafener Instituts für Familienunternehmen, die mich am Beginn meines Studiums ursprünglich für die Forschung zu Familienunternehmen begeistert hatten. Dass mir meine akademische Leidenschaft bei meinem Berufseinstieg erhalten bleiben konnte, ist Peter Längle zu verdanken. Er hat seit unserer ersten Begegnung an dieses Projekt geglaubt, es begeistert und vor allem ohne jeden Zweifel durchgehend all die Jahre unterstützt.

Aus tiefem Herzen danke ich meiner Partnerin Hannah Löffler, die mich die ganze Zeit trotz meiner monatelangen Abwesenheit und Doppelbelastung durchgehend unterstützt, angespornt, aufgeheitert und mit ihrer Güte beschenkt hat. Ich kann mich sehr glücklich schätzen, sie an meiner Seite zu haben.

Mein größter persönlicher Dank gilt meiner Familie, meinem lieben Bruder Luca und vor allem meinen Eltern Suzana und Ewald Franzoi. Sie haben mich in allem was ich mache mein ganzes Leben unterstützt und dass ich es bis zu dem Punkt geschafft habe, diese Zeilen zu schreiben, ist in großen Teilen ihnen zu verdanken. Sie könnten in dem was sie tun und wie sie sind keine besseren Vorbilder für mich sein. Ihnen sei diese Arbeit gewidmet.

# Abstract

The four papers of this dissertation investigate the influence of large family shareholders on financial decisions and the performance of listed firms in Germany. This country is especially interesting, as the German corporate governance system is considered less investor friendly with a limited influence of shareholders on managerial decisions. Based on this environment this dissertation offers a novel approach to analyzing the financial behavior of family firms, based on the incentive structure of family blockholders and the degree of family influence in corporate boards. The first paper focusses on short-term financial management and demonstrates that particularly the share of family members on the management board slows down the cash conversion cycle in working capital management. The second paper analyzes the financial reporting behavior of family-controlled firms towards outside non-controlling shareholders. It demonstrates that the degree of family involvement in management significantly increases earnings management activities, particularly in a way that may not hurt long-term financial success. The third paper argues that the incentive structure of large family blockholders to actively engage in corporate governance substantially differentiates them from other large shareholders on the capital market. It estimates that portfolios of family firms record significant positive abnormal stock returns compared to non-family firms, indicating a positive effect of family influence on governance and control. Actively engaged family shareholders and the financial behavior of family firms in Germany suggest that these firms may particularly differ in their performance during financial crises. The fourth paper finds that the operative crisis reaction of family firms appears to avoid strategies that may endanger long-term success, such as cuts in personnel or R&D expenses. Family firms appear to profit from the influence of family blockholders as they record a superior performance on the stock market compared to non-family firms no later than three years after the beginning of financial crises. This dissertation uses a hand-collected panel dataset identifying blockholders and every board position in 278 corporations. It demonstrates that the degree of family involvement in boards significantly influences financial and earnings management as well as stock market performance and provides contributions for both academia and practitioners.

**Keywords**: Family Firms, Family Ownership, Blockholders, Board Composition, Family Management, Corporate Governance, Working Capital, Earnings Management, Shareholder Activism, Stock Market Performance, Abnormal Returns, Financial Crisis

# Contents

# List of Abbreviations

| | |
|---|---|
| **ABEM** | Accrual-based Earnings Management |
| **Ajd.** | Adjusted |
| **AktG** | Aktiengesetz (German Stock Corporation Act) |
| **Avg.** | Average |
| **BHR** | Buy-and-Hold Return |
| **CCC** | Cash Conversion Cycle |
| **CDAX** | Composite Deutscher Aktienindex |
| **CEO** | Chief Executive Officer |
| **COGS** | Cost of Goods Sold |
| **COVID** | Coronavirus Disease |
| **cf.** | Confer |
| **CAPEX** | Capital Expenditures |
| **CF** | Cash-flow |
| **DebtEqu** | Debt to Equity Ratio |
| **DIO** | Days Inventory Outstanding |
| **DOI** | Digital Object Identifier |
| **DPO** | Days Payables Outstanding |
| **DSO** | Days Sales Outstanding |
| **Dum** | Dummy Variable |
| **DrittelbG** | Drittelbeteiligungsgesetz |
| **e.g.** | Exempli gratia |
| **EBIT** | Earnings before Interest & Taxes |
| **EBITDA** | Earnings before Interest, Taxes, Depreciation & Amortization |
| **EC** | European Council |
| **EU** | European Union |
| **EUR** | Euro |
| **Et al.** | Et alii |
| **ExBo** | Executive/Management Board |
| **FE** | Fixed Effects |
| **FF** | Family Firm |
| **GAAP** | Generally Accepted Accounting Principles |
| **HGB** | Handelsgesetzbuch (German Commercial Code) |
| **HHI** | Herfindahl-Hirschman-Index |
| **HML** | High-minus-low |
| **i.a.** | Inter alia |

| | |
|---|---|
| **i.e.** | Id est |
| **IFRS** | International Financial Reporting Standards |
| **k** | Thousand |
| **KapAEG** | Kapitalaufnahmeerleichterungsgesetz |
| **KonTraG** | Gesetz zur Kontrolle und Transparenz im Unternehmensbereich |
| **KPI** | Key Performance Indicator |
| **m** | Million |
| **Max.** | Maximum |
| **MCap** | Market Capitalization |
| **MgVG** | Gesetz über die Mitbestimmung der Arbeitnehmer bei einer grenz-überschreitenden Verschmelzung |
| **Min.** | Minimum |
| **Mio** | Millions |
| **MitbestG** | Mitbestimmungsgesetz |
| **MontanMitbestG** | Montan-Mitbestimmungsgesetz |
| **N** | Number of Observations |
| **No.** | Number |
| **NF** | Non-family Firm |
| **NTC** | Net Trade Cycle |
| **OLS** | Ordinary Least Squares |
| **OPEX** | Operating Expenditures |
| **p** | Probability (Significance) |
| **PPE** | Property, Plant and Equipment |
| **R&D** | Research & Development Expense |
| **SEW** | Socioemotional Wealth |
| **SD** | Standard Deviation |
| **SG&A** | Selling, General & Administrative Expense |
| **SIC** | Standard Industrial Classification |
| **SupBo** | Supervisory Board |
| **S&P** | Standard & Poor's |
| **SMB** | Small-minus-big |
| **$R^2$** | Coefficient of Determination |
| **RE** | Random Effects |
| **REM** | Real Earnings Management |
| **RMRF** | Market Excess Return over Risk-free Rate |
| **ROA** | Return on Assets |
| **ROE** | Return on Equity |
| **UK** | United Kingdom |

**US** United States of America
**WC** Working Capital
**WML** Winners-minus-losers
**WpHG** Wertpapier Handelsgesetz (German Securities Trade Act)

# 1 Introduction

## 1.1 General Introduction

Family firms are very common in Germany and contribute significantly to the German economy (Gottschalk et al., 2019). Though the German capital market is smaller compared to that of Anglo-Saxon countries such as the US or UK (La Porta et al., 1997), even among listed firms in Germany, individuals or families still on average represent the most common type of large shareholder (Faccio and Lang, 2002; Ampenberger et al., 2013). Prominent examples of listed firms with blocks of shares held by families are the consumer goods company Beiersdorf controlled by the Herz family or the automotive supplier Continental controlled by the Schaeffler family.

Anecdotal evidence suggests that these family blockholders substantially influence the financial behavior of the firms they are invested in. In 2020, BMW's largest shareholder – the Quandt family – received a dividend of around 770 million Euros based on a majority vote at BMW's Annual Shareholder Meeting. This led to significant media attention as the dividend was distributed despite the outbreak of the COVID-19 pandemic, short-time working and the onset of an economic crisis (e.g. Financial Times, 2020a). While this may be a debatable decision from a moral or even economic perspective, other public references by contrast suggest that family-controlled firms lay off fewer employees or wait longer with regards to cuts in workforce during times of crises (e.g. Financial Times, 2020b). Another example is the company Fielmann substantially controlled by the Fielmann family – while the company pursued a comparatively conservative dividend policy ranging below their peer group in the last five years before 2020, Fielmann was able to strongly benefit from the liquidity buffer it had built-up during the economic impact of the COVID-19 pandemic (Handelsblatt, 2020).

What however are the mechanisms determining the financial behavior of firms controlled by family blockholders? What drives the financial decisions in family firms in Germany and by which means do family blockholders influence these financial decisions? Is it mere size of their voting block? Or is it the influence of family blockholders in corporate boards to which they are often appointed?

Research on the financial behavior of family firms confirms that they differ from non-family firms in many aspects: In Germany family firms exhibit a higher equity ratio than non-family firms (Schmid, 2013). Their policies in cutting jobs in times of economic crises are indeed more restrained compared to non-family firms (Sraer and Thesmar, 2007; Mietzner and Tyrell, 2012) and among family firms in other European countries, they are also found to maintain higher cash holdings than their counterparts (Durán et al., 2016). Existing literature already suggests that such differences in financial behavior are partly connected to the presence of family members in the management of the firm – specifically in Germany (e.g. Andres, 2008; Ampenberger, 2013).

Stock listed corporations in Germany have a specific framework of corporate governance, that significantly differs from those of other countries (Becht and Boehmer, 2003). For example, shareholders cannot directly appoint or remove members of the management board and the number of supervisory board members appointed by shareholders is limited by the German co-determination system with a significant number of board seats reserved for employees. This dissertation posits that the question whether the assessment of family influence in research properly reflects the characteristics of this corporate governance system is highly important to understand the impact of family blockholders on the financial behavior of family firms.

The research motivation for this dissertation and its geographic focus on Germany is two-fold. First, due to a lower level of shareholder protection as well as the German two-tier board system, the incentives and abilities for large shareholders to closely monitor and actively engage in corporate governance bodies are increased (Gugler and Yurtoglu, 2003). Large family shareholders by contrast have an additional incentive to do so, as usually a high share of family wealth is invested in the firm (Anderson and Reeb, 2003a) and one of their central entrepreneurial goals is to bequeath the firm to the following generation (Berrone et al., 2012). The motives of these families and their desired financial behavior of the firm may substantially diverge from those of other investors (e.g. Achleitner et al., 2014). Controlling for the influence of family members on financial decisions is important but must account for the peculiarities local German corporate governance system.

Second, existing literature and empirical research on the financial behavior of family firms in Germany insufficiently accounts for family blockholders' influence. This is presumably the case, as hardly any replicable, fine-graded governance data on family involvement is publicly available and individual data collection is highly time consuming and costly[1]. Yet, given the prevalence of

1 Kaserer and Moldenhauer (2008) among other authors for example describe the "enormous effort" that would be required for the construction of a comprehensive dataset in Germany.

family firms and the significance of their economic contribution to the German economy, gaining a better understanding of the influence of family governance involvement on the financial behavior of these firms is highly suggested.

The following subsections illustrate the significance of family firms around the world and demonstrate why family-controlled firms play a pronounced role in the German economy. After the introduction of the theoretical frameworks for this thesis, implications of the idiosyncratic corporate governance system in Germany on the assessment of family influence are discussed. Finally, the research objectives and structure of this publication-based dissertation are introduced.

## 1.2 Economic Relevance

The economic relevance of family firms was brought into mainstream research spotlight by a number of highly recognized publications around the millennial (i.e. La Porta et al., 1999; Claessens et al., 2000). Their contributions mainly built on prior work by Shleifer and Vishny (1986) and other scholars who investigated the significance of large shareholders on corporate ownership and control as a result of the legal origin and framework of shareholder protection in countries around the world (i.e. Shleifer and Vishny, 1997; La Porta et al., 1998). Following these publications, twenty years of research on family firms unfolded documenting manifold differences in the financial behavior between family controlled, and non-family firms (Amit and Villalonga, 2020) emerging as a leading area of research in management and financial economics (Villalonga et al., 2015).

The macroeconomic relevance of family firms specifically in Germany is well documented by studies on both listed and non-listed family-controlled firms (e.g. Faccio and Lang, 2002, Gottschalk et al., 2019; Achleitner et al., 2019; Aminadav and Papaioannou, 2020). Besides of existing contributions in research on the peculiarities of the financial behavior of family firms (e.g. Anderes, 2008; Kaserer and Moldenhauer, 2008; Schmid, 2013) the following subsections describe the institutional setting and prevalence of family controlled firms in Germany as well as selected financial aspects.

### 1.2.1 Prevalence of Family Firms

Most firms around the world are substantially owned by families (Burkhart et al., 2003; Villalonga and Amit, 2020). As La Porta et al. (1999) note, firms worldwide are usually not widely held, but controlled by large shareholders – often by the state, bust mostly by families. For example, even in the US, a country commonly associated with widely held firms, more than one third of the largest firms in the S&P500 and Fortune500 exhibit a significant level of family control (Anderson and Reeb, 2003a; Villalonga and Amit, 2006; 2009). In Eastern Asia by contrast, Claessens et al. (2000) find family control in more than half of the researched firms in nine different countries.

In Europe Laeven and Levine (2008) find that large shareholders are very common, and that nearly half of the firms exhibit one controlling owner[2]. Barontini and Caprio (2006) demonstrate, that according to their sample, families are the largest shareholder in 52.6 % of the firms in their specific sample. Franks et al. (2012) find that between 30 % (listed) and 41 % (private) of the firms in selected European countries are family controlled. Faccio and Lang (2002) thereby report that the average level of voting rights of identified families in listed firms amounts to 44.3 %.

Bridging twenty years of research from the first major publication on global ownership structures by La Porta et al. (1999), Aminadav and Papaioannou (2020) just recently published a study on corporate control in the *Journal of Finance* that introduces the largest sample of publicly traded firms so far applied in this research field: Analyzing 26,843 firms in 84 countries around the world (including industrial, emerging as well as developing countries) they find that about 45.7 % of all firms are controlled by families, the most common type of shareholder[3] in the sample (20 % voting rights threshold). The fact that the firms in the sample cover a median market capitalization of 83.1 % across all countries underlines the significance of firms controlled by families around the world.

Most of the studies on corporate control around the world apply certain ownership/voting right thresholds to account for the fact that a firm may be regarded as "controlled" by a certain shareholder (Villalong and Amit, 2020). These thresholds vary according to the regional focuses of the respective studies to account for the level of control required to substantially influence corporate policies as a shareholder in a specific region (Aminadav and Papaioannou, 2020). Hence, comparing the distribution of family-controlled firms across different studies must be done with caution. However, the frequency of large blockholders or certain regional levels of block-ownership for example by family shareholders

2 The authors define controlling shareholders as those exceeding a threshold of 10 % in voting rights.

3 The authors identify private firms as the second largest shareholder type (31.3 %) followed by mutual or pension funds/nominees/trusts (14.9 %).

are not coincidental, but in large parts the endogenous result of the history of law and governance rules in different parts of the world (La Porta et al., 1998, 1999).

### 1.2.2 Ownership Concentration and Family Control in Germany

Apart from political theories of corporate control, the degree of shareholder protection largely determines the level of ownership concentration in a country (Aminadav and Papaioannou, 2020). According to La Porta et al. (1998) shareholder protection is largely based on the legal origin of a specific continent or nation[4]: According to their publication, the level of ownership protection is much lower in civil-law countries, than in common-law countries. Accordingly, though Germany provides for a high level of law enforcement, investor rights are rather limited compared to countries such as the US or UK (La Porta et al., 1998). As a substitutional mechanism for a less protective environment for investors (La Porta et al., 1998), voting blocks are rather concentrated as for example Becht and Boehmer (2003) find that 82 % of all listed corporations in Germany have a minority blockholder[5]. In Germany, the controlling shareholder is most likely a family – the founder of the firm or his descendants (La Porta et al., 1999).

Quantifying the economic influence of family firms in Germany is not an easy task to do, as for example no comprehensive, federal statistics about the ownership structures of registered companies exist and the availability of respective official data is limited (Schraml, 2010). Nevertheless, different studies approach a quantitative assessment by building on representative samples, alternative sources and their own definitions of family-controlled firms. While these studies allow an insight on the economic significance or frequency of family firms at large, quantifications of individual studies have a limited comparability.

Table 1.1 provides an overview of the distribution of family-controlled firms among all firms in general as well as among listed firms in Germany. Haunschild and Wolter (2010) estimate that 95,3 % of the German companies belong to families or individuals. Accordingly, among all active companies in Germany, Gottschalk et al. (2019) extrapolate that about 90 % of all firms are controlled by

4 In this publication La Porta et al. (1998) introduce their "Antidirector Rights Index" on shareholder protection in 49 countries around the world. While years of following research built on their main contributions, the index and the conclusions drawn based on it have also been challenged (i.e. Spamann, 2010). The recent publication by Aminadav and Papaioannou (2020) by contrast support the findings of La Porta et al. (1998) on a large sample basis.

5 Controlling more than 25 % of the voting rights.

families accounting for 54 % of all employees and 45 % of sales in 2017[6]. Their study furthermore estimates, that 86 % of all companies in Germany are owner managed.

**Table 1.1:** Distribution of Family-controlled Firms in Germany

| **Study (Authors)** | **Sample size** | **Family Firm Definition** | **Family-controlled (%)** | **Firm Status** |
|---|---|---|---|---|
| Haunschild and Wolter (2010) | 14,679 | 50 % ownership / family managed | 95,3 % | Unlisted |
| Gottschalk et al. (2019) | 3,292k* | 50 % ownership / family managed | 90 % | Unlisted |
| Franks et al. (2012) | 923 | 25 % voting-rights | 38.6 % | Unlisted/ Listed |
| Faccio and Lang (2002) | 704 | 20 % voting-rights | 64.6 % | Listed |
| Aminadav and Papaioannou (2020) | 722 | 20 % voting-rights | 51.5 % | Listed |
| Barontini and Caprio (2006) | 119 | 10 % voting rights | 48.3 % | Listed |
| Ampenberger et al. (2013) | 660 | 25 % voting rights and/or family board presence | 47 % | Listed |
| Achleitner et al. (2019) | 475 | 25 % voting-rights and/or family board presence | 41 % | Listed |

The table presents selected studies on the distribution of family firms in Germany. Please note that comparability of the studies among each other is limited, as some include (a) financial firms in which families are usually less present as shareholders, (b) require to meet certain thresholds in firm size to be included in the sample or (c) apply broader or narrower ownership/voting control definitions including family board presence or only founding family ownership. Analogous to Faccio and Lang (2002) the share of family-controlled firms reported for Aminadav and Papaioannou (2020) includes private firms that are not widely held as ultimate owners. The selected studies are largely based on (ultimate) ownership/voting-rights-definitions and do not consider alternative definitions such as the SFI- or F-PEC-Index. For a discussion of family business definitions see respective chapter; * extrapolated based on the Mannheim Enterprise Panel.

6 The sectors of agriculture, forestry, fishing, public administration, defense, social security, kindergartens and schools, interest groups as well as church and other religious associations, private households, extraterritorial organizations as well as companies in the legal form of registered associations are excluded.

### 1.2.3 Listed Family Firms in Germany

Following La Porta et al. (1997, 1998) a lower level of shareholder protection, is not only associated with higher ownership concentration but also with smaller capital markets. Accordingly, the German stock market is significantly smaller than for example in the US (La Porta et al., 1997). While ownership concentration among listed firms ranges at a higher level than in Anglo-Saxon countries (Faccio and Lang, 2002), large shareholders are also found to align their voting shares with relevant controlling thresholds (Becht and Boehmer, 2003; Ampenberger, 2010). For example, Stefan Quandt, member of the Quandt family owning substantial parts of BMW, holds about 25.6 % of the voting rights that equals a blocking minority with regards to the German Stock Corporation Act.

Different publications document, that families represent the largest type of shareholder among listed firms in Germany. In their study of the largest one thousand both listed and unlisted firms in Germany[7], Franks et al. (2012) find that 38.6 % of all sample firms are controlled families. In their large study of ownership structures in Western European countries, Faccio and Lang (2002) document that about 64.6 % of all firms in Germany are controlled by families of private firms owned by individuals.

Ampenberger et al. (2013) and Achleitner et al. (2019) apply a family firm definition that requires a blocking minority by founding families and/or the presence of any family member on the board. The reported share of family firms among all firm years in their studies ranges from 41–47 %. Considering the prime standard alone, which prescribes higher transparency standards than the general standard, the share of family firms is even higher and amounts to 69 % (Ampenberger, 2010). In conclusion, all publications, including Barontini and Caprio (2006) and the latest contribution by Aminadav an Papaioannou (2020) confirm that the share of family firms among listed firms is substantially above the average found for Western Europe (Faccio and Lang, 2002). The only large European economies exhibiting higher shares of family-controlled firms are France and Italy (Franks et al., 2012; Aminadav and Papaiannou, 2020)[8].

Despite of the finding, that family firms represent a high share of the listed firms in Germany and that family ownership is persistent over time (Franks et al., 2012), various publications document that these firms also differ in

---

7 77 firms could not be identified.

8 Please see respective publications for a detailed discussion of the impact of the differences among French civil-law and German civil-law origin on ownership concentration in Germany, France and Italy.

several financial aspects some of which are mentioned here in short by way of example:

Empirical studies on family- and non-family firms initially focused on the performance of these firm-types (Ampenberger, 2010). Apart from studies on different international settings[9] or specific countries[10], family-controlled firms in Germany are found to have a superior performance compared to non-family firms (e.g. Barontini and Caprio, 2006; Andres, 2008; Achleitner et al., 2019).

As previously described, the German economy exhibits not just a lower level of market financing compared to for example in Anglo-Saxon countries (La Porta et al., 1997), but an economic system that is largely based on bank financing (e.g. Gorton and Schmid, 2000). International studies on debt structures suggest, that family firms in most countries maintain higher debt levels (Schmid, 2013), presumably to avoid dilution of their own control (for example by capital increases). In Germany by contrast, family firms are found to have significantly lower debt-levels than non-family firms (e.g. Ampenberger et al., 2013).

Furthermore, family firms in Germany are found to differ from non-family firms in size, (Achleitner et al., 2019) as they are found to be smaller with regards to total assets, sales and the number of employees (Andres, 2008). In addition, their financial management techniques diverge from non-family firms as they are for example more engaged in earnings management (Achleitner et al., 2014). Lastly, family firms in Western Europe including Germany maintain higher levels of cash holdings (Durán et al., 2016).

With regards to corporate control, family blockholders differ from other large shareholders insofar as they are frequently present on the boards of the firms (Ampenberger, 2010) and this is confirmed by multiple studies who control for the fact that any member of the board is part of a family blockholder via dummy variable (e.g. Andres, 2008; Ampenberger et al., 2013). In one of the few more precise assessments of the corporate governance involvement of

9 e.g. Maury (2006), Van Essen et al. (2015) and Barontini and Caprio (2006) in Europe, Wang and Shailer (2017), Duran et al. (2018) in emerging markets or Claessens et al. (2002) in Asia; for meta-studies across countries on the performance of family firms please relate for example to O'Boyle et al (2012), Wagner et al. (2015), Taras et al. (2018) and Hansen and Block (2020).

10 e.g. Anderson and Reeb (2003a), Villalonga and Amit (2006) and Miller et al. (2007) in the US, Chu (2011) in Taiwan, Minichilli et al. (2016) in Italy, Sraer and Thesmar (2007) in France or Miralles-Marcelo et al. (2014) in Portugal and Spain.

family shareholders, Achleitner et al. (2012) show that 18 % of all board seats in the listed firms of their panel are occupied by the founder or members of the founding family (median 16.7 %).

This fact is notable in that the management presence of family shareholders appears to substantially influence the financial behavior of these companies: For example, the lower debt-ratio of listed family firms in Germany is driven by family-management-presence (Ampenberger et al., 2013). In addition, Andres (2008) shows that the increased profitability of family firms compared to non-family firms is due to the presence of a member of the founding family on the board – otherwise their performance is indistinguishable from other types of companies. The same positive influence is found for Founder CEOs in Germany (Barontini and Caprio, 2006). Furthermore, the higher cash levels in family firms (Durán et al., 2016) appear to be primarily determined by the fact if the CEOs is a family member (Caprio et al., 2020).

The previously described literature review on family firms explains the general economic relevance of family firms in German. Most important for this dissertation, it underlines the relevance of family firms among all listed firms on the German stock market. Hence, understanding the financial decision making and the impact of family shareholders in these firms is of high relevance for the German economy. As listed, family-controlled firms are so prevalent and allow for a control group of non-family-controlled or widely held firms of almost the same size, Germany offers an ideal setting to analyze listed family firms (Ampenberger, 2010).

The literature review shows that listed family firms are by far no homogenous group (Achleitner et al., 2919). As indicated by several studies, family shareholders are frequently involved in the governing bodies of these firms. Yet, in firms that are owned by multiple shareholders or that are at least partly widely held, the degree of corporate governance involvement of selective blockholders such as by family shareholders has several consequences for the question of who is in meaningful control of these firms.

## 1.3 Theoretical Framework

Family firms feature several governance and control aspects that differentiate them from companies without family shareholders, such as anonymous widely held public corporations (Villalonga and Amit, 2020). The following sub-sections describe the theoretical context in which research on the performance and financing of German listed family businesses is embedded. The two presented theories (Principle Agent Theory and Socioemotional Wealth Theory) are the main frameworks for the motivation of the hypotheses on the selected financial aspects investigated in the subsequent main chapters of this dissertation[11].

### 1.3.1 Principle Agent Theory

Most companies in Germany are privately held (not listed) and among all these firms, about 86 % of them are also owner-managed (Gottschalk et al., 2019). However, this is not always the case: Particularly as companies for example age it becomes increasingly difficult to find enough (sufficiently qualified) owner-managers to succeed in managerial positions of the firm and as a result non-family managers may take over operational control in the company (see Burkart et al., 2003 for a collection of reasons). Furthermore, firms may for example grow and finance their entrepreneurial activities by increasing their capital base via selling shares to new and additional shareholders – probably even by going public on the stock market (Volk, 2013).

Principal-agent theory is among the most frequently used theoretical concepts in corporate governance (Mazzi, 2011) to explain conflicts that arise from such a separation of ownership from control (Berle and Means, 1932). The framework is a substantial part of new institutional economics and describes the relations among (economic) institutions under bounded rationality (Williamson, 1975a, b) with given information asymmetries[12] and conflicts of interest among them (Jensen and Meckling, 1976; Fama and Jensen, 1983).

A principal (i.e. shareholder) engages an agent (i.e. manager) and delegates decision making power to the agent (Jensen and Meckling, 1976). Managers may subsequently not act according to the interests of shareholder, as their individual incentives and utility functions may diverge from those of the shareholder (Fama and Jensen, 1983; Demsetz and Lehn, 1985). A manager for example, may be more risk-averse in his corporate decisions than preferred by the shareholder, as he or she can hardly diversify human-capital specific risk on the individual level,

11 The relevant aspects of the theories are discussed with regards to family firms and the investigated research objectives in the respective following main chapters and may not serve as a general introduction to the individual theory. Furthermore, this motivation section focusses on the main theoretical frameworks for this thesis and does not represent a thorough assessment of all existing theories on the financial behavior of family firms.

12 Such information asymmetries may concern (ex-ante) adverse selection due to hidden characteristics (Akerlov, 1970) or ex-post moral hazard due to hidden action and/or hidden intention (Jensen and Meckling, 1976; Eisenhardt, 1989).

while a shareholder may diversify his individual investment risk by portfolio diversification (Amihud and Lev, 1981).

The costs arising due to agency conflicts may result in monitoring expenses for the principal (e.g. effective incentives for the agent, engaging in monitoring via financial reporting), bonding expenditures by the agent (e.g. contractual commitments to stay on board in case of a transaction), and a residual loss in welfare (losses that occur despite of monitoring and bonding expenditures) (Jensen and Meckling, 1976; Eisenhardt, 1989). Villalonga and Amit (2006) refers to the agency relation among shareholders and managers as agency problem I (see Figure 1.1 for an illustration)[13].

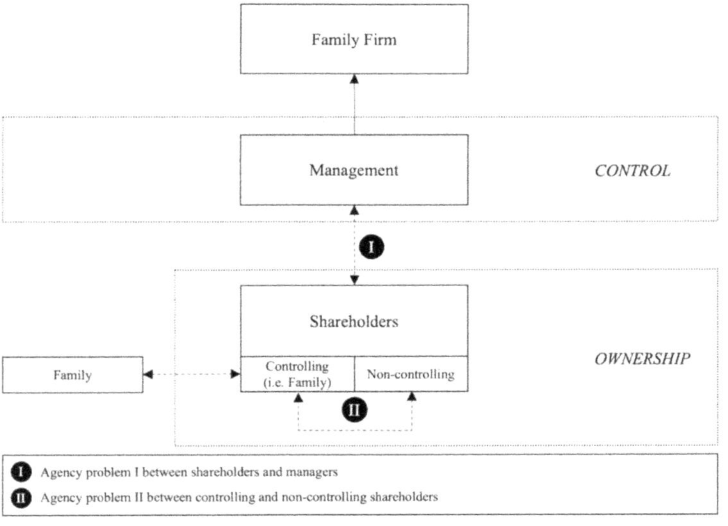


**Figure 1.1:** Agency Problem I and II in Family Firms

13 Please note that with regards to the research objective of this dissertation the discussed principal agent relations focus on Type 1 and Type 2 agency problems but do not cover specific agency problems between creditors and shareholders (Type 3) or among family members (Type 4; such as agency problems between family shareholders and family outsiders) (Villalonga and Amit, 2015).

Large blockholders may effectively reduce agency problems as they have increased incentives and abilities to monitor managers and hence may add value to corporate governance for example by reducing free-rider problems (Shleifer and Vishny, 1986; Gugler and Yurtoglu, 2003, Villalonga and Amit, 2006). Family blockholders in family firms are found to be particularly efficient in reducing agency problems with managers (Demsetz and Lehn, 1985; Villalonga and Amit, 2006; Maury, 2006): They have a high incentive for monitoring as usually a high share of their family wealth is invested in the firm (Anderson and Reeb, 2003a). Family shareholders possess a superior knowledge about the firm and the business (Klein, 2000; Anderson and Reeb, 2003a). Furthermore, they have an increased ability to monitor the firm, as they are frequently engaged on the board of directors of the firm (Fama and Jensen, 1983, Andres, 2008). As family shareholder members are often present in such management roles, the interests and utility functions among shareholders and managers substantially overlap and hence reduce agency problems arising from the separation of ownership and control (O'Boyle et al., 2012).

As previously described, due to its comparably low level of shareholder protection, Germany exhibits a high level of ownership concentration (i.a. Faccio and Lang, 2002; Becht and Boehmer, 2003). While large shareholder may be more successful in solving agency problems among managers and investors, they may lead to a different agency problem (agency problem II) as they may also distribute wealth from other (smaller) investors to themselves (Morck et al., 1988; Shleifer and Vishny, 1997; Burkart et al., 2003; Villalonga and Amit, 2006; Maury, 2006). This may be the case if a large majority shareholder takes decisions to the detriment of smaller shareholders or when control rights of large shareholders exceed cash-flow rights (Barontini and Captrio, 2006). Such a phenomenon is supported by weak minority shareholder protection (Gugler and Yurtoglu, 2003).

Relatively wealthy family investors holding significant blocks of voting rights for example may decide to keep earnings in the company for future investments instead of paying dividends that benefit minority shareholders. One possibility to lower agency costs arising from this problem is to engage independent managers in executive positions or non-shareholder individuals among the board of directors (Volk, 2013). In order to increase their monitoring abilities (Fama and Jensen, 1983), members of family blockholders by contrast are often present in managerial roles of the firm (Villalonga and Amit, 2006). As private benefits in case of banks, investment funds or widely held corporations are distributed among many independent owners, their incentives for both the monitoring of managers as well as the expropriation of minority investors are lower than in case of large family shareholders (Villalonga and Amit, 2006). Hence, family blockholders might partly shift agency problems from the shareholder-manager to the large shareholder-small shareholder level[14].

Studies on listed family firms are frequently based on agency theory, suggesting that the share of equity owned by family blockholders moderates conflicts between large family shareholders and minority shareholders (Taras et al., 2018). A prominent example that is also investigated for Germany later in thesis, is the entrenchment of minority shareholders by misleading financial accounting and reporting of large, influential family shareholders (e.g. Achleitner et al., 2014). Furthermore, early performance studies on the performance of family firms apply agency problems on both the manager/shareholder-level as among shareholders itself as an explanatory framework (e.g. Anderson and Reeb, 2003a; Villalonga and Amit, 2006).

Capturing the influence of family shareholders including their presence on the board(s) of the firm may hence be relevant for assessing both the ability of family members to monitor managers or executive actions according to the family blockholders' interests as well as the level of potential agency conflicts with minority shareholders (e.g. Fan and Wong, 2002; Andres, 2008) and subsequent financial consequences of their blockholder-presence.

### 1.3.2 Socioemotional Wealth Theory

Though limited by bounded rationality, agency theory presumes a value and utility maximization of both principals and agents under individual but given risk preferences (Jensen and Meckling, 1976; Shleifer and Vishny, 1997). Behavioral theory by contrast suggests that the risk preferences of decision makers are not consistent but depend on the framing of a problem and that they prefer to "avoid a loss if this implies taking a higher risk" (Stankiewicz, 2016). Family firms for example are argued to pursue not only economic, but also non-economic goals (e.g. Lee and Rogoff, 1996; Chrisman et al., 2004; Berrone et al., 2012). Returning to the illustration in Figure 1, objective functions of the family (as a whole or via outside family members) such as its legacy and reputation, values or promotion of family members may influence family shareholders in their decisions (Villalonga and Amit, 2015).

One of the most prevalent frameworks of assessing non-economic goals in family firms is the concept of socioemotional wealth (SEW). The theory was primarily introduced in a prominent article by Gomez-Mejia et al. in 2007 by

---

14 For a more detailed discussion of agency relations and consequences in family firms see Burkhart et al., 2003; Chrisman et al., 2004; Block, 2009; Ampenberger, 2010.

studying the risk-behavior of families owning Spanish olive oil mills: In their study they showed that family firms are not necessarily more risk-averse under economic means, as previously assumed for family businesses in academia, but may take more risk in specific business situations to protect their socioemotional wealth, such as their entrepreneurial independence. Following the concept, for family firms protecting their socioemotional endowment such as control over the firm, influence on the business or the identification with the firm and its name may be prioritized over decisions that might otherwise be driven in a different direction by economic logic (Gomez-Mejia et al., 2007; 2011).

In a review article based on the theoretical origin and empirical evidence, Berrone et al. (2012) identify five different dimensions (referred to as "FIBER") of the SEW-Concept (Wagner, 2016): (1) *Family control and influence* captures the direct or indirect influence of family members in the firm (i.e. management positions, founder involvement, dominant family coalition) regardless of financial considerations. (2) *Family members' identification with the firm* describes the level to which the family is tied to the firm and affects the firm's behavior but also the external perception of the firm as part of the family itself. (3) *Binding social ties* accounts for the family's social relationship with stakeholders, networks, or communities that may result for example in a higher commitment of employees to the family and the firm or a higher level of trust by stakeholders. (4) *Emotional attachment* describes the fact that as the family and the firm is more interwoven, emotions may both positively and negatively amplify corporate behavior and decision making compared to non-family firms, for example in periods of economic crises or succession (Stankiewitcz, 2016). Lastly, (5) *Renewal of family bonds to the firm through succession* refers to the family shareholders' desire to pass-on the family business to the succeeding family generation as one of the pivotal reference points in the framework of socioemotional wealth affecting for example the long-term planning and decision horizons or the willingness and purchase price expectation of family shareholders to sell the business (Berrone et al., 2012; Zellweger et al, 2012).

Empirical evidence on the concept of socioemotional wealth is growing in recent years and unveils its addition and contribution to previously existing theories on family firms: Gottardo and Moisello (2014, 2019) for example attach the higher leverage ratios of Italian family(-managed) firms to their desire of non-opening up the capital of the firm to non-family shareholders to protect their family influence and control. Sun et al. (2019) show that family firms invest more into R&D during crises than non-family firms to protect their family social networks and perpetuate the family dynasty and long-term success. Hauck and Prügl (2015) show that specific dimensions of SEW moderate the innovation activities of family firms during intra-family succession periods while Gomez-Mejia et al.

(2010) argue that the same is the case with diversification decisions of family firms. Furthermore, various publications retrace the differences in earnings management among family and non-family firms to the former protecting their socioemotional wealth (Stockmans et al., 2010; Gomez-Mejia, 2014; Achleitner et al., 2014; Martin et al., 2016). Finally, the fact that family firms in polluting-intense sectors tend to soil less is in line with families protecting their image and hence socioemotional wealth (Berrone et al., 2010, 2012).

## 1.4 Assessment of Family Influence

### 1.4.1 Family Business Definition Dilemma

Ever since research on family businesses gained attention in literature, the discussion evolved around how to adequately define family businesses (i.a. Chua et al., 1999; Habbershon and Williams, 1999). Research lacks a common definition of family businesses (Astrachan et al., 2002; Wirsching, 2017) which is referred to as the "family business definition dilemma" since the introduction of the term by Klein et al. (2005). The existing family firm definition-concepts applied in research thereby developed at large following the general streams and trends in research on this type of enterprises (Taras et al., 2018).

While most publications on the general prevalence of family firms across countries apply an ultimate ownership definition of family firms (e.g. La Porta et al., 1999; Faccio and Lang, 2002; see Section 1.2), scholars investigating specific research aspects of family firms suggested numerous definition approaches evolving around the assessment of significant and meaningful family influence in the firm (e.g. family management presence, founder presence, generational stage, self-perception of potential family businesses).

In the past, there was hardly any standardization of the definitions used (Wirsching, 2017). Yet, there have been approaches at least to provide an overview of the various definitions of family businesses in literature (e.g. Chrisman et al., 2005; Westhead and Howorth, 2007; Hernández-Linarez et al.,2018). In a review study of 267 journal articles, Harms (2014) systematically analyzes family firm definitions applied in literature by frequency. Doing so, he identifies six clusters of family business definitions (Taras et al., 2018): The (1) *components of involvement/essence approach* by Chua et al. (1999) initially argues that the essence of families for the firm such as the vision across generations should be combined with the components of involvement such as ownership stakes and management participation. This approach anticipates many ideas that are also applied in later definitional concepts. (2) *Self-developed definitions* account for independent definitions of scholars neglecting established streams creating additional micro-definitions of family businesses on their own. (3) *Other definitions* account for those who were either applied before established concepts of definitions were available (and are therefore not explicitly met) or that are chosen for particular methodological research designs. Articles *without explicit definition* (4) apply own definitions without even referring to other established approaches or even mentioning the own definition. Clusters (3) and (4) are the most prevalent ones according to Harms (2014).

The (5) *F-PEC/familyness approach* by contrast is based on a measure initially developed by Astrachan et al. (2002) and Klein et al. (2005) after their notion of the challenges in family business definition (the "family business definition dilemma"). It combines elements of Power (e.g. ownership, management)[15], Experience (generational control) and Culture (family vs. business values) and therefore "hard" and "soft" aspects of definitions to develop a scale of family characteristics. It furthermore considers behavioral and resource-based-view aspects of the familyness concept that was introduced by Habbershon and Williams (1999) and provides a framework for the assessment of the assumed competitive advantages of family firms (Harms, 2014). On the one hand, the F-PEC-Scale has the advantage of assessing the influence of family members in the bords more accurately than other approaches and in summary provides for a continuous scale of family characteristics of a family firm (Klein et al., 2005). On the other hand, the approach is based on the self-assessment of CEOs (in all of its dimensions) and therefore raises issues of self-selection bias and replicability of the approach in defining family businesses. The same restrictions apply to other developments such the FIBER scale[16] (Berrone et al., 2012) or subsequent variants (e.g. Hauck et al., 2016) proposing a measure of family influence based on the socioemotional wealth of family firms (Gomez-Mejia et al., 2007).

The family business definition dilemma is particularly severe in empirical research on financial and performance aspects of family firms, as empirical results are highly driven by sample selection criteria (Mazzi, 2011). Since the methodological introduction by the early performance studies of Anderson and Reeb (2003a) and Villalonga and Amit (2006) *empirical definitions* (6) based

15 Aspects of the elements included in Power-dimension build on the previously developed SFI- (Substantial Family Influence-) Index by Klein (2000), Ampenberger (2010).

16 See chapter on socioemotional wealth for a description of the dimensions assessed by the FIBER-scale by Berrone et al. (2012).

on measurable variables (Harms, 2014) are most frequently used for empirical research on family businesses – particularly in case of performance studies and publicly listed companies (Taras et al., 2018).

Apart from collecting data on ownership levels of family shareholders or definitions based on exceeded voting/ownership thresholds (e.g. Faccio and Lang, 2002; Sraer and Thesmar, 2007), the application of dummy variables to control for the management influence of family members has become the main approach in empirical family busines research to further access heterogeneity among family firms (Harms, 2014). Variations of controlling for the management influence of families range from dummies capturing if the CEO is a member of the family (e.g. Ali et al., 2007; Achleitner et al., 2014;) over the fact that a member of the family is appointed to the board in general (e.g. Anderson and Reeb, 2003a; Cella, 2009; Ampenberger et al., 2013) to the fact that the founder is still involved in management (e.g. Villalonga and Amit, 2006; Andres 2008, Ampenberger, 2010).

## 1.4.2 Implications of the German Dual Board System

As described various empirical studies on listed family firms control for family firm heterogeneity by assessing the presence of a family member in a management function via dummy variable. Given empirical findings of this approach on the consequences of family board presence for example on financing structures or performance (Ampenberger et al., 2013; Schmid, 2013; Andres, 2008) underline the need to assess family management influence in Germany. Yet, previously applied measures and tools largely do not sufficiently account for the means of this influence. The reasons are grounded in the peculiarities of the German corporate governance system as these rules have significant consequences for agency problems between owners and managers as well es among owners itself (Becht and Boehmer, 2003; Gugler and Yurtoglu, 2003):

The German corporate governance system for listed stock corporation companies differs substantially from those in Anglo-Saxon countries such as the US or UK, but also from those of other European countries such as Spain, Sweden, Greece or Switzerland (Klein, 2000; Becht and Boehmer, 2003). While most countries worldwide provide for a one-tier board system, the German Stock Corporation Act prescribes a two-tier board system consisting of a management[17] and a supervisory board (Gugler and Yurtoglu, 2003; Du Plessis, 2004)[18].

17 The terms management and executive board are used as synonyms in this dissertation.

18 For a more detailed overview on the historical development of the general German corporate governance and corporate finance environment see e.g. Kauf (2014) or Volk

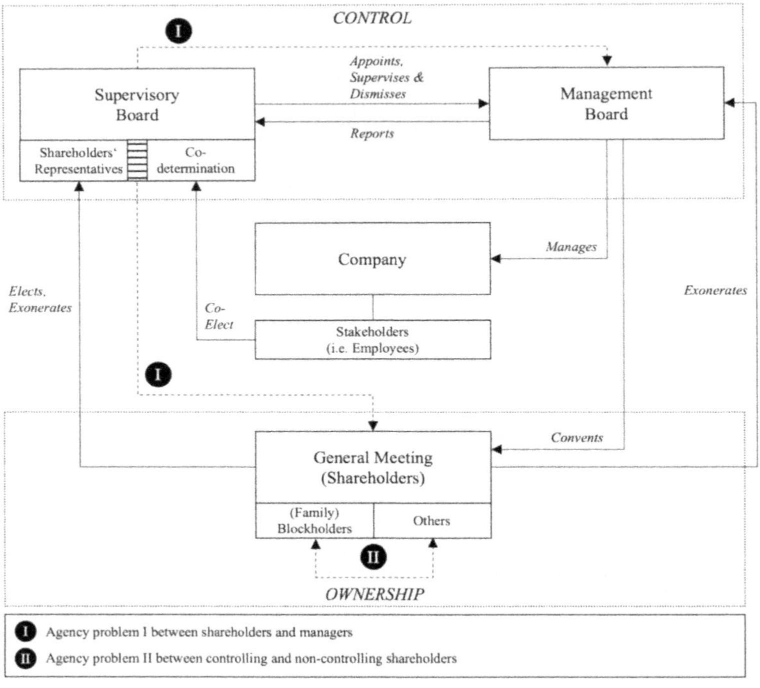


**Figure 1.2:** Agency Problems in the German Two-tier Board System

Figure 1.2 features the most important aspects of the German two-tier system and consequences for selected agency relations. On the one hand, the management board ("Vorstand") is jointly in charge of managing the company on its own responsibility[19]. The board members are appointed and dismissed by the supervisory board for a period of maximum five years[20]. The executive board is obliged to report to the supervisory board on a regular basis on significant

(2013). Since 2004, as per Council Regulation (EC) No 2157/2001 and the German Act on the Introduction of the European Company (Gesetz zur Einführung der Europäischen Gesellschaft (SEEG)), listed companies in Germany can also have the legal form of a Societas Europeaea (SE). In this case the adoption of a one-tier board system is possible.

19 § 76, 77 AktG (German Stock Corporation Act).

20 § 84 AktG (German Stock Corporation Act).

governing aspects, financial performance such as the development of sales and profitability as well as business aspects and transactions with a significant impact on the profitability or liquidity of the company[21].

The supervisory board („Aufsichtsrat") on the other hand is in charge of controlling and supervising the management board[22] as well as appointing and dismissing the management board (Gorton and Schmid, 2000; Rieckers and Spindler, 2004). Members of the management board may only be dismissed for grave cause[23]. By contrast to single board corporate governance regimes, in which the CEO may also be the chairman of the board ("CEO Duality"), in Germany a member of the supervisory board may not be a member of the management board or execute any other authorized representative/agent or officer with full commercial power of attorney of the company[24]. Furthermore, management measures of the executive board must not be transferred to the supervisory board[25].

Shareholders shall exercise their rights primarily at the Annual General Meeting[26]. Those rights include (among others) the appointment of the members of the supervisory board, the decision on the appropriation of the net income, the general approval of the actions taken by the management and supervisory board (exoneration), the appointment of the auditor of the annual accounts, decisions about amendments of the by-laws as well as measures on the procurement of capital and reduction of capital[27]. Shareholders, however, may not directly appoint or dismiss members of the management board. Furthermore, the exoneration of the supervisory and management board by the General Meeting is without direct legal consequence.[28]

---

21 § 90 AktG (German Stock Corporation Act).

22 § 111 AkG (German Stock Corporation Act).

23 § 84 (3) AktG (German Stock Corporation Act), grave causes shall consist of, in particular, gross dereliction of duties, inability to properly manage the company's affairs, or a vote of no confidence by the General Meeting, unless the confidence has been withdrawn on grounds that are manifestly irrelevant.

24 § 105 AktG (German Stock Corporation Act).

25 § 111 (4) AktG (German Stock Corporation Act).

26 § 118 AktG (German Stock Corporation Act).

27 § 101, 119, 120 AktG (German Stock Corporation Act).

28 According to § 120 (2) AktG (German Stock Corporation Act) the approval and discharge does not entail any waiver of claims to compensation and supervisory board members can only be removed from office by the General Meeting in a separate voting procedure with a majority of at least three quarters of the votes cast (§ 103 (1, S. 2) AktG).

By contrast to other countries with one-tier board systems this two-tier system substantially limits the influence of shareholders over top management:

Firstly, while the shareholders in the General Meeting have the right to appoint members of the supervisory board, this is limited by the German co-determination concept prescribing that either one third or even the same amount of board seats as those of appointees by the shareholders must be held by representatives elected by employees (Gorton and Schmid, 2000)[29]. There are exceptions from this law in case of family businesses with fewer than 500 employees having with a single owner or in which all shareholders are related to each other[30], which is not the case for listed companies. Hence, even when a shareholder such as a family owns more than 50 % of the voting rights, control may not be complete and ownership influence is substantially limited (Gugler and Yurtoglu, 2003).

Secondly, members of the supervisory board, that are appointed for a maximum period of four Annual General Meetings after their appointment, may only be removed from office by the General Meeting with a majority of at least three quarters of the votes cast.[31]

Thirdly, while the General Meeting is usually convened by the management board or in special cases by the supervisory board, shareholders have the right to call the executive board to convent a General Meeting and to set items to the agenda if they own at least 5 % of the share capital[32]. Furthermore, they may ask questions to the executive board during the General Meeting[33]. But, unlike for example in the US, the General Meeting may only decide on measures of

---

29 § 96, AktG (German Stock Corporation Act); If the company has between 500 and 2,000 employees, one third of the supervisory board members is appointed by employees (Act on One-third Employee Representation in the Supervisory Board, DrittelbG), in case of more than 2,000 employees one half of the board positions (Co-determination Act, MitbestG). In case of corporations belonging to the mining, coal or steel sector, the supervisory board consists of the same amount of employee and shareholder board members as well as one neutral member to break ties (Amending Act on Employee Co-Determination in the Iron- and Steel-Producing Industry, MontanMitbestGErgG) (Gorton and Schmid, 2000; Ampenberger, 2010). Additional regulations are prescribed by the Act on Employee Co-Determination in the Case of a Cross-Border Merger (MgVG).

30 § 1 (1, Nr. 1) DrittelbG (Act on One-Third Employee Representation in the Supervisory Board).

31 § 103 (1, S. 2) AktG (German Stock Corporation Act).

32 § 121, 111 (3), 122 AktG (German Stock Corporation Act).

33 § 131 AktG (German Stock Corporation Act).

the management on company affairs if the executive board demands such a decision[34].

Fourthly, even though one of these grave causes for the dismissal of a member of the management board by the supervisory board is a vote of no confidence by the General Meeting[35], the withdrawal of confidence must not be "on grounds that are manifestly irrelevant". Furthermore, such a vote of no confidence requires to be put on the agenda of the General Meeting by shareholders 30 days in advance of the meeting[36] and requires a majority vote in the General Meeting.

Due to the given leeway of the management board, limited influence of shareholders in the supervisory board and a comparably lower level of shareholder rights (La Porta et al., 1998, 1999; Leuz et all, 2003), large shareholders have high incentives to control and monitor the firm via presence among the boards of the firm (Gugler and Yurtoglu, 2003). As Germany faces a high level of ownership concentration, particularly in form of voting blocks held by family shareholders, family members also have the ability to be frequently present in the management and supervisory board (Becht and Boehmer, 2003; Achleitner et al., 2019). As the management board is generally jointly in charge of managing the company on its own responsibility (while primarily reporting to the supervisory board), power on the supervisory board is substantially limited by co-determination of employees (Gorton and Schmid, 2000) and the direct influence of shareholders is basically limited to the Annual Meeting, such a governance setting calls for a detailed assessment of the influence of family members throughout all bodies and positions in order of capturing the real influence of family shareholders on financial decisions of the firm.

### 1.4.3 Collection of Governance Data

While all publications of this dissertation include financial data from different providers such as Thomson Reuters Datastream or S&P Capital IQ, data on the corporate governance influence family shareholders is the result of a year-long collection process. The starting point of the methodological approach of this dissertation is the observation that previous financial research under the German corporate governance system of listed firms only roughly considers the influence of family shareholders in the corporate governance bodies of the firm.

---

34 § 119 (2) AktG (German Stock Corporation Act).
35 § 84 (3, S. 2) AktG (German Stock Corporation Act).
36 § 122 (3) AktG (German Stock Corporation Act).

Scholars are indeed aware of the peculiarities of the given two-tier board system and control for family influence for example by integrating a dummy variable controlling for the fact that a family member is on the executive and/ or supervisory board (e.g. Cella, 2009; Achleitner et al., 2014) or by identifying family/founder-CEOs (e.g. Ali et al., 2007; Ampenberger et al., 2013). Yet, as the previous subsection demonstrated, this approach may be insufficient and too imprecise, depending on the considered financial aspect. Notably, to the best of my knowledge, no more precise governance data on a transparent and replicable basis is available via data providers and no publication on financial aspects of listed family firms in Germany considers the precise influence of these family members[37].

Research on family firms always somewhat struggles to collect reliable and detailed governance data and information that also fits the given corporate governance system of a country, as family firms and family firm owners are naturally secrete with such information (Kormann, 2017). As previously described many applied definitions, scales or assessments of family influence may be subjective or based on self-assessment thereby producing a potential observer, reporting or selection bias (e.g. F-PEC-Scale, FIBER-Scale).

Listed companies are obliged by law to regularly publish certain governance data such as exceeded ownership thresholds[38], appointments to the firm's boards or information on related parties, board-ownership or conflicts of interest that are relevant to be reported to the market. As publicly listed family firms of course have the same obligations to publish such information, this allows to draw a more accurate picture of family involvement among these firms (Ampenberger, 2010). The guideline for such a data collection process must be the prescriptions of the German Stock Corporation Law and the two-tier corporate governance

37 To the best of my knowledge, Achleitner et al. (2009, 2019) are the only authors describing the composition of management boards in their general study on listed family firms in Germany, however, without considering the precise influence of family managers in peer-reviewed publications for example on performance or financing structures (Ampenberger et al., 2013). Achleitner et al. (2012) are the only scholars applying a similar dataset in their investigation of voter ownership dynamics in listed German family firms.

38 According to the German Securities Trading Act (WpHG) shareholdings must be disclosed when exceeding voting rights thresholds of 3/5/10/15/20/25/30/50 or 75 %. The German Stock Corporation Act (AktG) provides for control thresholds of 25 %, 50 % of 75 % of outstanding voting capital (see section 1.3.4 for information of selective shareholder rights connected to these control thresholds).

system that may separate the methodological approaches in family business research on the governance influence of family blockholders in Germany from other international context.

The dataset applied for the corporate governance variables in this dissertation is based on 278 firms listed in the general and prime standard of the German CDAX stock market index. Over a period from 2000 to 2013 every available annual financial statement and management report was investigated to hand-collect all relevant governance data. First, every shareholder holding a share larger than 5 % (common shares) was identified (analogous to Achleitner et al., 2012). This threshold accounts for specific shareholder rights such as the right to call the executive board to convene a General Meeting or adding items to the agenda of the General Meeting[39]. Second, the background of each and every board position in the executive and supervisory board in each firm and year was detected. In connection with the total board size, this allows to assess the relative power of family members among boards. Third, the approach also captures the presence of a family who also founded the firm as well as the presence of a founder or his/her family in person on the board(s). If necessary supplementary information from company websites, Bureau van Dijk's Dafne database publicly available sources was consulted for clarification purposes.

The retrieved panel dataset hence provides for a thorough mapping of family influence in the investigated companies over time. Most important, this dataset allows to estimate empirical models that may explain relevant influences of members of the shareholding family in accordance with German stock corporation law, while being transparent and replicable in the best possible way.

## 1.5 Research Objectives

As presented before, literature suggests that the financial behavior of family firms is significantly driven by the management presence of family shareholders. This dissertation argues that research on family firms in Germany needs to gain a deeper understanding of the means of family influence and applies the hand-collected dataset previously described to four objectives of financial research.

First, a better understanding of family influence is for example particularly required in case of short-term financial decisions as these decisions are assumed to be primarily driven by managers in the management board. Second, a thorough

39 § 122 AktG (German Stock Corporation Act).

assessment of family influence may be essential when investigating the reporting behavior of family firms, as the supply and demand of reporting information has already been shown to be moderated by the presence of large controlling shareholders in corporate boards (i.a. Fan and Wong, 2002; Achleitner et al., 2014). Third, such family board-presence may be relevant to the capital market by shaping a firm-specific form of corporate governance and influencing the ability to mitigate agency problems in the firm. Forth, the board-influence of family members and the specific economic and non-economic goals of family blockholders suggest, that family firms may exhibit a different financial behavior specifically in times of economic crises. The following sections motivate the selected research objectives in more detail and describes how they build on each other.

## Research Objective 1 – Working Capital Management

The first research question deals with the influence of family shareholders on a financial aspect that is largely under researched in family business literature. While for example many publications explore the long-term debt structure of family firms, there is a remarkable lack of studies on short-term investment decisions and working capital management specifically (Autukaite and Molay, 2013; Motylska-Kuzma, 2017).

This is notable for several reasons: First, working capital management in general may increase shareholder value (Shin and Soehnen, 1998) and was shown to increase corporate profitability in Germany (Meyer and Lüdtke, 2006; Wöhrmann et al., 2012). Second, the German economy is largely based on family firms in the manufacturing, building and wholesale/retail sector (Gottschalk et al., 2019; Achleitner et al., 2019) and effective working capital management is a crucial part of business success for these sectors (Knauer and Wöhrmann, 2013). Third, as working capital management is one of the key resources to utilize internal financial resources (Shin and Soehnen, 1998; Richards and Laughlin, 1980) the lower level of debt-financing of family firms in a bank-based economy like in Germany (Schmid, 2013) may potentially increase the relevance of internal financing resources such as effective working capital handling.

Most important, several theoretical and empirical contributions on the influence of family ownership and management on other financial aspects suggest that working capital management as well may differ between family firms and non-family firms. The assumed risk-aversion of family shareholders (Andres, 2008; Anderson et al., 2012) for example might lead to less efficient inventory management as higher levels of inventory may prevent production disruptions. On the other side, the same effect could be triggered by family-managers that might be just less professional as outside-managers are recruited from a larger pool of talent (Anderson and Reeb, 2003a). A different example affecting working capital management could be that family firms may be more cautious with aggressive collection of outstanding receivables to protect their socioemotional wealth and maintain a positive relation with their stakeholders (Zellweger and Nason, 2008; Cennamo et al., 2012).

Against the background of the corporate governance system of Germany one may even more expect an impact of the presence of family members in the management boards: Existing literature already proves for example, that the lower level of debt in German family firms is particularly due the presence of a family member on the board. Working capital management by contrast is expected to be far more subject to daily management decisions of the executive board. Hence, if family ownership matters in terms of shareholder incentives, decision horizons or just the level of professionalization on financial issues among shareholding family members, the degree of family involvement in management should be of high relevance for working capital management in German family firms. Thus, the first research question asks:

*How does the level of family ownership and specifically the degree of family involvement in the management and supervisory board affect working capital efficiency?*

## Research Objective 2 – Earnings Management

After assessing the influence of family blockholders on working capital management by considering the presence of family members among management boards, the second research question turns to earnings management. While the former research objective allows to access the influence of family members on current assets and current liabilities management techniques within the firm, the second research question also allows to gain insights on the agency conflicts between controlling minority shareholders (such as family blockholders) and minority shareholders.

The reasons for earnings management are manifold and range from private rent-seeking by managers over smoothing swings in earnings to the avoidance of debt covenant violations (e.g. Healy and Wahlen, 1999; Myers et al., 2007; Jaggi and Lee, 2002) and are primarily due to the separation of ownership from control typical in widely-held companies. Financial reporting in general can serve as a mechanism to overcome agency problems by reducing information asymmetries among managers, shareholders or creditors (Wang, 2006). Yet, at the same time, large shareholders may also use such techniques to mislead and expropriate minority shareholders (Leuz et al., 2003), for example to reduce the demand for dividend distributions (Gugler and Yurtoglu, 2003).

Family blockholders may affect earnings management practices as they have a superior incentive (family wealth concentration) and ability (firm knowledge, board presence) to monitor managers on earnings management. At the same time their powerful position in the company may cause additional information asymmetries leading to more earnings management (for expropriation purposes) on the one hand or less earnings management (due to increased pressure for appropriate financial reporting by other shareholders) on the other hand (Ali et al., 2007; Wang, 2007).

The quality of financial reporting by family firms has been extensively researched worldwide due to the prevalence of this ownership type. But despite of the specialties of the corporate governance system, there are hardly any publications for the German context. Achleitner et al. (2014) were the first scholars presenting broader evidence that family firms indeed differ in earnings management also in Germany. Yet, to the best of my knowledge, no publication has differentiated the means of family influence on earnings management techniques. Under the German two-tier corporate governance framework for listed firms, family shareholders are highly incentivized to be engaged among the management boards as their influence as "pure" shareholders is otherwise limited by law. If family blockholders influence earnings management techniques it is expected that this is primarily the case via board-involvement of family members. Hence, the second main research question investigates:

*How does the level of family ownership and involvement in the executive and supervisory board, i.e. the overall family influence, affect earnings management?*

## Research Objective 3 – Stock Market Performance

The prior two research questions investigate to which extend the degree of influence of family shareholders in corporate boards affects financial management. The answers to these questions allow to assess the influence of family members on day-to-day financial management practices as well as to gain an understanding not only about which earnings management techniques family firms prefer (some techniques are more harmful to long-term success than others) but to discuss the incentives of family blockholders on earnings management and their relation to other shareholders.

If family blockholders affect financial aspects by the degree of management influence, this adds to existing findings on family firms and supplements general studies highlighting differences among large blockholders in their effect on corporate policies and performance (Cronqvist and Fahlenbrach, 2009; Andres, 2008).

All firms included in the applied dataset are listed on the German stock exchange. Recent studies note that the market reacts differently on shareholders actively handling agency problems in firms (Mietzner and Schweizer, 2014). As previously described, following the inherent interest of family shareholders to monitor the firm in which the largest part of their (undiversified) family wealth is invested in (Anderson and Reeb, 2003a), and due to the German two-tier corporate governance system, many family members are present in the companies' executive and supervisory boards (Andres, 2008; Ampenberger et al., 2013).

As family firms are so widespread (Villalonga and Amit, 2020), literature already extensively analyzes performance differences compared to non-family firms (e.g. Wagner et al., 2015; Taras et al., 2018 and other meta-studies on performance). While the question of management involvement may be less relevant in countries with higher ownership protection, the actual influence of family shareholders in the corporate boards and thus in corporate governance is not sufficiently considered in such studies for Germany – despite of the fact that due to the corporate governance system family members often belong to management.

The fact that this influence is not properly assessed in performance studies is particularly notable, as scholars show that the market performance of listed corporations may be significantly driven by corporate governance differences among firms (Gompers et al., 2003; Bebchuk et al., 2009). Hence, it is assumed that the corporate governance as shaped by the incentives and monitoring ability of family shareholders to control the firm may explain differences in market performance compared to non-family firms.

To fully reflect the means of corporate governance influence of family blockholders in Germany, the respective methodology of the paper suggests a new, transparent and replicable index of family influence capturing ownership, the executive and supervisory board, as well as the founder presence. Hence the third research question asks:

*How does the corporate governance involvement of family shareholders explain long-term stock market return differences between portfolios of family- and non-family-influenced firms?*

## Research Objective 4 – Financial Crises Performance

The previous research question examines to what extend the corporate governance involvement of family blockholders helps to explain stock return differences between family and non-family firms. While a precise measure of family involvement has been neglected until now in research on performance differences, an assessment and thorough understanding of performance differences among family and non-family firms is of great relevance for the German economy (Ampenberger, 2010; Gottschalk et al., 2019).

Though not finally resolved, prior research suggest that family firms exhibit a higher operative performance compared to non-family firms (i.a. Wagner et al., 2015; Hansen and Block, 2020). Yet at the same time we find family firms to maintain a lower level of debt financing (Ampenberger et al., 2013) corroborating the assumption of increased risk avoidance by family firms (Mishra and McConaughy, 1999) that is extensively discussed by scholars by itself.

The superior operative performance of family firms in Germany (Andres, 2008), their more conservative capital structures and the notion of a significantly different behavior of family firms compared to non-family firms (such as for example with regards to working capital management) raise the question if such firms may profit from their ownership structure and precondition in phases of economic recession. Due to their inter-generational long-term orientation (Zellweger et al., 2012; Arrondo-Garcia et al., 2016) and the high concentration of wealth of family shareholders in the firm (Anderson et al., 2003), family firms and non-family firms are expected to differ in their crisis behavior and incentive structure. As observed by Sraer and Thesmar (2007), Mietzner and Tyrell (2012) or Gottschalk et al. (2019), family firms for example could afford to hold their employees longer during recessions before laying them off, as they are less indebted (Schmid, 2013). Doing so, family firms might protect their employees as stakeholders of the firm (Zellweger and Nason, 2008), but also profit immediately from full intellectual and production capacities in recovery phases.

Despite of all these observations and the given relevance of family firms in Germany, there are notably few publications on the performance of family firms in periods of economic crises. Existing studies on the market performance for example mostly cover phases of general economic growth and largely find the stock return performance of family firms in Germany at least on the same level or above non-family firms (Corstjens et al., 2006; Cella, 2009). But for Germany, to the best of my knowledge, there are no specific studies on the performance of family firms during financial crisis available. Yet, the few existing studies from in other countries confirm that in phases of recessions both the reaction as well as the performance of family firms differs from non-family firms (i.a. Lins et al., 2013; Minichilli et al., 2016; Sun et al., 2019).

If all the noted idiosyncrasies of family firms in Germany are assumed as advantageous in and after economic downturns, one could expect that the capital market anticipates such features of family firms and prices them into stock market performance. Applying the two past economic crises as an exogenous shock to all firms (Minichilli et al., 2016; Aldamen et al., 2020) would allow to observe such differences in the performance of family and non-family firms during such phases and afterwards. Against the backdrop of the current ongoing economic turmoil due to the COVID-19 pandemic answering this research question may also allow to assess questions of general economic resilience among states and their particular economic structure – with a high share of family businesses in case of Germany (Faccio and Lang, 2002; Gottschalk et al., 2019). Thus, the fourth research question is:

> *How does the stock market performance of firms with and without family blockholders differ in and after the world financial crisis and the Euro crisis?*

## 1.6 Dissertation Structure

This cumulative dissertation includes four stand-alone papers. Each of the papers represents one of the following chapters and investigates one of the research objectives discussed in the prior section (see Figure 1.3 below). Every publication exhibits its own structure consisting of an introduction, literature review and hypothesis, data/methodology, empirical results, discussion, and conclusion section. Tables are presented within the respective paper-section, the appendices of the publications are presented at the end of each chapter, respectively.

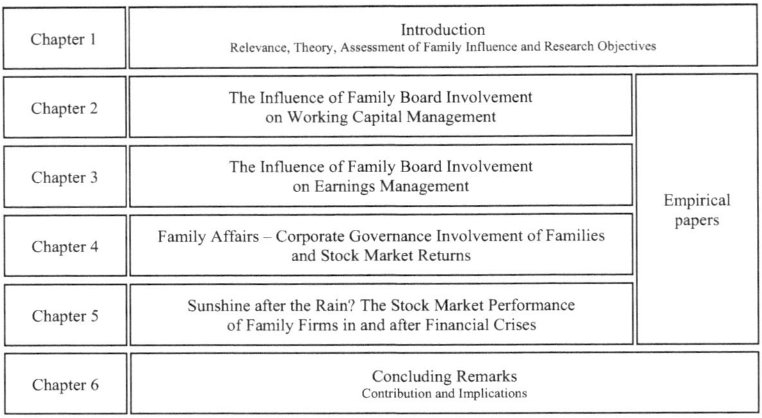


**Figure 1.3:** Overview of the Key Elements of this Dissertation

All papers are either published in an international journal or currently under review for publication. In case of the former the publications are available via the websites of the respective journals following the noted Digital Object Identifiers (DOI). The background of each paper, respective co-authorships as well as the current status of publication are described in the footnotes at the beginning of each of the following four chapters. The last Chapter 6 summarizes the overall aim of this thesis and notes concluding remarks across all four publications on the influence of families on financing aspects and performance of family firms of this thesis. Furthermore, this chapter discusses implications for scholars in research as well as practitioners derived from the research objectives of this dissertation.

# 2 The Influence of Family Board Involvement on Working Capital Management

**Abstract:*** While research on long-term capital structures of family and non-family firms is well established, differences in current assets- and liabilities-management are largely under-researched. The aim of the study is to examine whether the type and degree of family involvement in the firm affect the efficiency of working capital management. Employing a partially hand-collected panel of 278 listed firms from 2000 to 2013 this paper analyzes the impact of family shareholders as owners, managers, and supervisors on working capital handling in Germany. The results show that primarily the share of family members in the executive board increases the length of the cash conversion cycle (CCC), particularly in smaller and non-service firms. Most notably, family management increases the inventory period (DIO). The higher average equity ratio of family firms suggests that family firms may face reduced financing pressure to address such inefficiencies in current assets and current liabilities management. Furthermore, family-managed firms may be less professional in their working capital management. The findings contribute to the literature by showing that in a country with a less investor-friendly corporate governance system, family influences on working capital management are primarily due to management presence, not plain shareholder influence. The results stress the need for researchers to consider the degree of family management involvement when analyzing the financial aspects of family firms.

## 2.1 Introduction

The German economy is largely based on listed and privately held family firms (Faccio and Lang, 2002; Achleitner et al., 2019; Gottschalk et al., 2019). Family shareholders represent a unique type of shareholder (Andres, 2008), as they often have a significant amount of family assets invested in the firm (Anderson and Reeb, 2003b), want to keep the firm in the family across generations (Arrondo- García et al., 2016) and are frequently present on the management boards (Achleitner et al., 2019). Due to their ownership structure, family firms differ from non-family firms in various financial aspects (Filbeck and Lee, 2000; Michiels and Molly, 2017; Motylska-Kuzman, 2017). Family firms in Germany are found to be less leveraged (Schmid, 2013), have a higher operative

---

* This article is published in *Corporate Board: Roles, Duties and Composition*, Vol. 17 No. 3, Franzoi, F., The Influence of Family Board Involvement on Working Capital Management, 42–60, Copyright: Franzoi, F. (2021).

and market performance (Andres, 2008; Franzoi and Mietzner, 2021a), differ in their earnings management techniques (Achleitner et al., 2014) and in their behavior towards other stakeholders such as employees (Mietzner and Tyrell, 2012).

Working capital management is a key instrument to utilize internal financial resources and create shareholder value while avoiding short-run liquidity needs (Richards and Laughlin, 1980; Shin and Soenen, 1998; Boisjoly et al., 2020). Analogous to the differences in other financial aspects between family and non-family firms mentioned above, various arguments suggest that one may also expect such differences in the handling of working capital. As family shareholders, for example, are often also appointees in the boards of the firm in Germany (Franzoi et al., 2021), they have a superior ability to control managers in executing efficient working capital management. Further, the lower leverage ratio in family firms might increase the importance of internal financing sources such as optimized cash-to-cash cycles (Baños-Caballero et al., 2014). The long-term orientation (Gómez-Mejía et al., 2007; Block, 2009), risk-aversion (Anderson et al., 2012), and social endowment of family firm owners (Miller et al., 2008; Mueller and Philippon, 2011; Chua et al., 2011) might, on the other hand, also lead to less efficient working capital handling as family shareholders, for example, may prefer higher levels of inventory or offer more generous payment conditions to customers. Another reason for the lack of efficiency could be that the natural succession in family firms results in less suited managers holding key positions (Bennedsen et al., 2007). Therefore, the main purpose of this paper is to examine whether the type and degree of family involvement affect the efficiency of working capital management exchange-listed firms in Germany.

While various financial peculiarities of family firms are well-represented in literature, academic emphasis on the management of current assets and liabilities in family firms is rather weak (Autukaite and Molay, 2013; Motylska-Kuzman, 2017). At the same time, working capital management becomes increasingly important: firstly, production, procurement, and delivery processes in economies worldwide became more interwoven and streamlined while working capital efficiency tended to decline (Windhaus et al., 2018). Secondly, the economic impact of the global COVID-19 pandemic increased pressure specifically on manufacturing and retail firms to maintain effective working capital management (Hofmann and Wetzel, 2020; Zimon and Tarigi, 2021; Kortman et al., 2021). This is particularly severe in Germany, as the economy is based on family firms in the building, manufacturing as well as trade sector and the largest part of the listed firms belongs to the manufacturing sector (Gottschalk et al., 2019; Achleitner et al., 2019). Thirdly, as German firms are typically bank-financed (Gorton and Schmid, 2000) and the corporate sector's access to financing is increasingly affected by regulations and capital requirements (Fidrmuc et al., 2015), internal sources of financing become more important.

Summary statistics of studies on other financing means or on working capital handling in general indicate differences among family and non-family firms in Germany (Eiben and Redlefsen, 2006; Sure, 2014; Holzamer and Wendt, 2018; Ahrens et al., 2019). Yet, no article has shed an empirical spotlight on these differences. In addition to the general lack of research, it is particularly under-researched by which means family shareholders might influence working capital management. Germany, for example, has a specific corporate governance framework for public companies in which the influence of shareholders is largely limited to the annual general meeting, where shareholders appoint parts of the supervisory board that subsequently names and controls the executive board (Gorton and Schmid, 2000; Franzoi and Mietzner, 2021a). Research on the long-term financing structure of family firms, for example, already shows that it is particularly influenced by the involvement of the family in management (Ampenberger et al., 2013). As working capital handling is, even more, subject to day-to-day decisions in management, this study expects that the effective influence of family shareholders may be primarily executed through family member presence in the executive board.

This article investigates the influence of family ownership and management involvement on working capital efficiency in 278 listed German firms. The empirical models apply the cash conversion cycle (CCC) and its components of days inventory outstanding (DIO), days sales outstanding (DSO), and days payables outstanding (DPO) as proxies for the working capital management efficiency among firms. The observation period from 2000 to 2013 excludes major effects on the financing of companies and current assets due to the EU capital requirement directive (Basel III) coming into effect in 2014. The study contributes to the literature by showing that family shareholders indeed determine working capital management. The empirical models, however, show that not family ownership, but the degree of family influence in management increases the CCC. Against the backdrop of the German corporate governance system, the results are reasonable as the day-to-day working capital management is expected to be influenced mainly via the executive board. The effects are mainly observable in non-service firms and smaller companies and are primarily caused by slower inventory turnover (more DIO) in family-managed firms. The paper follows that these effects may be less due to risk aversion of families but more due to a lower level of professionalization in the working capital management of family-managed firms. Furthermore, due to the higher equity ratio of family firms, these firms may face less pressure to address, for example, inefficiencies in inventory management.

The structure of this paper is as follows. Section 2 reviews the literature and formulates hypotheses while Section 3 explains the methodology. The results of the study are presented in Section 4. After the discussion in Section 5, Section 6 concludes the findings.

## 2.2 Literature Review

### 2.2.1 Working Capital Management

A static view on working capital comprises the difference between a firm's current assets and current liabilities (Richards and Laughlin, 1980; Autukaite and Molay, 2013). By contrast, an operating cash-flow-oriented perspective on working capital focusses on the time span from expenditures for thepurchase of materials to the collection of payments for the sale of finished products – thereby covering the flow of cash from suppliers to inventory to accounts receivable and back into cash (Richards and Laughlin, 1980; Shin and Soenen, 1998). A popular measure of working capital in this sense is the cash conversion cycle (CCC) (Gitman, 1974; Deloof, 2003). Working capital management of days inventory-, sales- and payables outstanding (CCC) may therefore be described as the trade-off between the dual goals of working capital, i.e. liquidity (e.g. to buy inventory/pay trade liabilities) and profitability (e.g. avoiding unnecessarily deployed cash that needs to be financed) (Shin and Soenen, 1998).

Despite other financial factors such as the capital structure policy of the firm, the working capital management policy is among the most important factors directly impacting the financial performance as well as shareholder wealth (Gill et al., 2014). Different publications find a negative (Shin and Soenen, 1998; Deloof, 2003; García-Teruel and Martínez-Solano, 2007), a positive (Gill et al., 2010), or a concave/convex relationship between net trade cycle or CCC and corporate performance (Baños-Caballero et al., 2012; Afrifa, 2016). Furthermore, efficient management of working capital appears to have a positive impact on (firm) market value for both large corporations (Wang, 2002), as well as small and medium-sized enterprises (SMEs) (Afrifa, 2016). According to Gill (2013), the same holds for family businesses in Canada, in particular. For Germany, two publications confirm a positive relationship between DIO and profitability (Meyer and Lüdtke, 2006) as well as between the net trade cycle and profitability (Wöhrmann et al., 2012).

### 2.2.2 Family Firms and Working Capital

Few studies on working capital in Germany distinguish between family and non-family firms. Some recent publications, however, hint at differences in working capital handling. Sure (2014), for example, finds deficits in family firms, especially in small-sized enterprises. A survey-based study by Eiben and Redlefsen (2006) shows that only half of the responding family firms applies active working capital management. Holzamer and Wendt (2018, p. 18) find that family firms in Germany have 14 days longer CCC than their non-family counterparts, whereas in the industrial segment the CCC is even 23 days longer than in non-family firms.

The long-term orientation of family firms (Block, 2009; Lumpkin and Brigham, 2011) and their given incentive structure provide indications for a different working capital management compared to non-family firms. Business interaction with customers and suppliers, in general, can be seen as one of the key parts of stakeholder management (Freeman, 1984; Hill and Jones, 1992). Family firms are perceived to possess superior stakeholder and network management (Zellweger and Nason, 2008). The credibility and long-term commitment in their stakeholder management also affect suppliers and customers (Cornell and Shapiro, 1987) and hence trade working capital management. Family firms may be motivated to hinder working capital practices that are economically efficient in the short-term, like collecting receivables fast or paying suppliers with delay (Gill et al., 2014), but might damage long-term business survival and their socioemotional wealth (Gómez-Mejía et al., 2007) or that are too risky in terms of their supply chain anyways (such as minimal stock holdings to avoid warehouse costs).

Consequently, Gottardo and Moisello (2014) find significantly higher inventory levels in the case of Italian family firms. Among less professionalization, they attribute this finding to a more conservative risk behavior of family firms regarding their supply chain and inventory. In Germany, the Institute for SME Research observes similar effects: family firms exhibit higher working capital ratios than non-family firms and this is mainly due to higher levels of inventory (Ahrens et al., 2019). In addition, their study argues that the higher asset coverage ratio and the higher level of general liquidity they observe may be potential signs for increased risk aversion and for the family's desire to keep their firm flexible.

### 2.2.3 Corporate Governance and Working Capital

Recent publications indicate that not only the ownership structure but also corporate governance aspects may influence working capital practices. Akram et al. (2018) find evidence that the specific national and firm-individual corporate governance framework such as the number of independent directors on the board has an impact on the general efficiency of working capital handling. Findings come from Canada showing that board composition regarding CEO duality or gender may affect working capital management practices in small family businesses (Gill and Biger, 2013; Gill et al., 2014). Fiador (2016) provides an additional indication, that board size, board independence, and CEO duality affect working capital efficiency assessed by the CCC. Regarding Germany, there is only one publication suggesting similar results for the general level of liquid assets. In their descriptive study comparing two economically strong regions, the authors find ahigher level of liquidity in firms with family management (Ahrens et al., 2019).

Though the literature review suggests structurally different working capital management in family firms, no other studies on the corporate governance influence of family members via ownership, management, and control on working capital are available. With regards to the German economic structure, legal system, and the specific corporate governance framework the aim of this paper is to gain a deeper understanding by which means of influence family shareholders affect working capital management in listed family firms.

## 2.3 Hypothesis

Due to the economic environment of low shareholder protection (La Porta et al., 1998), German firms are typically bank-financed (Gorton and Schmid, 2000). The economic desire to safeguard invested assets and mitigate agency problems (Shleifer and Vishny, 1997) results in an increased ownership concentration (Becht and Boehmer, 2003). The prominent ownership and management influence of families thereby substantially influences the financial decisions (Schmid, 2013; Ampenberger et al., 2013) as well as the corporate performance of family firms (Kaserer and Moldenhauer, 2008; Andres, 2008; Mazzi, 2011).

Based on the premises of Germany and the idiosyncratic features of family shareholders it is expected that family ownership significantly influences working capital management. The undiversified concentration of invested family wealth and the superior knowledge of family members in their firm (Anderson and Reeb, 2003a) equals a large incentive and ability to control managers (Demsetz and Lehn, 1985; Andres, 2008) in their management of short-term assets and liabilities. Inefficient working capital handling may equal a higher dependence on external financing (Baños-Caballero et al., 2014; Afrifa and Padachi, 2016). Since family firms in Germany exhibit a lower level of leverage too, this may imply stricter working capital management, as family blockholders tend to avoid too much control by external debtholders (Schmid, 2013). Furthermore, lower levels of working capital to be financed equals the risk-averse attitude of family firms (Andres, 2008) in reducing bankruptcy risks (e.g. efficient cash collection from customers) and financing costs (e.g. for trade credits or inventory storage costs).

By contrast, various arguments also suggest less efficient working capital handling. Higher levels of working capital generally correspond with the assumed risk-aversion of families. For example, conservative handling of inventory may prevent disruptions in the supply chain and production as well as negative price fluctuations through more available stock. As a second aspect, the instant payment of trade liabilities might decrease financing costs through discounts and avoid additional external financing of family firms by banks. With regards to the different stakeholder management of family firms that accounts for the long-term orientation and socioemotional wealth of family shareholders (Gómez-Mejía et al., 2007), aggressive management of trade receivables towards customers or trade payables towards suppliers appears less likely (Gill et al., 2014). In summary, the incentive structure of family shareholders, their risk aversion, financing preferences as well as their stakeholder orientation suggest significant effects on the working capital handling of these family firms. Hence, hypothesis 1 assumes: *Family and non-family firms differ in their working capital management.*

As revealed by the literature review, the first results indicate that the specific corporate governance influence of family firms may as well determine working capital handling. In Germany's mandatory corporate governance framework for stock-corporation law, the governance of companies is split into an executive/management board (i.e. for day-to-day active management) and a controlling supervisory board. Against this backdrop and the German co-determination system, the influence of shareholders (and therefore also families) is mainly limited to the annual shareholders' meeting (Gorton and Schmid, 2000; Mietzner and Schweizer, 2014; Franzoi et al., 2021). Successfully influencing the financial decisions of firms, therefore, requires family appointees in the executive board. Hence, in Germany, a high share of family members in family-owned firms belong to the executive board (Achleitner et al., 2019). Accordingly, Ampenberger et al. (2013) show that the influence of families on the capital structure is primarily executed via management involvement.

Working capital management is largely due to day-to-day management decisions in the firm. These decisions affect all aspects of working capital including negotiations with suppliers, purchasing, stockpiling, changing invoice payment terms and granting cash discounts to customers, collecting cash from overdue trade receivables outstanding, or executing optimization measures (e.g. warehouse optimizations). If family ownership of firms matters with regards to working capital all these factors may be primarily influenced by family members being appointed to the executive board. Consequently, if family members succeeding their predecessors through nepotism may be less qualified to lead the company (Burkart et al., 2003; Bennedsen et al., 2007; Eugster and Isakov, 2019), working capital management may be directly affected. Following these arguments, hypothesis 2 assumes that: *Working capital management is affected by the share of family members in the executive board.*

In the German corporate governance system, the supervisory board is in charge of appointing and controlling the executive board as well as approving certain strategic decisions of the executive board. Therefore, the direct influence of supervisory board members on daily working capital decisions is rather limited. Nevertheless, it may affect guidelines and major decisions in working capital management such as the change of strategic suppliers or the approval of larger efficiency or restructuring programs to be executed by the executive board (such as improved procurement processes or investments in warehousing). Though listed, many firms listed on the German stock exchange are small- or medium-sized (Achleitner et al., 2019) with family members appointed to the supervisory board (Franzoi and Mietzner, 2021a)[40]. Hypothesis 3 therefore assumes that: *Working capital management is affected by the share of family members in the supervisory board.*

## 2.4 Methodology

### 2.4.1 Data

Previous publications apply surveys (Eiben and Redlefsen, 2006), interviews (Holzamer and Wendt, 2018), or case studies (Sure, 2014) as research methods to investigate working capital management practices in German family firms. The current study broadens existing research by applying a quantitative panel

40 Current challenges of digitalization, more efficient supply chains or working capitl financing tools might be too difficult to handle for family members in the executive board. Filbeck and Lee (2000) support this argument by finding larger family businesses with non-family members in the financial decision-making role more likely than their smaller counterparts to employ sophisticated financial management techniques (incl. working capital management).

regression methodology and differentiating ownership and management influences of families. To investigate the hypothesis the analysis is based on a largely hand-collected panel data set that is also used by Franzoi and Mietzner (2021a, b) and Franzoi et al. (2021)[41]. The dataset contains 278 randomly chosen firms listed at the German stock market (CDAX-index, general and prime standard) covering a period from 2000 to 2013[42]. The specific time frame of the panel dataset allows to exclude major organizational and regulatory effects on working capital/current asset management. As shown by Boisjoly et al. (2020), the year 2000 marks a cornerstone in a two-decade previous improvement of current asset and working capital management (e.g. six sigma or lean management). On the other hand, by the effect of January 2014, the EU issued its capital requirement directive on the implementation of Basel III and other financial regulations, thereby affecting lending access and conditions for the financing of companies (Fidrmuc et al., 2015) and current assets.

As listed firms are forced to regularly publish financial and firm information, the ownership and management structure of these firms has been manually collected for every firm and year from annual reports/financial statements and publicly available information. Financial and insurance firms are excluded from the sample and the ownership data covers common stock holdings (no preferred shares). All financial information has been collected from Standard & Poor's Capital IQ platform.[43]

---

41 These publications address different research questions. While the former two investigate the impact of family influence on stock market performance, the latter examines earnings management practices in family firms.

42 The 278 sample firms were randomly chosen among all firms listed in the General and Prime Standard of the CDAX-index. Covering more than half of all firms, the sample is regarded as representative to listed firms in Germany (478 at period-end of the investigation). The number of employed firms is limited by the extremely time-costly hand-collection process of required, reliable governance data over all time periods of the panel (such as investigating every single management or supervisory board position or every shareholder holding more than 5 % of the voting rights in every firm year).

43 As analysis and results may potentially be affected by outliers, data for financial variables are winsorized at the 1 % and 99 % level, analogous to other publications (e.g. Toilo et al., 2019, Ampenberger et al., 2013).

### 2.4.2 Model Specification and Dependent Variables

The main focus of this paper lies in the analysis of the family-influence on the efficiency of trade working capital management. Analogous to other publications (Baños-Caballero et al., 2014; Fiador, 2016) this study applies the cash conversion cycle (CCC) as a proxy to identify differences in working capital efficiency between family owned/managed and non-family affected firms. The CCC is defined by the net of Days Inventory Outstanding (DIO i.e. Inventory/COGS*365) plus Days Sales Outstanding (DSO i.e. Trade Receivables/Total Sales*365) minus Days Payables Outstanding (DPO i.e. Trade Payables/COGS*365). The model also employs a working capital efficiency measure that is more robust to individual annual outliers, the two-year average CCC ($t_{-1}$ and $t_0$) as provided by Capital IQ as a default variable output option. The fully detailed definition of the average CCC can be found in appendix in Table 2.12. As governance influences in firms may affect parts of the CCC differently (Fiador, 2016), the individual components of the CCC are also estimated separately. The following general regression model is applied (for individual model specification please refer to respective table):

$$\begin{aligned} WC_{it} &= \alpha + \beta_1 Family_{it} + \beta_2 Mgmt\,Family_{it} + \beta_{3-7} Shareholders_{it} \\ &\quad + \beta_8 Board\,Size_{it} + \beta_j Controls_{it} + e_{it} \end{aligned} \qquad (1)$$

where *WC* refers to the working capital measures of (a) the cash conversion cycle (CCC), (b) the two-year average cash conversion cycle, and the CCC-components (c) DIO, (d) DSO, and (e) DPO (as well as the two-year averages of the components). Following the results of the F-test and Breusch-Pagan test (fixed/random effects vs. Pooled OLS) and the Hausman test (fixed- vs. random effects), the study applies a fixed-effects regression model. The fixed effects regression method allows the applied models to control for firm-specific time-invariant firm heterogeneity. All models apply robust standard errors to account for heteroscedasticity and autocorrelation.

### 2.4.3 Independent Variables

While the variable *Family* in Equation 1 refers to the percentage of family stock ownership, *Mgmt Family* captures (a) the family management influence via dummy variable (presence of family members on the boards) as well as (b) the share of family members on the board. To control for the influence of other large shareholders besides *Shareholders* equals a vector of the ownership variables covering shareholdings of *Other corporations*, *Banks*, *Financial institutions*, *Employees* and the *Government*. As in the case of family ownership, every shareholder with an ownership stake of >5 % is identified.

Some of the existing publications on governance influences show that board size may affect the CCC (Fiador, 2016). Hence, *Board Size* (i.e. the number of board members) controls for the fact that on the one hand larger boards may increase control over single-manager decisions in working capital handling and that on the other hand smaller boards may be more effective in decision making processes and controlling (Gill and Biger, 2013).

The vector of *Controls* in Equation 1 accounts for the following independent variables: Firm size may positively affect working capital management by lowering financial constraints through better access to different forms of financing, lower financing costs and higher market power for example towards suppliers (Baños-Caballeros et al., 2014; Warner et al., 2019; Boisjoly et al., 2020). Hence, *MCap* (market capitalization) accounts for size. *Age* accounts for firm age. Older firms may have better relationships with stakeholders (e.g. Petersen and Rajan, 1997; Niskanen and Niskanen, 2006; Zellweger and Nason, 2008) and better access to external financing (Baños-Caballero et al., 2010). On the other side, older firms might be inflexible in applying advanced financial management techniques (Filbeck and Lee, 2000).

Among corporate earnings and other financial institutions (e.g. trade credits), bank financing may influence working capital levels/management (Troilo et al., 2019). The debt-to-equity ratio (*DebtEqu*), is expected to have a negative influence on working capital management. Even during low interest rates, already highly leveraged firms may be forced to squeeze-out internal financial resources such as working capital. Under imperfect market conditions, costs of funding for of CCC may be higher for firms with larger leverage as they have to pay higher risk premiums (Baños-Caballero et al., 2010). In order to account for the ability to generate financial resources the model includes the Cashflow-margin (*CF*). Higher cashflows are expected to increase the CCC as firms may be less likely to face financial constraints in working capital management (Baños-Caballero et al., 2014; Afrifa, 2016).

Firm performance may affect working capital management by extended access to external financing or higher market dominance and connected bargaining power (Baños-Caballero et al., 2010). The model accounts for this influence via return on assets (*ROA*). Furthermore, the model controls for a company's *Growth* in sales. While with regards to expected future growth companies might stockpile additional inventory for example, such growth phases might also be accompanied by larger trade credits to boost sales levels (Baños-Caballero et al., 2010; Elbadry, 2018). Lastly, the model controls for fixed tangible assets (PPE). Firms with more PPE may have difficulties in financing current assets in financially distressed situations (Fazzari and Petersen, 1993). On the other hand firms with more tangible instead of intangible assets may profit from fewer information asymmetries and lower funding costs (Baños-Caballeros et al., 2010).

## 2.5 Results

### 2.5.1 Descriptive Statistics

Table 2.1 describes the summary statistics of the main governance variables. In more than half of the companies a family held more than 25 % of the voting rights. Under German stock corporation law shareholders larger than this threshold have a blocking minority for most of the relevant decisions of the shareholder's committee (such as appointing managers or family members to the boards). The high prevalence of family shareholders is even more crucial as in nearly every third company 50 % or more of the voting rights are attributable to a family. The family stake amounts to 28 % (median) of the voting rights.

**Table 2.1:** Descriptive Statistics on Governance Variables

| | **Family Ownership** | | | **Family Management** | | | **Board Size** | |
|---|---|---|---|---|---|---|---|---|
| | **25 %** | **50 %** | **Avg.** | **Dum** | **ExBo %** | **SupBo %** | **ExBo** | **SupBo** |
| Mean | 0.53 | 0.32 | 0.31 | 0.35 | 0.18 | 0.09 | 3.32 | 6.99 |
| Median | 1.00 | 0.00 | 0.28 | 0.00 | 0.00 | 0.00 | 3.00 | 6.00 |
| SD | 0.50 | 0.47 | 0.29 | 0.48 | 0.29 | 0.16 | 1.71 | 5.37 |
| N (firm years) | 2936 | 2936 | 2936 | 2917 | 2917 | 2889 | 2917 | 2905 |

This table presents the mean, median, standard deviation and n of the main governance variables of interest across the sample from 2000–2013. A list of all variables can be found in the Appendix.

As shareholder influence is limited in Germany, family managers are present in 35 % of all executive boards. About 18 % of all executive board positions are occupied by family members and even in the supervisory board nearly 10 % of all positions belong to family members. The high level of active management involvement by family shareholders in Germany matches with the findings of other publications (Achleitner et al., 2019; Franzoi et al., 2021).

Turning to working capital management, Figure 2.1 illustrates the CCC of family- and non-family-firms (by ownership and management) over time. The general length of the cash conversion cycle in the sample decreased over time, suggesting improvements in working capital management. In line with other observations in Germany (Ahrens et al., 2019) the CCC of the sample firms appears to be higher in family-influenced firms at most points in the observation period. Especially family-managed firms (executive board) exhibit a similar or higher level of CCC since 2006.

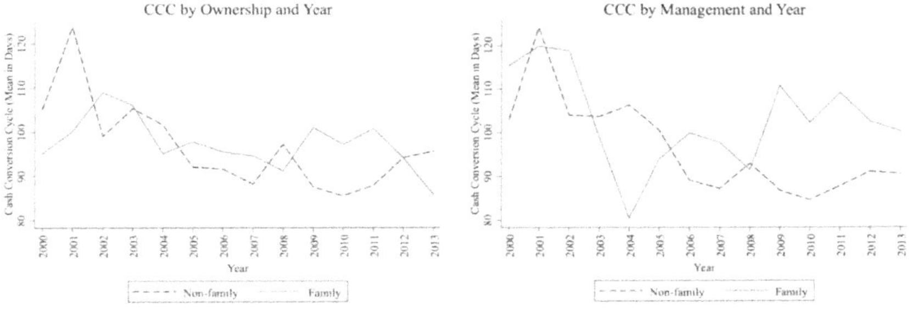


**Figure 2.1:** CCC by Ownership and Management

The graphs present the annual cash conversion cycle by ownership (min. 25 % blocking minority by families) and family management presence (Dummy) in executive boards.

**Table 2.2:** Summary Statistics and Differences in Means by Management Type

| | Family Management | | | Non-family Management | | | Sign. of Dif. | |
|---|---|---|---|---|---|---|---|---|
| | **Mean** | **Median** | **N** | **Mean** | **Median** | **N** | **Mean** | **Median** |
| CCC | 102.18 | 90.63 | 858 | 94.02 | 84.22 | 1732 | ** | ** |
| DIO | 91.90 | 85.50 | 866 | 90.80 | 75.62 | 1742 | n.s. | n.s. |
| DSO | 72.51 | 59.05 | 1012 | 62.12 | 56.99 | 1853 | *** | *** |
| DPO | 71.27 | 45.54 | 1003 | 64.42 | 45.98 | 1830 | n.s. | n.s. |
| ExBo Size | 2.95 | 3.00 | 1033 | 3.53 | 3.00 | 1884 | *** | *** |
| SupBo Size | 4.81 | 3.00 | 1024 | 8.19 | 6.00 | 1876 | *** | *** |
| Mcap | 407.26 | 64.24 | 901 | 4,153.01 | 256.69 | 1582 | *** | *** |
| DebtEqu | 0.80 | 0.32 | 886 | 0.78 | 0.48 | 1650 | n.s. | *** |
| Age | 43.19 | 23.00 | 1033 | 61.93 | 37.00 | 1884 | *** | *** |
| ROA | 0.03 | 0.03 | 1001 | 0.03 | 0.04 | 1834 | ** | ** |
| CF | 0.01 | 0.02 | 961 | 0.02 | 0.03 | 1762 | * | *** |
| Growth | 0.12 | 0.06 | 1000 | 0.08 | 0.05 | 1826 | *** | ** |
| PPE | 0.17 | 0.12 | 1015 | 0.21 | 0.18 | 1862 | *** | *** |

This table presents the summary statistics for the variables employed in the main regression models (pooled). Significance of differences is based on the t-test (means) and the Wilcoxon/Mann-Whitney test (median). A list of all variables can be found in the Appendix. Significance of differences at the 10 %, 5 % and 1 % levels is indicated by *, ** and ***, respectively.

Table 2.2 reports the summary statistics and differences in means/medians of family/non-family firms by family executive board management presence (dummy). Variations in the number of firms years (N) compared to governance statistics in Table 2.1 are due to the availability of respective accounting data[44]. Family-managed firms appear to have a slower mean turnover in inventory (DIO), days sales outstanding as well as days payables outstanding. Temporal trends neglected, the overall picture of pooled summary statistics provide a first (albeit significant) indication that the cash conversion cycle of firms with family management is about six days longer than without family management both in (both mean and median). Interestingly and in line with theory, a significant difference in the CCC could however only found with regards to family management, not family ownership (see Table 2.6 in Appendix).

44 The availability of respective accounting data for for the research purpose of this study is not affected by the application of different accounting standards. The general impact of accounting standards is addressed in the robustness section.

Regarding other variables, family-managed firms are significantly smaller (MCap) and are 14 years younger (median). While their cashflow margin amounts below non-family-managed firms, sales growth rates are higher. The level of PPE is lower in family-led firms in the sample. Summary statistics furthermore confirm that the leverage of German family firms is significantly lower (Schmid, 2013). Figure 2.2 in the Appendix plots the median debt-to-equity-ratios (DebtEqu) of family/non-family-owned firms (continuous lines) and family/non-family-managed firms (dashed lines) over time. While the overall average level of leverage is decreasing over time, the sample supports the findings of other studies, that at least long-term financing decisions in family firms are substantially driven by family management involvement (Ampenberger et al., 2013). Against the general trend of the sample, firms with family management involvement exhibit a similar or lower median debt-equity-ratio over the years.

The correlation matrix is presented in Table 2.7 in the Appendix. As assumed the influence of families is correlated with working capital KPIs. While family ownership only exhibits a significant correlation with DSO, the management influence of family members in the executive and supervisory board is positively and significantly correlated with the cash conversion cycle. In case of family managers on the executive board this correlation is also significant in case of DIO and DSO. As expected, size and the debt-to-equity-ratio both show a significant negative correlation with the cash conversion cycle.

## 2.5.2 Regression Results

Table 2.3 reports the results of the regression models on the CCC and the influence of the family as shareholders and as executive board members. Models 1 and 4 focus on the ownership structure and do not show a significant effect on the length of the CCC. A constant significant impact of family shareholding cannot be observed as only two of the six models exhibit a positive influence on a 10 % level. By contrast, the presence of family managers on the executive board (Models 2 and 5) significantly increases the (average) CCC confirming the results of previous differences in means testing. Models 3 and 6 reveal, that not only the presence of family managers, but more strongly the share of family delegates among the members of the executive board significantly increases the length of the CCC. This finding is found to be robust on 1 % level and supports Hypothesis 2.

The size of the executive board did not reveal any stable, significant results. The finding of negative coefficients by Fiador (2016) and Gill and Biger (2013) could not be confirmed for Germany. Regarding control variables, leverage

(DebtEqu) has a negative effect in all models, however only significant in case of the average CCC. The negative effect of ROA supports other publications that assume an increased bargaining power against customers/suppliers in case of increased profitability (Baños-Caballeros et al., 2010; Shin and Soenen, 1998). The negative effects of sales growth supports the notion, that fast-growing companies follow aggressive working capital policies (Baños-Caballeros et al., 2010; Elbadry, 2018).

Table 2.4 presents the regression results on the CCC-components. As reported by Model 1 and 4 the positive influence of family management on the CCC appears to be due to slower inventory management. In both models DIO increase with the share of family managers. Model 6 suggests that firms with more family managers also exhibit more days payables outstanding (DPO)[45]. This effect is only observable on the two-year average length of the CCC. Since the effect is smaller than in case of DIO, the overall increase in CCC reported in Table 2.3 appears therefore reasonable. As presented in Model 2 and 5, the share of family management does not have any significant effect on the days sales outstanding (DSO). Notably, family ownership has no significant effect on the components of the CCC either.

The regression results on the supervisory board are shown in Table 2.5. As reported previously, the share of family ownership has no significant effect in any of the models. Models 1–4 suggest that the size of the supervisory board has a positive effect on the CCC and that this effect is primarily driven by more DIO. The positive effect of the influence of the family in the supervisory board (Model 1) also appears to be driven by the influence of the family in the executive board (Models 2–3). No such CCC-increasing effect of the family-share in the supervisory board could be found regarding DIO, DSO and DPO. The positive influence of family-members in the executive board (as reported by Table 2.3–2.4) remains stable when controlling for supervisory board involvement of family members. Results on the two-year-average CCC and its components are similar and can be found in Table 2.8 (Appendix).

45 While the dummy for family management has a significant, positive effect on the CCC (see Table 2.3), in case of the CCC-components it only reveals a significant positive influence on average DSO and DPO.

**Table 2.3:** Cash Conversion Cycle (Executive Board)

| | (1) CCC | (2) CCC | (3) CCC | (4) Avg. CCC | (5) Avg. CCC | (6) Avg. CCC |
|---|---|---|---|---|---|---|
| Exec Family (Dum) | | 19.76** | | | 19.13*** | |
| | | (8.60) | | | (7.18) | |
| Exec Family (%) | | | 53.06*** | | | 44.66*** |
| | | | (20.32) | | | (15.78) |
| Family (%) | 25.02 | 27.72 | 28.26 | 13.91 | 15.80* | 16.52* |
| | (22.32) | (23.56) | (23.66) | (9.69) | (9.16) | (9.39) |
| Corporation (%) | 33.61** | 26.63* | 28.30* | 23.10** | 17.38 | 18.44* |
| | (15.69) | (15.45) | (15.45) | (11.07) | (11.00) | (11.12) |
| Bank (%) | 18.59 | 14.05 | 15.21 | -12.75 | -16.87 | -15.72 |
| | (58.38) | (60.06) | (59.82) | (54.11) | (54.29) | (54.04) |
| Finance (%) | 13.02 | 9.347 | 9.719 | 1.276 | -1.067 | -0.688 |
| | (14.78) | (14.94) | (14.76) | (13.20) | (13.89) | (13.72) |
| Employees (%) | 39.30 | 26.59 | 26.39 | 13.36 | 8.708 | 9.465 |
| | (37.38) | (39.25) | (37.73) | (32.24) | (32.01) | (30.77) |
| Government (%) | 27.66 | 43.32 | 46.60 | 13.27 | 33.89 | 35.92 |
| | (56.23) | (50.76) | (50.56) | (35.36) | (28.71) | (29.05) |
| Exec Board Size | | 1.925 | 3.120** | | 1.435 | 2.495* |
| | | (1.43) | (1.56) | | (1.25) | (1.36) |
| MCap | 2.490 | 0.697 | 0.577 | 2.017 | -0.0416 | -0.0884 |
| | (2.56) | (2.78) | (2.77) | (2.37) | (2.45) | (2.45) |
| DebtEqu | -0.242 | -0.661 | -0.748 | -0.260 | -0.654* | -0.695* |
| | (0.47) | (0.50) | (0.51) | (0.39) | (0.38) | (0.39) |
| Age | -7.971 | 0.677 | 1.878 | -9.808 | 0.442 | 1.058 |
| | (11.91) | (12.26) | (12.05) | (11.53) | (10.65) | (10.44) |
| ROA | -27.83 | -7.798 | -13.58 | -99.68*** | -91.27** | -95.12** |
| | (38.10) | (41.14) | (40.86) | (34.91) | (37.52) | (37.12) |
| CF | -33.29* | -31.47* | -31.89* | 4.115 | 12.55 | 12.04 |
| | (17.89) | (16.94) | (17.04) | (17.25) | (14.15) | (14.23) |
| Growth | -8.457* | -10.10* | -9.604* | -12.24*** | -14.41*** | -13.96*** |
| | (4.56) | (5.42) | (5.45) | (3.83) | (4.72) | (4.74) |
| PPE | -4.160 | -3.565 | -6.928 | 17.01 | 14.41 | 11.50 |
| | (34.70) | (38.19) | (38.71) | (22.57) | (24.36) | (24.93) |
| R2 | 0.0320 | 0.0374 | 0.0457 | 0.0392 | 0.0512 | 0.0563 |
| R2 (adj.) | 0.0257 | 0.0299 | 0.0382 | 0.0329 | 0.0437 | 0.0488 |
| N | 2030 | 1942 | 1942 | 1996 | 1911 | 1911 |
| FE | YES | YES | YES | YES | YES | YES |
| Robust | YES | YES | YES | YES | YES | YES |

This table presents the regression results of the cash conversion cycle (CCC) fixed effects regression models. Models apply robust standard errors, include a constant and cover the period from 2000 to 2013. Standard errors are presented in parentheses. A list of all variables can be found in the Appendix. Significance at the 10 %, 5 %, and 1 % levels is indicated by *, **, and ***, respectively.

**Table 2.4:** CCC-Components (Executive Board)

| | (1) DIO | (2) DSO | (3) DPO | (4) Avg. DIO | (5) Avg. DSO | (6) Avg. DPO |
|---|---|---|---|---|---|---|
| Exec Family (%) | 49.08** | 9.914 | 15.94 | 37.38** | 8.272 | 21.72*** |
| | (19.85) | (12.77) | (16.52) | (17.40) | (10.18) | (8.22) |
| Family (%) | 18.49 | -8.700 | 1.061 | 12.44 | -5.422 | 7.965 |
| | (13.30) | (8.27) | (13.14) | (10.15) | (6.27) | (7.65) |
| Corporation (%) | 16.70 | -16.36* | -15.69 | 14.79 | -13.59* | -3.693 |
| | (13.61) | (8.79) | (11.69) | (13.90) | (7.00) | (7.29) |
| Bank (%) | -30.13 | -7.204 | -57.67 | -44.72 | 1.680 | -15.13 |
| | (42.93) | (17.20) | (35.11) | (42.26) | (18.24) | (21.99) |
| Finance (%) | 18.47 | -14.78** | -3.357 | 16.54 | -12.17** | 6.559 |
| | (12.05) | (6.39) | (9.36) | (11.57) | (5.97) | (8.32) |
| Employees (%) | 67.87 | -68.65** | -14.98 | 43.11 | -41.61 | 1.855 |
| | (47.04) | (31.44) | (28.82) | (41.19) | (33.76) | (23.99) |
| Government (%) | 12.25 | -12.95 | -19.43 | 22.70 | 25.65 | -20.56 |
| | (28.67) | (38.98) | (60.86) | (33.14) | (53.26) | (36.76) |
| Exec Board Size | -0.0449 | 1.056 | -1.468 | 1.059 | 1.017 | -0.0723 |
| | (1.00) | (1.18) | (1.28) | (1.07) | (0.81) | (0.77) |
| MCap | 4.344* | -0.0855 | 0.965 | 2.978 | -0.575 | -0.290 |
| | (2.46) | (1.11) | (1.80) | (2.41) | (1.01) | (1.43) |
| DebtEqu | -0.297 | -0.288 | -0.489 | 0.0651 | -0.0771 | -0.138 |
| | (0.37) | (0.36) | (0.68) | (0.51) | (0.27) | (0.31) |
| Age | -0.0850 | -8.946* | -12.33** | 1.364 | -6.664 | -2.521 |
| | (7.45) | (5.41) | (5.12) | (7.42) | (5.43) | (4.27) |
| ROA | -76.02* | -34.89* | -93.21*** | -107.9*** | -95.01*** | -78.75*** |
| | (44.25) | (18.78) | (32.50) | (39.12) | (21.08) | (20.22) |
| CF | -27.71** | -25.12** | -28.31* | -11.15 | 6.372 | -12.11* |
| | (12.04) | (11.24) | (16.86) | (10.04) | (9.22) | (7.10) |
| Growth | -6.390 | -4.468 | -3.928 | -16.98*** | -15.56*** | -13.17*** |
| | (4.77) | (2.80) | (4.88) | (4.85) | (3.23) | (3.51) |
| PPE | 36.44* | -57.85** | -41.35 | 45.76** | -44.38*** | -34.60* |
| | (20.15) | (24.69) | (27.06) | (21.65) | (15.44) | (19.07) |
| R2 | 0.0520 | 0.0770 | 0.0391 | 0.0880 | 0.136 | 0.0892 |
| R2 (adj.) | 0.0447 | 0.0702 | 0.0319 | 0.0809 | 0.130 | 0.0822 |
| N | 1950 | 2052 | 2039 | 1930 | 2051 | 1977 |
| FE | YES | YES | YES | YES | YES | YES |
| Robust | YES | YES | YES | YES | YES | YES |

This table presents the regression results of the cash conversion cycle-components (DIO/DSO/DPO) fixed effects regression models. Models apply robust standard errors, include a constant and cover the period from 2000 to 2013. Standard errors are presented in parentheses. A list of all variables can be found in the Appendix. Significance at the 10 %, 5 %, and 1 % levels is indicated by *, **, and ***, respectively.

**Table 2.5:** Cash Conversion Cycle / CCC-Components (Supervisory Board)

| | (1) CCC | (2) CCC | (3) CCC | (4) DIO | (5) DSO | (6) DPO |
|---|---|---|---|---|---|---|
| Sup Family (%) | 54.00* | | 63.72** | 29.01 | 9.632 | -11.53 |
| | (27.73) | | (29.45) | (24.63) | (18.25) | (12.58) |
| SuF(%) X Exec(Dum) | | 64.65*** | | | | |
| | | (20.02) | | | | |
| Exec Family (%) | | | 56.29*** | 50.41** | 12.63 | 17.36 |
| | | | (20.99) | (20.46) | (13.98) | (17.21) |
| Family (%) | 28.34 | 30.87 | 24.25 | 16.06 | -10.20 | 1.305 |
| | (20.94) | (24.22) | (20.58) | (12.19) | (8.56) | (13.40) |
| Corporation (%) | 25.28* | 27.07* | 27.36* | 15.71 | -17.11* | -15.94 |
| | (14.96) | (15.69) | (15.19) | (14.02) | (8.88) | (11.81) |
| Bank (%) | 22.34 | 20.39 | 18.79 | -28.20 | -7.177 | -57.91* |
| | (58.00) | (58.62) | (59.19) | (42.25) | (17.34) | (34.86) |
| Finance (%) | 10.71 | 10.60 | 10.58 | 18.41 | -14.60** | -2.587 |
| | (14.81) | (15.11) | (14.50) | (11.54) | (6.45) | (9.36) |
| Employees (%) | 19.48 | 28.03 | 3.567 | 55.97 | -69.92** | -7.111 |
| | (36.69) | (38.18) | (36.88) | (45.02) | (32.06) | (29.04) |
| Government (%) | 28.88 | 33.33 | 42.00 | 5.077 | -10.94 | -17.52 |
| | (53.42) | (51.21) | (50.42) | (26.55) | (39.94) | (61.44) |
| Exec Board Size | | | 3.180** | -0.284 | 1.192 | -1.556 |
| | | | (1.58) | (1.03) | (1.26) | (1.24) |
| Sup Board Size | 1.984*** | 1.520** | 1.781** | 2.122*** | -0.564 | -0.707 |
| | (0.75) | (0.68) | (0.75) | (0.79) | (0.58) | (0.77) |
| R2 | 0.0366 | 0.0364 | 0.0576 | 0.0599 | 0.0806 | 0.0414 |
| R2 (adj.) | 0.0290 | 0.0288 | 0.0491 | 0.0515 | 0.0728 | 0.0332 |
| N | 1924 | 1922 | 1922 | 1930 | 2031 | 2018 |
| Controls | YES | YES | YES | YES | YES | YES |
| FE | YES | YES | YES | YES | YES | YES |
| Robust | YES | YES | YES | YES | YES | YES |

This table presents the regression results of the cash conversion cycle (CCC) fixed effects regression models. Models apply robust standard errors, include a constant and cover the period from 2000 to 2013. Standard errors are presented in parentheses. A list of all variables can be found in the appendix. Significance at the 10 %, 5 %, and 1 % levels is indicated by *, **, and ***, respectively.

## 2.6 Discussion and Robustness

### 2.6.1 Discussion

Results support existing research findings, that governance structures in firms do indeed matter with regards to working capital management (Akram et al., 2018; Gill and Biger, 2013; Gill et al., 2014; Fiador 2016). In his study on capital structures in Germany, Schmid (2013) highlights the influence of families in family firms. The current empirical results on working capital management point in a similar direction. The influence of families appears to be primarily driven by active management involvement and not by ownership. These results appear reasonable with regards to the German corporate governance system that limits the shareholders' influence to the annual shareholders' meeting and the appointment of the supervisory board. Results demonstrate that when family members serve as executives, the working capital efficiency decreases and the length of the CCC increases..

Can this influence be isolated to the lead positions in the board(s)? Family CEOs substantially influence many financial aspects in family-owned firms (Anderson and Reeb, 2003a, 2004; Villalonga and Amit, 2006; Michiels and Molly, 2017; Andres, 2008). The CEO position in general may also be relevant for working capital management (Gill et al., 2014; Fiador; 2016). Table 2.9 in the Appendix presents regression models controlling for board-lead positions. Model 1–2 show no significant effect on the CCC in case of a family-CEO. Model 3 furthermore demonstrates that it does not make a difference in terms of working capital management if the CEO is also the founder of the firm and so does the general involvement of the founder in the board (Model 4). Model 5 shows that it also does not matter whether the chairman of the supervisory board is a family member. The driver with regards to family influence on working capital management appears to be the presence and relative family influence in the executive board.

What are the notable effects in working capital? Firstly, results suggest that the share of family management slows down inventory turnover (DIO). This is in line with Holzamer and Wendt (2018) who find higher CCCs for family firms, primarily driven by higher DIO. While Ahrens et al. (2019) find a generally higher inventory intensity (inventory/total assets) in family firms in Germany, the sample of the present study does not reveal such differences among family owned/-managed firms (results not reported). It appears to be less likely that the higher level of DIO is due to the assumed risk aversion of families (for example by preventing disruptions in supply chains or price fluctuations through higher inventory levels). It appears more likely that higher DIOs are due to less professional inventory management: Family successors might have gained their position rather through nepotism than by qualification (Burkart et al., 2003; Eugster and Isakov, 2019). This may be supported by findings that only half of the family firms in a survey-based study apply active working capital management (Eiben and Redlefsen, 2006) and that family firms lack professionalization with regards to working capital handling (Sure, 2014). Since family firms have a higher equity-ratio, the financial pressure due to financing needs or due to external control by debtholders to address inefficiencies in inventory turnover may furthermore be reduced.

Secondly, estimations reveal a limited effect on the trade payables period, as a positive effect of family management is only significant for the average level of DPO[46]. Generally, more DPO may support to finance working capital, as trade payables are settled later. If DPO in family firms proof to be longer in future publications, one reason could be a superior stakeholder-management of family firms towards suppliers (Zellweger and Nason, 2008), for example by more generous credit terms. Lappaleinen and Niskanen (2013) suggest that family firms generally prefer the use of trade credits as a financing source, which is in line with the avoidance of external financing costs or increased leverage.

Thirdly, family management has no significant effect on DSO. Either the efficiency of credit management is unaffected by family members, or the perception of family firms as more caring towards stakeholders (i.e. customers) cannot be confirmed. If the latter holds to be true in future analyses, this in line with Achleitner et al. (2014) and Franzoi et al. (2021) who find increased real earnings management by discretionary expenses in family firms, but none by boosting sales, for example, through more lenient credit terms to customers.

Empirical findings on the family influence on the supervisory board is rather weak and appears to be driven by the simultaneous executive board presence. No significant effect on any of the CCC-components can be observed. This finding is in line with Ampenberger et al. (2013) who could not observe significant effects in the supervisory board on the capital structure in family firms either. While the alignment of interest between family shareholders and the firm increases when family members serve on boards of the company (Fama and Jensen, 1983; Jensen, 1986; Anderson and Reeb, 2003a), the results on working capital management

46 As in case of inventory, trade payables/total assets are not significantly higher in family firms of the sample.

show that within the German corporate governance system, families need to be engaged particularly in the executive board to affect financial decisions.

### 2.6.2 Robustness

The results raise a number of robustness questions: Firstly, regarding the insignificance of family ownership it might be insufficient to consider ownership stakes held by families in general (including families that acquired, but not necessarily founded companies). Founding families in particular may be poorly diversified and have a large share of wealth invested in their firm (Anderson and Reeb, 2003a). Hence, their influence, motives and alignment with the company may differ from family investors who seek to diversify on a portfolio level (Zellweger, 2006; Andres, 2008). Results remain insignificant considering solely the ownership shares of founding families. It may as well be relevant from a stewardship- and agency- (Le Breton-Miller et al., 2011) as well as from a legal- and governance-perspective (i.e. a family does not always exceed the minority blocking threshold of 25 %) if the family is also the largest shareholder. Like before, results show that the shareholder rank has no significant influence on the CCC either. Furthermore, families may also control their shares via family offices or family foundations. Regression results remain largely unchanged when considering these two aspects in addition to the initially applied definition of family ownership.

Secondly, some studies on working capital efficiency apply the net trade cycle (NTC) instead of the CCC as the dependent variable where the denominator of DIO and DPO is sales instead of COGS (Shin and Soenen, 1998; Baños-Caballero et al., 2014). Despite of a certain loss in accuracy, this approach has the advantage that it is applicable for companies that adopted total cost accounting in the past (Knauer and Wöhrmann, 2013). Historically, listed companies in Germany were allowed to apply national, instead of international GAAP (i.e. HGB vs. IFRS).[47] However, the general findings remain unchanged when applying the NTC instead of the CCC. Findings furthermore remain unchanged in additional robustness tests after (a) controlling for international accounting standards via

47 In 2002, the EU adopted a regulation on the application of international accounting standards (No 1606/2002) for publicly traded, consolidated companies coming into effect in 2005 for the latest. For the sample this may raise misspecification issues regarding asset valuation (i.e. variables based on total assets), cost accounting (e.g. Cost of Goods Sold) or the financial reporting processes (application of international standards).

IFRS dummy variable, (b) cutting off panel data in the year of the introduction of the respective regulation or (c) generally integrating year-dummies in all fixed effect models. Finally results remain stable after applying alternative proxies for size (total assets and revenue), performance (return on equity, EBITDA-margin and net income-margin) or cash flow (levered/unlevered free cash flow and free cash flow excl. change in trade working capital). The results of all robustness tests are available upon request.

Thirdly, working capital management practices may vary across industries (Hawawini et al., 1986; Warner et al., 2019). The manufacturing and service industries are among the most common general branches in the CDAX (Achleitner et al., 2019). Based on primary four-digit SIC codes, 55.8 % of the firms in the sample belong to the manufacturing industry and 29.5 % to the service industry[48]. While regression models already control for firm-specific fixed effects in working capital management, Table 2.10 in the Appendix estimates regression models specifically for the largest industries in the sample (analogous to Shin and Soenen, 1998). Models 3–5 further account for the cases that the manufacturing, or the service, or both industries are excluded from the model. The increase in CCC due to additional family managers on the executive board remains significant at least on a 10 %-level throughout four of five models. Model 4 demonstrates, that the positive influence on the CCC is driven by non-service firms, consistently no significant effect is observable when solely considering service firms. Furthermore, as previously shown, the share of family ownership remains insignificant in all industries.

Fourthly, firm size may affect the governance influence of families: Companies listed in the German CDAX in general and family and non-family firms in particular differ significantly in size (Ampenberger et al., 2013), as family ownership decreases with size (Faccio and Lang, 2002). As presented in Table 2.1 (and Table 2.6 in the Appendix), family-influenced firms in the sample are significantly smaller. While previous models do not support a general size effect on the CCC, the question arises whether family members might have an increased leverage on working capital management in smaller firms. Table 2.11 in the Appendix presents results on a sample split alongside median firm size. As Model 1 shows, the family management influence on the CCC is only significant in firms below the sample median size (mEUR 193.6 of revenue). This finding is

48 Branches and industries are not identified on a more fine-graded level because the number of firms would be insufficient for statistically reliable regression estimations.

robust on the other median size measures such as market capitalization (model 3) and total assets (model 5) and also holds for DIO (not reported).

## 2.7 Conclusion

This article contributes to the literature by being among the first to investigate differences in working capital management across family and non-family firms, particularly in Germany. A detailed measure of family influence via ownership, executive board, and supervisory board is provided in order to analyze the means of determination against the backdrop of the specifics of the German corporate governance system. Understanding working capital management in family firms is of crucial importance in Germany as (1) it may increase shareholder value (Shin and Soenen, 1998) and corporate profitability (Meyer and Lüdtke, 2006; Wöhrmann et al., 2012); (2) these firms are regarded to embody the backbone of the country's economy active in working capital-intense sectors (Gottschalk et al., 2019; Achleitner et al., 2019), and (3) effective working capital management can serve as an important source of internal financing (Richards and Laughlin, 1980) in Germany's bank-based financial system.

The empirical models employ a sample of 278 listed firms in Germany from 2000 to 2013. While financial data is retrieved from a database, ownership and governance data is manually collected on a single board-position level. The results reveal that family firms exhibit a significantly longer CCC than non-family firms. Specifically, regression models show that in terms of working capital efficiency, not family ownership, but the involvement of family members and the share of family managers in the executive board is crucial in increasing the CCC. A theoretical explanation for these results is Germany's specific corporate governance system in which shareholders' influences on management are limited. If family ownership matters in terms of shareholder incentives, decision horizons, or just the level of professionalization on financial issues among shareholding family members, the degree of family involvement in management is a crucial factor regarding working capital management in family firms.

Results show that the longer CCC is primarily driven by more DIO (i.e. slower inventory turnover in family-managed companies). The absence of significant differences in total inventory levels between family- and non-family firms suggests that the reason for higher DIO, however, is more lack of professionalization and less due to the assumed risk aversion of families. While no effect on the days sales outstanding (DSO) is observable, the models provide limited results that family management involvement may also increase days payables outstanding (DPO), for example, through more lenient credit terms of suppliers. The latter would be in line with the avoidance of additional external financing by family firms and the superior stakeholder management towards suppliers suggested by the literature. In summary, results further suggest that due to the higher equity ratio of family firms, they may face reduced pressure to tackle inefficiencies in working capital handling.

The findings of this article are relevant for future research as they demonstrate that the degree of family management involvement is a key determinant in the management of working capital. On the other side, the influence of plain family ownership on day-to-day management decisions appears to be limited. Challenges in collecting high-resolution governance data necessary for empirical analyses might explain the relatively low number of publications on working capital practices in family firms. This study is important for future research as it demonstrates that time-costly hand-collection of differentiated governance data on family firms can provide additional insights on operative aspects of corporate management in these firms. It finds that specifically in the case of working capital management the presence of family managers is a crucial driver of firm performance. Hence, with regards to the family business definition dilemma (Mazzi, 2011), the results demand caution in applying plain ownership definitions for family firms when studying current asset management practices. It is highly demanded to enhance controlling for family members in management positions in future publications.

This study has some limitations which could provide additional opportunities for research. As it investigates listed corporations in Germany, the findings are limited to similar corporate governance systems (as, for example, in Austria) and listed family firms. Future research may hence focus on the international comparison of working capital practices in family firms to differentiate the impact of the German corporate governance framework on these findings. Furthermore, non-listed firms need to be analyzed to account for the transferability of the results to non-listed family firms. In addition, the findings on CCC-components need to be confirmed by empirically accessing the drivers of inventory and payables management in family firms.

Lastly, this article has implications for practitioners and investors in family firms. While the results that the longer CCC in family-managed firms is primarily due to a slower inventory cycle (DIO), active working capital management may offer the potential for lower operative and financing costs. Minority investors in family firms may therefore focus on potential hidden firm value in smaller, family-managed firms as optimizing inventory turnover, in particular, has been shown by previous studies to positively influence firm profitability in Germany.

## 2.8 Appendix

**Table 2.6:** Summary Statistics and Differences in Means by Firm Ownership

| | Family Firms (25 %) | | | Non-family Firms | | | Diff | |
|---|---|---|---|---|---|---|---|---|
| | **Mean** | **Median** | **N** | **Mean** | **Median** | **N** | **Mean** | **Median** |
| CCC | 97.03 | 85.84 | 1344 | 94.49 | 85.06 | 1234 | n.s. | n.s. |
| DIO | 92.99 | 79.46 | 1350 | 89.39 | 75.75 | 1244 | n.s. | n.s. |
| DSO | 67.12 | 58.66 | 1513 | 63.60 | 56.62 | 1334 | ** | * |
| DPO | 69.99 | 46.26 | 1505 | 65.07 | 46.02 | 1317 | n.s. | n.s. |
| ExBo Size | 3.06 | 3.00 | 1478 | 3.62 | 3.00 | 1298 | *** | *** |
| SupBo Size | 5.77 | 4.00 | 1475 | 8.47 | 6.00 | 1289 | *** | *** |
| Mcap | 1520.42 | 97.39 | 1360 | 4323.03 | 228.62 | 1117 | *** | *** |
| DebtEqu | 0.76 | 0.38 | 1365 | 0.851 | 0.47 | 1169 | n.s. | *** |
| Age | 49.17 | 27.00 | 1558 | 62.708 | 36.00 | 1378 | *** | *** |
| ROA | 0.04 | 0.04 | 1505 | 0.028 | 0.03 | 1307 | ** | *** |
| CF | 0.02 | 0.02 | 1454 | 0.012 | 0.02 | 1239 | n.s. | * |
| Growth | 0.10 | 0.05 | 1501 | 0.089 | 0.05 | 1301 | n.s. | n.s. |
| PPE | 0.19 | 0.17 | 1526 | 0.201 | 0.16 | 1335 | n.s. | n.s. |

This table presents the summary statistics for the variables employed in the main regression models (pooled). A definition of all variables can be found in the Appendix. Significance of differences is based on the t-test (means) as well as the Wilcoxon/Mann-Whitney test (median). Significance of differences at the 10 %, 5 % and 1 % levels is indicated by *, ** and ***, respectively.

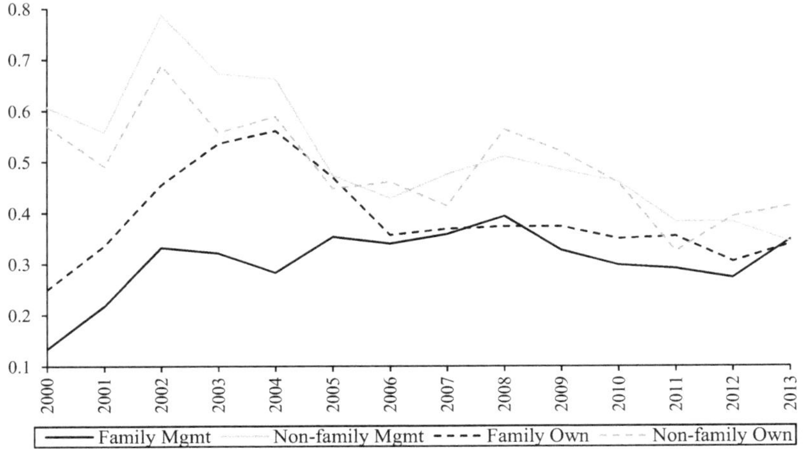


**Figure 2.2:** Debt-Equity-Ratio (Median by Year)

This graph presents the annual median debt-to-equity-ratio by ownership (min. 25 % blocking minority held by families) and family management presence (Dummy) in executive boards.

**Table 2.7:** Pierson/Spearman Correlation Matrix

| | (1) | (2) | (3) | (4) | (5) | (6) | (7) | (8) | (9) | (10) | (11) | (12) | (13) | (14) | (15) | (16) | (17) | (18) | (19) | (20) | (21) | (22) | (23) |
|---|---|---|---|---|---|---|---|---|---|---|---|---|---|---|---|---|---|---|---|---|---|---|---|
| (1) CCC | | 0.799* | 0.373* | 0.044 | 0.1* | 0.092* | 0.095* | -0.134* | 0.097* | -0.09* | -0.01 | -0.158* | -0.062* | 0.014 | 0.085* | -0.118* | -0.121* | -0.121* | 0.123* | 0.031 | -0.114* | -0.014 | -0.029 |
| (2) DIO | 0.819* | | 0.074* | 0.358* | 0.123* | 0.058* | 0.056* | -0.067* | 0.101* | -0.011 | 0.016 | -0.104* | -0.06* | -0.001 | -0.054* | -0.077* | -0.027 | -0.039 | 0.199* | 0.01 | -0.101* | -0.028 | 0.131* |
| (3) DSO | 0.353* | 0.085* | | 0.302* | 0.042 | 0.069* | 0.092* | -0.095* | 0.001 | -0.072* | -0.054* | -0.1* | -0.007 | 0.052* | 0.136* | -0.119* | -0.105* | -0.147* | -0.146* | -0.099* | -0.108* | 0.022 | -0.351* |
| (4) DPO | -0.12* | 0.269* | 0.267* | | 0.154* | 0.021 | 0.031 | 0.115* | -0.023 | 0.119* | -0.038 | -0.015 | -0.023 | 0.046* | -0.111* | -0.018 | 0.149* | -0.001 | 0.021 | -0.124* | -0.086* | 0.009 | -0.08* |
| (5) TWC | 0.049* | 0.049* | -0.001 | -0.034 | | -0.345* | -0.381* | 0.559* | -0.052* | 0.556* | -0.224* | -0.096* | 0.105* | 0.093* | -0.188* | 0.217* | 0.855* | 0.222* | 0.464* | 0.189* | 0.051* | 0.042 | 0.196* |
| (6) Exec Fam (Dum) | 0.082* | 0.057* | 0.108* | 0.017 | -0.344* | | 0.974* | -0.162* | 0.047* | -0.289* | 0.351* | -0.098* | -0.082* | -0.168* | 0.089* | -0.111* | -0.342* | -0.134* | -0.171* | -0.053* | -0.102* | 0.059* | -0.131* |
| (7) Exec Fam (%) | 0.083* | 0.08* | 0.128* | 0.071* | -0.374* | 0.841* | | -0.247* | 0.047* | -0.324* | 0.339* | -0.1* | -0.095* | -0.165* | 0.088* | -0.106* | -0.386* | -0.114* | -0.192* | -0.072* | -0.11* | 0.053* | -0.147* |
| (8) ExBo Size | -0.142* | -0.118* | -0.096* | -0.038 | 0.589* | -0.195* | -0.304* | | -0.076* | 0.425* | -0.153* | -0.002 | 0.092* | 0.058* | -0.079* | 0.206* | 0.612* | 0.05* | 0.127* | 0.092* | 0.067* | 0.066* | 0.102* |
| (9) Sup Fam (%) | 0.075* | 0.052* | 0.003 | -0.04 | -0.135* | 0.034 | 0.075* | -0.111* | | -0.051* | 0.399* | -0.152* | -0.114* | -0.134* | -0.032 | -0.104* | -0.078* | -0.006 | 0.115* | 0.062* | 0.003 | -0.013 | 0.084* |
| (10) SupBo Size | -0.155* | -0.084* | -0.134* | 0.018 | 0.625* | -0.314* | -0.327* | 0.566* | -0.213* | | -0.248* | 0.015 | 0.137* | 0.064* | -0.139* | 0.278* | 0.511* | 0.207* | 0.287* | 0.043 | 0.02 | -0.035 | 0.214* |
| (11) Family (%) | 0.019 | 0.036 | -0.064* | -0.029 | -0.216* | 0.339* | 0.283* | -0.183* | 0.351* | -0.283* | | -0.294* | -0.15* | -0.266* | 0.013 | -0.193* | -0.217* | -0.081* | -0.028 | 0.075* | 0.014 | -0.015 | 0.04 |
| (12) Corporation (%) | -0.104* | -0.076* | -0.081* | 0.007 | -0.073* | -0.104* | -0.098* | -0.016 | -0.115* | -0.012 | -0.296* | | -0.014 | -0.082* | -0.007 | 0.047* | -0.032 | 0.07* | 0.101* | -0.087* | -0.065* | 0.006 | 0.113* |
| (13) Bank (%) | -0.061* | -0.071* | -0.016 | -0.007 | 0.103* | -0.065* | -0.088* | 0.196* | -0.097* | 0.181* | -0.128* | -0.041 | | 0.145* | 0.043 | 0.117* | 0.102* | 0.066* | -0.037 | -0.05* | -0.009 | 0.004 | 0.043 |
| (14) Finance (%) | -0.012 | -0.008 | -0.001 | 0.001 | 0.08* | -0.177* | -0.161* | 0.034 | -0.16* | 0.111* | -0.287* | -0.099* | 0.075* | | -0.012 | 0.048* | 0.041 | 0.063* | -0.063* | -0.076* | -0.014 | -0.026 | -0.089* |
| (15) Employee (%) | 0.04 | -0.055* | 0.122* | -0.064* | -0.121* | 0.064* | 0.033 | -0.016 | -0.059* | -0.078* | -0.079* | -0.039 | 0.01 | -0.028 | | -0.048* | -0.158* | -0.195* | -0.191* | -0.024 | 0.031 | 0.031 | -0.217* |
| (16) Government (%) | -0.092* | -0.08* | -0.092* | -0.03 | 0.191* | -0.107* | -0.091* | 0.225* | -0.08* | 0.379* | -0.165* | 0.027 | 0.121* | 0.053* | -0.035 | | 0.224* | 0.136* | -0.008 | -0.107* | -0.05* | 0.001 | 0.016 |
| (17) MCap | -0.14* | -0.077* | -0.129* | -0.004 | 0.867* | -0.349* | -0.401* | 0.631* | -0.134* | 0.608* | -0.199* | -0.033 | 0.125* | 0.047* | -0.13* | 0.21* | | 0.056* | 0.35* | 0.344* | 0.156* | 0.13* | 0.189* |
| (18) DebtEqu | -0.073* | -0.049* | -0.071* | -0.008 | 0.071* | -0.006 | 0.026 | 0.057* | -0.017 | 0.064* | -0.046 | 0.018 | 0.058* | 0.069* | -0.033 | 0.11* | -0.046 | | 0.225* | -0.215* | -0.132* | -0.094* | 0.329* |
| (19) Age | 0.095* | 0.126* | -0.167* | -0.123* | 0.447* | -0.17* | -0.185* | 0.094* | 0.031 | 0.287* | -0.006 | 0.144* | -0.081* | -0.037 | -0.109* | 0.008 | 0.331* | 0.036 | | 0.096* | 0.024 | -0.092* | 0.402* |
| (20) ROA | -0.007 | -0.029 | -0.138* | -0.167* | 0.193* | -0.052* | -0.1* | 0.073* | 0.053* | 0.027 | 0.063* | -0.069* | -0.049* | -0.061* | -0.013 | -0.052* | 0.326* | -0.115* | 0.101* | | 0.279* | 0.331* | 0.07* |
| (21) CF | -0.112* | -0.121* | -0.177* | -0.158* | 0.049* | -0.083* | -0.089* | 0.043 | 0.003 | 0.011 | -0.01 | -0.015 | 0.024 | 0.032 | 0.009 | -0.059* | 0.094* | -0.03 | 0.075* | 0.239* | | -0.059* | -0.062* |
| (22) Growth | -0.049* | -0.032 | 0.015 | 0.029 | -0.047* | 0.092* | 0.056* | 0.025 | 0 | -0.061* | 0.027 | -0.049* | 0.003 | -0.029 | 0.003 | -0.003 | 0.009 | -0.051* | -0.139* | 0.16* | -0.142* | | -0.054* |
| (23) PPE | -0.129* | 0.006 | -0.35* | -0.013 | 0.062* | -0.121* | -0.131* | 0.016 | 0.024 | 0.175* | 0.032 | 0.175* | 0.015 | -0.084* | -0.1* | 0.062* | 0.083* | 0.064* | 0.344* | 0.045 | -0.003 | -0.071* | |

This table presents Pierson (lower half) and Spearman (upper half) correlation coefficients. Significance at the 5 % level is indicated by *.

**Table 2.8:** Average Cash Conversion Cycle / CCC-Components (Supervisory Board)

| | (1) Avg. CCC | (2) Avg. CCC | (3) Avg. CCC | (4) Avg. DIO | (5) Avg. DSO | (6) Avg. DPO |
|---|---|---|---|---|---|---|
| Sup Family (%) | 33.27** | | 40.25*** | 3.088 | 0.295 | -11.64 |
| | (13.51) | | (14.65) | (21.24) | (11.82) | (11.34) |
| SuF(%) X Exec(Dum) | | 64.57*** | | | | |
| | | (13.64) | | | | |
| Exec Family (%) | | | 46.18*** | 36.34** | 9.237 | 20.74** |
| | | | (16.25) | (17.95) | (10.90) | (8.59) |
| Family (%) | 16.75* | 17.66* | 13.35 | 12.93 | -6.135 | 9.039 |
| | (9.36) | (9.35) | (8.90) | (10.61) | (6.55) | (7.88) |
| Corporation (%) | 15.51 | 16.95 | 17.05 | 14.55 | -14.75** | -3.711 |
| | (10.89) | (10.94) | (11.56) | (14.50) | (7.10) | (7.47) |
| Bank (%) | -10.55 | -11.25 | -13.54 | -44.39 | 1.424 | -15.68 |
| | (53.30) | (53.72) | (53.32) | (42.03) | (18.28) | (21.86) |
| Finance (%) | -0.370 | -0.126 | -0.539 | 16.07 | -12.51** | 6.507 |
| | (13.76) | (13.95) | (13.49) | (11.13) | (6.03) | (8.35) |
| Employees (%) | 7.919 | 11.43 | -4.435 | 37.39 | -41.68 | 5.405 |
| | (31.33) | (30.71) | (32.24) | (40.09) | (33.86) | (23.78) |
| Government (%) | 21.80 | 24.92 | 32.09 | 15.99 | 26.18 | -20.51 |
| | (30.05) | (29.60) | (29.02) | (30.10) | (53.19) | (36.79) |
| Exec Board Size | | | 2.390* | 0.747 | 1.047 | -0.126 |
| | | | (1.36) | (1.08) | (0.83) | (0.77) |
| Sup Board Size | 1.739*** | 1.541** | 1.547** | 1.822*** | -0.0627 | -0.217 |
| | (0.66) | (0.63) | (0.65) | (0.68) | (0.43) | (0.42) |
| R2 | 0.0475 | 0.0538 | 0.0661 | 0.0968 | 0.138 | 0.0911 |
| R2 (adj.) | 0.0399 | 0.0463 | 0.0576 | 0.0887 | 0.130 | 0.0832 |
| N | 1893 | 1891 | 1891 | 1910 | 2030 | 1957 |
| Controls | YES | YES | YES | YES | YES | YES |
| FE | YES | YES | YES | YES | YES | YES |
| Robust | YES | YES | YES | YES | YES | YES |

This table presents the regression results of the CCC-components (CCC) fixed effects regression models. Models apply robust standard errors, include a constant and cover the period from 2000 to 2013. Standard errors are presented in parentheses. Significance at the 10 %, 5 %, and 1 % levels is indicated by *, **, and ***, respectively.

**Table 2.9:** Cash Conversion Cycle (CEO/Founder/Chairman Influence)

| | (1)<br>CCC | (2)<br>CCC | (3)<br>CCC | (4)<br>CCC | (5)<br>CCC |
|---|---|---|---|---|---|
| Family CEO | 14.62 | -2.121 | | | |
| | (10.18) | (12.02) | | | |
| Founder CEO | | | 13.44 | | |
| | | | (15.18) | | |
| Founder Inv | | | | 20.72 | |
| | | | | (12.88) | |
| Sup Family Chair | | | | | 11.81 |
| | | | | | (8.44) |
| Exec Family (%) | | 55.27** | | | |
| | | (25.31) | | | |
| Family (%) | 29.02 | 28.30 | 29.20 | 28.63 | 31.06 |
| | (23.73) | (23.68) | (23.90) | (23.73) | (23.66) |
| Corporation (%) | 25.65* | 28.34* | 25.71* | 25.59* | 25.60 |
| | (15.41) | (15.43) | (15.50) | (15.47) | (15.57) |
| Bank (%) | 14.08 | 15.40 | 13.45 | 8.590 | 22.28 |
| | (58.32) | (59.87) | (58.45) | (58.52) | (56.62) |
| Finance (%) | 8.823 | 9.858 | 8.861 | 8.416 | 10.26 |
| | (14.94) | (14.70) | (14.84) | (14.81) | (15.10) |
| Employees (%) | 25.08 | 27.26 | 28.04 | 23.87 | 28.87 |
| | (38.22) | (37.98) | (38.58) | (39.00) | (37.96) |
| Government (%) | 39.59 | 46.71 | 39.61 | 43.30 | 31.10 |
| | (52.09) | (50.62) | (52.00) | (50.55) | (53.19) |
| Exec Board Size | 2.142 | 3.168** | 2.292 | 2.217 | |
| | (1.49) | (1.53) | (1.52) | (1.47) | |
| Sup Board Size | | | | | 1.383* |
| | | | | | (0.71) |
| R2 | 0.0330 | 0.0457 | 0.0313 | 0.0351 | 0.0318 |
| R2 (adj.) | 0.0254 | 0.0378 | 0.0237 | 0.0275 | 0.0242 |
| N | 1942 | 1942 | 1938 | 1942 | 1924 |
| Controls | YES | YES | YES | YES | YES |
| FE | YES | YES | YES | YES | YES |
| Robust | YES | YES | YES | YES | YES |

This table presents the regression results of the cash conversion cycle (CCC) fixed effects regression models on board-lead positions. Models apply robust standard errors, include a constant and cover the period from 2000 to 2013. Standard errors are presented in parentheses. Significance at the 10 %, 5 %, and 1 % levels is indicated by *, **, and ***, respectively.

**Table 2.10:** Cash Conversion Cycle by Largest Industries (Executive Board)

| | (1) Manu | (2) Serv | (3) Non-Manu | (4) Non-Serv | (5) Non-Manu/ Serv |
|---|---|---|---|---|---|
| Exec Family (%) | 58.71*(30.48) | 31.57(30.27) | 47.06**(23.54) | 69.40***(24.49) | 86.48**(33.80) |
| Family (%) | 33.47(30.95) | -2.338(26.11) | 11.86(26.35) | 37.60(26.26) | 30.44(48.50) |
| Exec Board Size | 2.457(1.67) | 5.922*(3.20) | 5.675*(3.01) | 2.573(1.75) | 4.859(4.96) |
| R2 | 0.0625 | 0.0887 | 0.104 | 0.0669 | 0.197 |
| R2 (adj.) | 0.0505 | 0.0563 | 0.0854 | 0.0575 | 0.157 |
| N | 1186 | 438 | 756 | 1504 | 318 |
| FE | YES | YES | YES | YES | YES |
| Robust | YES | YES | YES | YES | YES |
| Ownership | YES | YES | YES | YES | YES |
| Controls | YES | YES | YES | YES | YES |

This table presents the regression results of the cash conversion cycle (CCC) fixed effects regression models by industry. Models apply robust standard errors, include a constant and cover the period from 2000 to 2013. Standard errors are presented in parentheses. Significance at the 10 %, 5 %, and 1 % levels is indicated by *, **, and ***, respectively.

**Table 2.11:** Cash Conversion Cycle by Median Size (Executive Board)

| | (1) | (2) | (3) | (4) | (5) | (6) |
|---|---|---|---|---|---|---|
| | **Revenue** | | **Market Capitalization** | | **Total Assets** | |
| | **<Median** | **≥Median** | **<Median** | **≥Median** | **<Median** | **≥Median** |
| Exec Family (%) | 81.41*** | 14.77 | 61.65** | 31.51 | 75.75** | 27.39 |
| | (28.91) | (13.08) | (29.50) | (23.51) | (29.11) | (22.19) |
| Family (%) | 47.48 | 4.342 | 51.12 | 16.19 | 41.32 | 21.42 |
| | (44.23) | (8.90) | (43.80) | (10.42) | (48.38) | (14.25) |
| Exec Board Size | 8.289** | 1.358 | 8.120** | 1.325 | 5.102* | 1.243 |
| | (3.77) | (1.14) | (3.90) | (1.21) | (2.93) | (1.38) |
| R2 | 0.0978 | 0.0727 | 0.106 | 0.0605 | 0.0825 | 0.0536 |
| R2 (adj.) | 0.0797 | 0.0608 | 0.0886 | 0.0481 | 0.0638 | 0.0415 |
| N | 763 | 1179 | 798 | 1144 | 754 | 1188 |
| FE | YES | YES | YES | YES | YES | YES |
| Robust | YES | YES | YES | YES | YES | YES |
| Ownership | YES | YES | YES | YES | YES | YES |
| Controls | YES | YES | YES | YES | YES | YES |

This table presents the regression results of the cash conversion cycle (CCC) fixed effects regression models of the sample split by size. Models apply robust standard errors and cover the period from 2000 to 2013. Standard errors are presented in parentheses. Significance at the 10 %, 5 %, and 1 % levels is indicated by *, **, and ***, respectively.

**Table 2.12:** Definition of Variables

| Variable | Definition |
|---|---|
| CCC | DIO + DSO – DPO |
| DIO | Inventory / Cost of Goods Sold + 365 |
| DSO | Accounts Receivable / Total Revenue * 365 |
| DPO | Accounts Payable / Cost of Goods Sold + 365 |
| Avg. CCC | Avg. DIO + Avg. DSO – Avg. DPO |
| Avg. DIO | ((Inventory(t) + Inventory(t-1)) / 2) / Cost of Goods Sold * 365 |
| Avg. DSO | ((Accounts Receivable(t) + Accounts Receivable(t-1)) /2) / Total Revenue * 365 |
| Avg. DPO | ((Accounts Payable(t) + Accounts Payable(t-1)) /2) / (Cost of Goods Sold – Inventory(t-1) + Inventory(t)) * 365 |
| Exec Family (Dum) | Dummy variable that take the value of 1 when a family member belongs to the executive board |
| Exec Family (%) | Number of family members on the executive board divided by the number of executive board members |
| Sup Family (%) | Number of family members on the supervisory board divided by the number of supervisory board members |
| SuF(%) X Exec(Dum) | Sup Family (%) * Exec Family (Dum) |
| Family (%) | Cumulative percentage of voting rights held by families (excl. family foundations or family offices) |
| Corporation (%) | Cumulative percentage of voting rights held by corporations |
| Bank (%) | Cumulative percentage of voting rights held by banks |
| Finance (%) | Cumulative percentage of voting rights held by other financial institutions |
| Employees (%) | Cumulative percentage of voting rights held by employees |
| Government (%) | Cumulative percentage of voting rights held by governments |
| Exec Board Size | Number of executive board members |
| Sup Board Size | Number of supervisory board members |
| MCap | Natural logarithm of the Last close shares outstanding * Last Close Price |
| DebtEqu | Total debt (excl. current/other liabilities) / Total equity |
| Age | Natural logarithm of the observation year minus the year of foundation |
| ROA | EBIT / ((Total Assets(t) + Total Assets(t-1)) /2) |
| CF | Levered Free Cash Flow / Total Revenues |
| Growth | Total Revenue(t) / Total Revenue(t-1) – 1 |
| PPE | Natural logarithm of Net Property, Plant and Equipment |

This table presents the definitions of the model employed in the general regression models. Variables employed in robustness models are described in the respective section.

# 3 The Influence of Family Board Involvement on Earnings Management

**Abstract***: This study explores the influence of family ownership and family board involvement on earnings management in German-listed firms. We extend existing research by applying a more precise measurement of family involvement that offers new insights into a family's effect on earnings management behavior. Our models suggest that the degree of management involvement of families is a significant driver of earnings management, a factor disregarded so far in the literature. Furthermore, the distinction between founding family and family ownership should be carefully considered. Employing a sample of 278 firms from 2000 to 2013, we find that greater family management presence on the executive board is associated with more earnings-decreasing accrual-based earnings management practices and more real earnings management activities via discretionary expenses. This is viewed as less value-destroying REM activity to meet earning targets. Overall, German family firms seem to use their powerful positions as shareholders and executive board members to expropriate shareholders and manage earnings to meet targets while maintaining family wealth.

## 3.1 Introduction

Top executives often use their managerial discretion to influence the reported earnings of their companies. The motives underlying earnings management decisions are quite varied and mostly rooted in agency conflicts that arise from the separation of ownership and control in widely held firms. The most common reasons cited in the extant literature are to obtain private benefits, reduce earnings variability (i.e. income smoothing), avoid covenant violations,

---

* This article is published in *Corporate Ownership and Control*, Vol. 18 No. 2, Franzoi, F., Mietzner, M. and Thelemann, F., The Influence of Family Board Involvement on Earnings Management, 106–123, Copyright: Franzoi, F., Mietzner, M. and Thelemann, F. (2021).

The article was presented at the 9th International Research Meeting in Business and Management 2018, Nice (France) as well as the 56th Annual Meeting of the Academy of Economics and Finance 2019, St. Petersburg, Florida (USA) and won the best PhD-Paper competition in finance at the latter. We are grateful to the participants of both conferences for many helpful suggestions.

or simply influence contractual provisions that depend on reported earnings (see, e.g. Healy and Wahlen, 1999)[49].

A concentrated ownership structure and the presence of large blockholders who have the incentive and the ability to monitor top executives are usually the most effective ways to reduce these types of agency problems between managers and owners (Shleifer and Vishny, 1986; Jensen and Meckling, 1976). However, major equity holdings by single investors can also create incentives to expropriate wealth from minority shareholders (Fama and Jensen, 1983; Morck et al., 1988; Shleifer and Vishny, 1997; Burkart et al., 2003). Ample evidence for the expropriation of outside investors comes from continental Europe, where dispersed ownership structures are less common, and firms tend to be controlled and managed by at least one dominant family[50]. Fan and Wong (2002), Leuz et al. (2003), and Ali et al. (2007), among others, document that family owners may try to influence financial reporting in order to mislead minority shareholders about earnings.

Given the dominance of family firms in continental Europe, it is not surprising that various studies have sought to disentangle the relation between family ownership and the earnings decision process (Prencipe and Bar-Yosef, 2011; Bhaumik and Gregoriou, 2010; Gomez-Mejia et al., 2014). Prior literature on earnings management and family ownership revealed significant differences between family and non-family firms in terms of earnings quality (Wang, 2006; Ali et al., 2007). However, the contradictory empirical results regarding a family's ability to influence reported earnings call for a deeper understanding of the mechanisms behind earnings management in family firms (Cascino et al., 2010; Prencipe, Bar-Yosef and Dekker, 2014).

Any potential influence individual stakeholders have on managerial decisions to protect their interests also requires considering the pertinent corporate governance system. Germany, for example, mandates a two-tiered board system for publicly listed firms. It consists of an executive board of inside directors, led by the CEO and responsible for the company's day-to-day operations, and

---

49 See, for example, Healy (1985), Dechow and Sloan (1991), Holthausen et al. (1995), and Guidry et al. (1999) on seeking private benefits; Trueman and Titman (1988), Hand (1989), and Myers et al. (2007) on reducing earnings variability, i.e., income smoothing; and Dechow et al. (1996), DeFond and Jiambalvo (1994), Sweeney (1994), and Jaggi and Lee (2002) on avoiding covenant violations.

50 Faccio and Lang (2002) and Becht and Boehmer (2003), among others, document that concentrated ownership structures with one or a few dominant, controlling shareholders are prevalent in many continental European countries.

a supervisory board with outside directors (i.e. shareholder, debtholder, and employee representatives) who are responsible for overseeing the executive board (Gorton and Schmid, 2000; Rieckers and Spindler, 2004). This institutional setting provides managers with significant leeway in running their businesses because they report solely to the supervisory boards. Nevertheless, both boards are involved in the determination of corporate actions (Rieckers and Spindler, 2004), so board members are generally able to affect firms' earnings decisions.

In contrast, and unlike in the US, shareholders cannot exercise direct control over top executives in Germany. Instead, according to the co-determination concept, they elect half the members of the supervisory board, which limits shareholder influence at annual meetings. Families have a "natural" interest in monitoring and influencing management and its decisions (Demsetz and Lehn, 1985). Thus, the German corporate governance system provides them with ample opportunities to either (1) directly influence reported earnings by actively participating in executive boards, or (2) exercising influence and control indirectly via voting rights or supervisory board membership[51].

We argue that focusing on the impact of ownership on company policies and management decisions in Germany will provide ambiguous results. Against the backdrop of German corporate governance, we propose instead to control explicitly for the different forms of family influence via ownership, management, and supervision when studying earnings management in family firms. Therefore, to increase the understanding of the impact of family influence on earnings management in German-listed family firms, we address the following research question:

How does the level of family ownership and involvement in the executive and supervisory board, i.e. the overall family influence, affect earnings management?

To the best of our knowledge, no prior study on earnings management in family firms has focused specifically on the various elements of the German corporate governance system and how they are interrelated. Therefore, we find it worthwhile to analyze the precise measures of family influence in Germany, as well as the effects of (1) concentrated ownership structures with heterogeneous blockholders, and (2) the stake of (founding) families in management and supervisory boards on corporate earnings decisions.

---

51 Family investment portfolios are often poorly diversified, with an overly large equity portion invested in their own firm (Anderson and Reeb, 2003a). Thus, families have a strong interest in influencing corporate decisions and managing for their own interests.

For this study, we construct a hand-collected panel dataset to explore the economic effects of how the ownership, management, and supervisory board involvement of families influence earnings decisions. We use a unique and comprehensive sample of 278 firms for the 2000–2013 period (2,936 firm-year observations), from which we can track all unique blockholders and their membership on the executive or supervisory boards among large German public firms. The results confirm our expectations.

First, family firms engage in earnings management, and family management presence is a key determinant of this phenomenon. Family management is associated with more earnings- decreasing accrual-based earnings management (ABEM) practices, and also leads to more real earnings management (REM) of discretionary expenses. Second, we find that families use their powerful positions as shareholders and executive board members to manage earnings by discretionary accruals and expenses. This is potentially done to reduce dividend pressure and avoid negative market reactions for not meeting earning targets. It also protects future family wealth.

We contribute to the literature by extending prior results along several dimensions. First, as we note earlier, this paper is the first to study the potential instruments through which families pursue their interests within the context of the German corporate governance system. It is these distinct features that set our results apart from those of Anglo-American countries.

Second, we follow the suggestions of earlier studies that called for greater understanding of the influence of blockholders (García-Meca and Sánchez-Ballesta, 2009) and family members on the executive board (Hutton, 2007; Jaggi et al., 2009; Salvato and Moores, 2010). Prior work on earnings management and family firms approached family influence by (1) applying dummy variables to control for family CEOs (Wang, 2006; Ali et al., 2007; Prencipe and Bar-Yosef, 2011; Achleitner et al., 2014), (2) labelling boards as overly family-controlled (Jaggi et al., 2009), or (3) counting the number of family members in C-suite roles (Ferramosca and Allegrini, 2018). We address the concerns raised in the literature by providing a thorough analysis of the specific effects of different levels of family control by explicitly considering the proportion of family members on the (1) management and (2) supervisory boards, and their attributed (3) voting rights (ownership stake)[52].

---

52 Our data collection approach follows the latest call for the identification and consideration of the family ties of individual board members (see, for example, García-Sánchez et al., 2020).

We confirm findings in existing research that management involvement of major blockholders in general, and families in particular, has consequences for the agency relations between managers and shareholders and controlling for, e.g. family and minority shareholders (Francis et al., 2005; Ali et al., 2007; Cronqvist and Fahlenbrach, 2009; Acero and Alcalde, 2016). In turn, ownership concentration and the level of separation of ownership and control (e.g. the level of family board involvement) have a significant effect on the informativeness of reported earnings (Fan and Wong, 2002).

The remainder of this paper is organized as follows. Section 2 discusses the related literature, while Section 3 introduces the data and describes the methodology of our empirical analysis. In Section 4 we present our results, Section 5 discusses them and Section 6 concludes.

## 3.2 Literature Review and Hypothesis Development

### 3.2.1 Large Shareholders, Corporate Governance, and Earnings Management

Agency conflicts in publicly listed companies can arise between both managers and shareholders (Type I) and controlling and non-controlling shareholders (Type II) (Demsetz and Lehn, 1985). The first may occur because of the separation of ownership from control and managers' incentives not to act in the interest of shareholders (Jensen and Meckling, 1976). The latter may arise when controlling shareholders seek benefits at the cost of non-controlling shareholders (Shleifer and Vishny, 1997). For example, they may attempt to influence financial reporting in order to mislead minority shareholders about earnings realities (Fan and Wong, 2002; Leuz et al., 2003; Ali et al., 2007).

Earnings and accounting information can be used to distort information asymmetries (Warfield et al., 1995; LaFond and Roychowdhury, 2008), or to overcome agency problems and align the interests of managers, shareholders, and creditors (Wang, 2006; Chen et al., 2014). On the one hand, large, actively engaged blockholders may lead to more reliable accounting earnings, because any potential opportunistic behavior is controlled by their monitoring ability (Dechow et al., 1996; Gárcia-Meca and Sánchez-Ballesta, 2009). On the other hand, greater ownership and voting rights concentration could give controlling shareholders incentives to expropriate and entrench minority shareholders (Fan and Wong, 2002; Leuz et al., 2003)[53]. Hence, ownership structure affects the supply and demand for quality financial reporting (Warfield et al., 1995; Leuz et al., 2003; Wang, 2006).

Due to the comparatively lower level of shareholder protection in civil law regimes, firms in many Continental European countries are marked by rather concentrated ownership structures with large blockholders (La Porta et al., 1999; Djankov et al., 2008). Most are controlled and/or managed by at least one dominant family (Faccio and Lang, 2002; Becht and Boehmer, 2003). Given this family firm prevalence and the increased level of earnings management caused by high ownership concentration (Leuz et al., 2003), various studies have tried to unwind the relation between family ownership and the earnings decisions process (Prencipe and Bar-Yosef, 2011; Bhaumik and Gregoriou, 2010; Gomez-Mejia et al., 2014). A somewhat contradictory picture has emerged.

For example, consider the literature on earnings management in the US Recent studies find better earnings quality and less earnings manipulation in family firms. These findings are attributable to, e.g. reduced agency problems of family firms (Wang, 2006; Ali et al., 2007; Tong, 2008; Jiraporn and Dadalt, 2009; Chen et al., 2014). However, given the stronger minority shareholder protection in the US (La Porta et al., 1998; Leuz et al., 2003), these results are not generally transferrable to continental Europe or Germany.

In contrast, family ownership in Spain has been found to be associated with better earnings quality and a lower level of earnings management (Bona-Sánchez et al., 2007). Thus, the positive aspects of family control appear to persist in the Spanish context of high ownership and voting rights concentration (Shleifer and Vishny, 1997). Similar results are obtained for Italy, a country more comparable overall to the German setting (Faccio and Lang, 2002). Cascino et al. (2010) show for Italy that earnings of family firms are of higher quality than those of non-family firms. And Prencipe and Bar-Yosef (2011) confirm that earnings management in Italy tends to be lower in family-controlled than non-family firms. The level of accrual-based earnings management in Italian family firms also appears to be related to the number of family members in C-suite positions (Ferramosca and Allegrini, 2018).

---

53 For example, La Porta et al. (1999) and Francis et al. (2005) show that concentrated ownership promotes share structures that allow for the separation of cash flow from voting rights (e.g., dual class shares).

Following Achleitner et al. (2014), we distinguish here between earnings manipulation in German family firms and specific earnings management techniques. This is important, because, relative to non-family firms, family firms avoid cash flow- effective real earnings management that might endanger their future success. Instead, they tend to engage in accrual-based earnings management – for example, as a way to avoid shareholder dividend pressure. According to Achleitner et al. (2014), this behavior is an expression of the long-term outlook of family firms to preserve future wealth and the family's control over the company.

Research on continental European firms suggests that understanding the potential influence of individual stakeholders on managerial decisions (in order to protect their interests), requires consideration of a country's specific corporate governance system (Leuz et al., 2003; Bhaumik and Gregoriou, 2010). For example, unlike the US, the UK, Switzerland, or Spain, the German corporate governance system mandates a two-tiered board system for publicly listed firms. A CEO-led executive board ("Vorstand") manages the day-to-day activities, while a supervisory board of outside directors ("Aufsichtsrat"), composed of shareholders, employee representatives, and debtholders, oversees the executive board (Gorton and Schmid, 2000; Rieckers and Spindler, 2004). Appointing the members of the supervisory board takes place at the shareholders' meeting.

Because the managers of the executive board report solely to the supervisory board, this specific setting allows for significant leeway in running the corporation. Nevertheless, both boards are involved in corporate actions (Rieckers and Spindler, 2004), and both sets of board members may affect the firm's earnings decision processes.

Some research finds that families have a greater ability to mitigate agency problems between shareholders and managers through better monitoring (Demsetz and Lehn, 1985; Ali et al., 2007). If family firms are recognized by shareholders or creditors as long-term success-oriented and poorly diversified (Anderson and Reeb, 2003a), overly reputation-sensitive (Anderson et al., 2003; Tong, 2008), or beneficial for corporate governance (Wang, 2006), the alignment effect may cause a reduced demand for better earnings quality. When the interests of minority shareholders are better aligned with those of the controlling family, the contracting terms for family firms may be less sensitive to the quality of financial information than those for non-family firms. Moreover, family firms may have fewer incentives to provide high-quality financial information (Wang, 2006).

On the other hand, Bhaumik and Gregoriou (2010) find that the presence of family firms can facilitate the shift from Type I to Type II agency problems that are already caused by weak minority shareholder rights (Leuz et al., 2003). Thus, in the German environment, we expect the entrenchment effect of family ownership to prevail for the following reasons (Becht and Boehmer, 2003).

First, the level of ownership concentration and earnings management is high (Leuz et al., 2003), and the agency conflict between controlling shareholders (including families) and minority shareholders is real (Gugler and Yurtoglu, 2003). Second, there is little inside competition for control, as most listed firms only have a small number of shareholders. Third, control thresholds drive the distribution of voting blocks[54]. Fourth, families/individuals hold the largest number of voting blocks that are larger than 5 %.

The entrenchment effect is likely to affect earnings management in two key ways. First, family shareholders may use their large power to expropriate minority shareholders and manage earnings up- or downward according to their interests[55]. In the case of Germany, this may happen, for example, to avoid dividend pressure[56] (Gugler and Yurtoglu, 2003; García Lara et al., 2005). Second, the Type II agency conflict with minority shareholders may create a strong demand for high earnings quality (Wang, 2006). At that point, the family as the controlling shareholder may be required to improve its reporting (less earnings management). This may happen, for example, to avoid potential negative consequences, such as sold shares of minority shareholders. Either way, we propose Hypothesis 1 as follows:

Hypothesis 1: Earnings management is related to family ownership.

### 3.2.2 Family Board Involvement

According to German corporate governance rules, corporate shareholders can exercise very little direct control over top executives. Because shareholders elect only half the members of the supervisory board (the

---

54 The German Securities Trade Act (WpHG) stipulates shareholding disclosure levels of 3/5/10/15/20/25/30/50 or 75 %. Company law prescribes corporate control thresholds of 25 %, 50 %, or 75 % of the voting capital outstanding.

55 We are aware that, if Type I agency conflicts dominate Type II, earnings management may be lower due to better monitoring. However, alternatively, it may be higher, since better alignment of shareholder interests reduces the demand of minority shareholders for high quality earnings. In the German setting, we assume the entrenchment effect on both supply and demand of earnings quality is dominant.

56 In different contexts, dividends may also serve as mechanisms to mitigate agency problems between controlling and minority shareholders (Faccio et al., 2001; Setia-Atmaja et al., 2009).

German concept of co-determination), their influence is limited mainly to the annual shareholder meeting. In general, they have no further rights[57].

In contrast, due to their concentration of family wealth within the family firm (Anderson and Reeb, 2003a) and their long investment horizon (Lumpkin and Brigham, 2011; Gomez-Mejia et al., 2014), families as shareholders have a natural interest and motivation in monitoring and influencing management and its decisions (Demsetz and Lehn, 1985). Therefore, through the German two-tiered board system, shareholding family members may influence earnings decisions and reporting by actively participating in executive boards or exercising influence and control indirectly via supervisory board and voting rights.

Research has found that German family firms exhibit a significant level of involvement, even in publicly listed firms (Andres, 2008; Ampenberger, 2010). Their involvement may also determine the level of alignment or – in the case of Germany – imminent entrenchment[58] between the family and minority shareholders. While increasing firms' monitoring ability, extensive family management and supervisory board presence enable and further motivate the potential entrenchment of minority shareholders.

So, on the one hand, family involvement may lead to greater earnings management of the family's interests. On the other hand, it may lead to less earnings management due to better monitoring of managers, or a higher demand for higher earnings quality by minority shareholders. Accordingly, family management involvement moderates both Types I and II agency problems and therefore affects earnings management. This leads to our Hypotheses 2a and 2b:

Hypothesis 2a: Earnings management in family firms is related to the level of family involvement in the executive board.

Hypothesis 2b: Earnings management in family firms is related to the level of family involvement in the supervisory board.

57 Para. 119 (2) of the German Stock Corporation Law ("Aktiengesetz") gives the executive board the opportunity, but not the obligation, to refer management issues and decisions to the shareholders' meeting.

58 For example, investors and the market have been found to value non-family management at a higher level than family management (Smith and Amoako-Adu, 1999). One reason is that family managers could be seen as less qualified, due to, e.g., nepotism (Lubatkin et al., 2005). Thus, transparency and firm performance are even more critical in family firms.

## 3.3 Sample Selection and Research Design

### 3.3.1 Sample

Our sample is comprised of 278 firms listed on the German Stock Exchange (CDAX), which contains all stocks listed on the General and Prime Standard of the Frankfurt Stock Exchange. We use 2000–2013 as our time frame. This ensures that the regulatory and institutional framework is stable, and not biased by significant changes in corporate governance regulations of prior years (in 1998, Germany issued two regulatory reforms affecting corporate governance and financial reporting practices, KonTraG and KapAEG). The sample excludes banks and insurance companies since these firms tend to follow their own operational logic and are governed by various financial regulations. Furthermore, our analysis only covers holdings of common shares, as we exclude preferred shares without voting rights.

The aim of our sample construction is to capture the influence of family ownership and management involvement on earnings management in Germany as precisely as possible. Our data incorporates information about shareholder structure, as well as the identity and origin of every executive and supervisory board member of every firm and year. To achieve this, we hand-collect the information using annual reports, company websites, and Bureau van Dijk's Dafne database. Financial and accounting data come from the Thomson Worldscope database.

Table 3.1 gives information on the total sample size and distribution of family firms for our sample period. We denote a firm as a family firm if the accumulated family ownership stake (voting rights) exceeds 25 %. As column 4 shows, the annual share of family firms declined from 63.90 % in 2003 to 55.21 % in 2013. On average, they account for 1,672, or 57.28 %, of our 2,936 firm-year observations. Hence, the proportion of family versus non-family firms remains fairly stable and balanced.

Column 5 shows that the average level of family ownership expanded from 53.47 % in 2000 to 57.68 % in 2013. For the pooled over time sample, families held 56.25 % of shares on average. Thus, the number of family firms decreased over 2003–2013, but their average voting rights stake increased slightly.

**Table 3.1:** Distribution of Family Firms

| Year | No. of firms | No. of family firms | Percentage of family firms | Family ownership |
|---|---|---|---|---|
| 2000 | 93 | 52 | 55.91 % | 58.21 % |
| 2001 | 116 | 67 | 57.75 % | 56.69 % |
| 2002 | 148 | 89 | 60.13 % | 57.09 % |
| 2003 | 169 | 108 | 63.90 % | 53.47 % |
| 2004 | 187 | 113 | 60.42 % | 54.43 % |
| 2005 | 211 | 127 | 60.18 % | 54.13 % |
| 2006 | 242 | 134 | 55.37 % | 54.14 % |
| 2007 | 258 | 143 | 55.42 % | 55.93 % |
| 2008 | 263 | 149 | 56.65 % | 56.15 % |
| 2009 | 262 | 146 | 55.72 % | 56.99 % |
| 2010 | 261 | 142 | 54.40 % | 57.56 % |
| 2011 | 251 | 139 | 55.37 % | 57.50 % |
| 2012 | 245 | 136 | 55.51 % | 57.53 % |
| 2013 | 230 | 127 | 55.21 % | 57.68 % |
| Total | 2936 | 1672 | 57.28 % | 56.25 % |

Notes: This table shows the time distribution of family firms and ownership shares. Family firms are identified using a measure that equals 1 if the family ownership percentage stake exceeds 25 %, and 0 otherwise. Family ownership is measured as the mean of common stock held by families in identified family firms. Total of percentage of family firms refers to the average year-on-year average of family firms.

### 3.3.2 Detecting Earnings Management

Firms manage earnings in two ways: the (legal) manipulation of accruals to affect earnings, referred to as accrual-based earnings management, or ABEM (Schipper, 1989), and real earnings manipulation, or REM (Hand, 1989; Fudenberg and Tirole, 1995; Dechow and Skinner, 2000; Roychowdhury, 2006). The first has no impact on real cash flows (e.g. changing the write-off policy of a firm); the latter directly affects cash flows (e.g. decreasing non-operational expenses, such as R&D costs). The detection of ABEM is the most commonly used method to investigate earnings management in research (Healy and Wahlen, 1999; Roychowdhury, 2006)[59]. REM has not been considered in investigating family

59 In general, firms use both methods as substitutes in different countries outside continental Europe (see, e.g., Cohen et al., 2008; Zang, 2012; and Chen et al., 2012).

firms previously. But family firms in Germany have been found to use both methods as substitutes rather than complementary (Achleitner et al., 2014).

### *3.3.2.1 Accrual-based Earnings Management*

In the financial reporting process, management is required to conduct accruals so that the firm's economic performance is clearly reflected in its financials (Dechow and Dichev, 2002). There is some discretion, for example, when deciding about the recognition and drawdown of provisions/reserves or asset write-offs (Dechow and Skinner, 2000, p. 239). These types of accruals are generally noted as discretionary or abnormal. The ability to choose how to handle these accruals gives management an opportunity to shift reported earnings in a specific direction, for example, for signaling or opportunism (Dechow, 1994). Thus, this is what we refer to as accrual-based earnings management.

To detect ABEM, we follow Wang (2006) and Achleitner et al. (2014) and use the model of Dechow and Dichev (2002), modified by Ball and Shivakumar (2005). One advantage of this approach is the increased explanatory power gained by the integration of the asymmetrical timely recognition of economic losses (Basu, 1997; Ball and Shivakumar, 2005). As a result, we can estimate the normal level of accruals for each industry-year by using the following model:

(1) Metric of ABEM:

$$\frac{ACC_t}{A_t} = \propto_0 + \propto_1 \frac{CFO_{t-1}}{A_{t-1}} + \propto_2 \frac{CFO_t}{A_t} + \propto_3 \frac{CFO_{t+1}}{A_{t+1}} + \propto_4 DCFO_t + \propto_5 DCFO_t \frac{CFO_t}{A_t} + \varepsilon_t$$

where $ACC_t$ is total accruals at time *t*, defined as income before extraordinary items less cash flow from operations at time *t*. Cash flow from operations is defined as net cash flows from operating activities less extraordinary items; $CFO_{t-1,\, t,\, t+1}$ is cash flow from operations at time *t-1, t, t+1*; $A_{t-1,\, t,\, t+1}$ is total assets at time *t-1, t, t+1*; $DCFO_t$ is an indicator that equals 1 if operating cash flow at time *t* is negative ($CFO_t - CFO_{t-1} < 0$), and 0 otherwise; and $DCFO_t{}^*CFO_t$ is a proxy for economic losses.

The residuals of equation (1) are our estimates for abnormal levels of (discretionary) accruals. We interpret more negative values, which implies that the actual observed accruals scaled by total assets are lower than the estimated industry-year specific normal level of discretionary accruals. This is evidence of more earnings-decreasing ABEM. We expect firms to have reported larger non-cash expenses within their discretion to lower net income (such as depreciation, estimates for bad debt reserves, or warranty expenses). Cash flow from operations is not affected.

#### *3.3.2.2 Real Earnings Management*

Note that ABEM only shifts the timing of earnings recognition by changing the accounting method or estimate for a specific transaction (Zang, 2012). In contrast, REM begins by adjusting real transactions (Liu et al., 2017), defined as "management actions that deviate from normal business practices, undertaken with the primary objective of meeting certain earnings thresholds" (Roychowdhury, 2006, p. 336).

Similarly to the empirical model of Achleitner et al. (2014) and the preliminary work by Roychowdhury (2006), we employ three measures to account for REM: abnormal level of cash flow from operations, abnormal level of production costs, and level of discretionary expenses. The validity of these measures has been proven in prior studies (e.g. Cohen et al., 2008; Cohen and Zarowin, 2010; Zang, 2012; Liu et al., 2017). Next, we specify these three methods of REM and their measurement in our models.

*Level of cash flow from operations*

Boosting sales before year-end closing is usually seen as a trigger for abnormal levels of cash flow from operations (Achleitner et al., 2014). Firms may offer price discounts or provide more lenient credit terms to temporarily increase sales, leading to higher current period earnings if margins are positive. However, in the current fiscal period, this will lead to a decrease in cash flows per dollar of sales. This intervention in real transactions is likely to negatively impact profitability in the next fiscal period, as sales typically drop as soon as the promotions end and the former prices and credit terms revert (Roychowdhury, 2006; Cohen and Zarowin, 2010; Achleitner et al., 2014). Following Roychowdhury (2006), the "normal" level of cash flow of operations (CFO) for each industry-year is measured by the following proxy:

(2) Normal level of CFO:

$$\frac{CFO_t}{A_{t-1}} = \alpha_0 + \alpha_1 \frac{1}{A_{t-1}} + \beta_1 \frac{S_t}{A_{t-1}} + \beta_2 \frac{\Delta S_t}{A_{t-1}} + \varepsilon_t$$

where $CFO_t$ is cash flow from operations at time $t$, defined as net cash flow from operating activities less extraordinary items; $A_{t-1}$ is lagged total assets at time $t-1$; $S_t$ is net sales at time $t$; and $\Delta S_t$ is change in net sales from time $t-1$ to time $t$ ($\Delta S_t = S_t - S_{t-1}$)

Note that we can assume earnings-increasing REM when the actual (observable) cash flow from operations is unusually low in the current period. The residual, i.e. the proxy for that abnormal level, turns negative. And this may signal that managers have accelerated sales to report higher earnings at year-end closing.

*Level of production cost*

Overproducing to lower the cost of goods sold (COGS) is another intervention used to accelerate earnings in the current period. Overproduction leads to a decline in fixed costs per unit, and thus reported COGS. As long as there are no increases in variable costs per unit, operating margins increase. The negative side effect, however, is an increase in inventory costs. This, in turn, leads to higher annual production costs relative to sales, while cash flow from operations given sales levels decrease. Because the increase in total production costs is not levelled out by a proportional increase in sales, positive abnormal levels of production costs are interpreted as evidence of earnings-increasing REM.

Consistent with prior literature, we estimate "normal" levels of production costs for each industry-year, as given in the equation below. Production costs consist of the sum of COGS and the change in inventory during the year.

(3) Normal of level of production costs:

$$\frac{PROD_t}{A_{t-1}} = \alpha_0 + \alpha_1 \frac{1}{A_{t-1}} + \beta_1 \frac{S_t}{A_{t-1}} + \beta_2 \frac{\Delta S_t}{A_{t-1}} + \beta_3 \frac{\Delta S_{t-1}}{A_{t-1}} + \varepsilon_t$$

where $PROD_t$ is production costs at time $t$, defined as the sum of $COGS_t$ and $\Delta INV_t = INV_t - INV_{t-1}$; $A_{t-1}$ is lagged total assets at time $t-1$; $S_t$ is net sales at time $t$; and $\Delta S_t$ is change in net sales from time $t-1$ to time $t$ ($\Delta S_t = S_t - S_{t-1}$).

The residuals of equation (3) are our estimates for abnormal levels of production costs. These represent the "normal" level of production costs estimated based on the year- and industry-specific coefficients, minus the actual (observed) production costs based on the firm-years' (lagged) sales and lagged assets. The more positive the values, the more earnings-increasing REM we can assume.

*Level of discretionary expenses*

A further regulating tool is discretionary or non- operating expenses, such as research and development (Baber et al., 1991; Dechow and Sloan, 1991), advertising, and selling, general, and administrative (SG&A) expenses. By cutting these expenses in the current period, cash flows increase (to the extent the discretionary expenses are paid for in cash), although future cash flows may decline (Achleitner et al., 2014; Cohen and Zarowin, 2010; Roychowdhury, 2006). We follow Roychowdhury (2006) in estimating normal levels of discretionary expenses, as a function of lagged sales scaled by lagged total assets. A function of current sales would be to bear the risk of capturing unusually low residuals in one year for a firm that has not necessarily cut discretionary expenses but has managed to increase sales in the current fiscal period. The estimation for "normal" levels of discretionary expenses for each industry-year is in equation (4).

(4) Normal level of discretionary expenses:

$$\frac{DISEXP_t}{A_{t-1}} = \alpha_0 + \alpha_1 \frac{1}{A_{t-1}} + \beta \frac{S_{t-1}}{A_{t-1}} + \varepsilon_t$$

where $DISEXP_t$ is discretionary expenses at year *t*, defined as the sum of R&D and selling, general, and administrative (SG&A) expenses (as long as SG&A expenses are available; R&D expenses are set to 0 if these items are missing, see Achleitner et al., 2014); $A_{t-1}$ is lagged total assets at time *t-1*; and $S_{t-1}$ is net sales at time *t-1*.

Abnormal level of discretionary expenses is obtained following the prior proxies for REM. Negative discretionary expenses in the current period are considered evidence of earnings-increasing REM actions. In this case, the actual (observed) level of discretionary expenses is lower than the "normal" level based on the estimated industry-year specific coefficients.

For interpretation purposes, we reverse the signs for abnormal levels of cash flows and abnormal levels of discretionary expenses. Thus, following Achleitner et al. (2014), larger (smaller) values of *REM_CFO*, *REM_PROD*, and *REM_DISC* indicate more (less) REM.

### 3.3.3 Accessing Family Influence

Family ownership is measured by the number of common shares held by family members. We, therefore, differentiate between founding families (the founder and subsequent generations), and families who did not found the company themselves but now hold a significant stake in the respective firm. For an example of founding family ownership, consider Henkel AG & Co. KGaA, founded in 1876 by Fritz Henkel. The members of the founding family still hold significant shares of the company, and are represented on the supervisory board. In contrast, BMW AG, founded in 1916, is no longer owned by the founding family. Today's largest blockholder in BMW is the Quandt/Klatten family, who began acquiring shares in the 1960s.

With respect to German corporate governance incentives, we capture shareholding families' board involvement within firms. Along with their voting power from common share holdings, families can actively and substantially influence the earnings management behavior of their firms. To obtain a specific and relative measure of family voting power on the executive board, and with respect to the German concept of co-determination on the supervisory board, we use the number of family members divided by total number of members on both boards.

### 3.3.4 Research Design

We use two models, one basic model, and one more advanced empirical model to estimate the effect of family influence on both ABEM (discretionary accruals) and REM. The basic model is in line with Achleitner et al. (2014). We add further control variables and use a random rather than a fixed effects model (as suggested by the Hausman test, which was performed over the course of our model analysis).

#### *3.3.4.1 Basic Model on Family Ownership*

To estimate the effect of family influence on discretionary accruals, we calculate:

$$\begin{aligned} ABEM_{it} = {} & \alpha_0 + \alpha_1\, FamOwn_{it} + \alpha_2\, LOSS_{it} + \alpha_3\, SIZE_{it} + \alpha_4\, GROWTH_{it} \\ & + \alpha_5\, PERF_{it} + \alpha_6\, HHI_{it} + \alpha_7\, EmplMgt_{it} + \alpha_8\, BIG4_{it} \\ & + \alpha_9\, INTACCTG_{it} + \alpha_{10}\, LEVERAGE_{it} + \alpha_{11}\, DivPayoutShs_{it} + \alpha_{12}\, LogAge_{it} \\ & + \alpha_{13}\, Crisis_{it} + \alpha_{14}\, PostCrisis_{it} + i.sic4d + \varepsilon_{it} \end{aligned}$$

$$\begin{aligned} ABEM_{it} = {} & \alpha_0 + \alpha_1\, FoundFamOwn_{it} + \alpha_2\, LOSS_{it} + \alpha_3\, SIZE_{it} + \alpha_4\, GROWTH_{it} \\ & + \alpha_5\, PERF_{it} + \alpha_6\, HHI_{it} + \alpha_7\, EmplMgt_{it} + \alpha_8\, BIG4_{it} \\ & + \alpha_9\, INTACCTG_{it} + \alpha_{10}\, LEVERAGE_{it} + \alpha_{11}\, DivPayoutShs_{it} + \alpha_{12}\, LogAge_{it} \\ & + \alpha_{13}\, Crisis_{it} + \alpha_{14}\, PostCrisis_{it} + i.sic4d + \varepsilon_{it} \end{aligned}$$

where *ABEM* is our metric for discretionary accruals; $FamOwn_{it}$ and $FoundFamOwn_{it}$ proxy for (founding) family involvement based on common shares held; $LOSS_{it}$ is a dummy variable that equals 1 if net income is less than 0; $SIZE_{it}$ is the natural logarithm of the market value of firm *i* at the end of fiscal year *t*; $GROWTH_{it}$ is change in sales for firm *i* from *t-1* to *t*; $PERF_{it}$ is net income at *t* divided by average total assets for firm *i* at *t*; $HHI_{it}$ is the sum of all squared blockholdings for firm *i* at *t*; $EmplMgt_{it}$ is firm *i*'s cumulative percentage of common shares held by management or employees that are not family members; $BIG4_{it}$ is a dummy variable that equals 1 if the firm is audited by one of the Big4 auditing companies (PwC, KPMG, Deloitte, or Ernst & Young), and 0 otherwise; $INTACCTG_{it}$ is a dummy variable that equals 1 if firm i uses US generally accepted accounting principles (GAAP) or international financial reporting standards (IFRS); $LEVERAGE_{it}$ is the leverage for firm i at time t (calculated as total liabilities scaled by total assets); $DivPayoutShs_{it}$ is the dividend payout ratio of firm *i* at *t*; $LogAge_{it}$ is the natural logarithm of firm *i*'s age at *t*, calculated as year t minus founding year; $Crisis_{it}$ controls for the years of the 2008–2009 financial crisis; $PostCrisis_{it}$ controls for the years after the financial crisis; and *i.sic4d* is the industry-dummy based on the four-digit SIC code (a list of varibales can be found in Table 3.5 in the Appendix).

We also analyze the relation between real earnings management activities and whether a firm is a family or non-family firm. This model is similar to the regression model employed for ABEM, except we do not include the control variable $BIG4_{it}$ because adjusted R-squared declined in the REM estimation models, as follows:

$$\begin{aligned} REM_{VARit} = {} & \alpha_0 + \alpha_1 FamOwn_{it} + \alpha_2 LOSS_{it} + \alpha_3 SIZE_{it} + \alpha_4 GROWTH_{it} \\ & + \alpha_5 PERF_{it} + \alpha_6 HHI_{it} + \alpha_7 EmplMgt_{it} + \alpha_8 INTACCTG_{it} \\ & + \alpha_9 LEVERAGE_{it} + \alpha_{10} DivPayoutShs_{it} + \alpha_{11} LogAge_{it} \\ & + \alpha_{12} Crisis_{it} + \alpha_{13} PostCrisis_{it} + i.sic4d + \varepsilon_{it} \end{aligned}$$

$$\begin{aligned} REM_{VARit} = {} & \alpha_0 + \alpha_1 FoundFamOwn_{it} + \alpha_2 LOSS_{it} + \alpha_3 SIZE_{it} + \alpha_4 GROWTH_{it} \\ & + \alpha_5 PERF_{it} + \alpha_6 HHI_{it} + \alpha_7 EmplMgt_{it} + \alpha_8 INTACCTG_{it} \\ & + \alpha_9 LEVERAGE_{it} + \alpha_{10} DivPayoutShs_{it} + \alpha_{11} LogAge_{it} \\ & + \alpha_{12} Crisis_{it} + \alpha_{13} PostCrisis_{it} + i.sic4d + \varepsilon_{it} \end{aligned}$$

where $REM_{VARit}$ equals the three REM metrics: $REM_{CFOit}$, $REM_{DISCit}$, and $\mathrm{REM}_{\mathrm{PRODit}}$.

In our random effects model, with robust standard errors, dummies for industry classifications (four-digit SIC code), and crisis and post-crisis years (following Höwer, 2016), we control for the following factors related to ABEM and REM: we incorporate *LOSS* and *LEVERAGE* as control variables to account for the firm-specific risk of bankruptcy. Following Albersmann and Hohenfels (2017), a negative net income (*LOSS*) could lead to more negative ("big bath" accounting) or more positive discretionary accruals (to, e.g. hide poor performance). Dyreng et al., (2012) further report a positive association between REM activities and negative net income. The results on *LEVERAGE* are mixed. More highly leveraged firms could have an incentive to engage in earnings management activities due to debt covenant constraints (DeFond and Jiambalvo, 1994; Sweeney, 1994; Roychowdhury, 2006). However, they could also face stricter monitoring by creditors and banks during financial distress, limiting their earnings management activities (Harris and Raviv, 1991).

We also include size (*SIZE*), growth (*GROWTH*), and profitability (*PERF*) in our models. Size could be positively (Lee et al., 2006; Martin et al., 2016) or negatively related to earnings management activities (Dechow and Dichev, 2002; Albersmann and Hohenfels, 2017). For growth, both Menon and Williams (2004) and Achleitner et al. (2014) find that growth firms engage in more ABEM. Roychowdhury (2006) also notes this for REM, because firms in a growth phase are especially pressured to meet earnings thresholds. In terms of firm performance, calculated as net income scaled by average total assets, Achleitner et al. (2014) find both effects, a positive association for ABEM and a negative association for REM.

To account for the effect of concentrated ownership, we incorporate the Herfindahl index (*HHI*). We also control for common stocks held by employees or management who do not belong to the family (*EmplMgt*). Here, we incorporate international accounting standards (*INTACCTG*), because tighter standards could increase the marginal benefit of REM compared to ABEM (Ewert and Wagenhofer, 2005). Note again that the dummy variable *BIG4* is only included in the ABEM model. Although Becker et al. (1998) and Ghosh et al. (2010) find a negative association with earnings management, European studies such as Maijoor and Vanstraelen (2006) and Albersmann and Hohenfels (2017) do not find any effects. Finally, we control for the dividend payout ratio (*DivPayoutShs*) and maturity of the firm (*LogAge*).

However, the focus of our Hypothesis 1 test is on the coefficient estimate of *FamOwn* and *FoundFamOwn*, which captures the relation between family firms and ABEM versus REM.

#### *3.3.4.2 Advanced Model on Family Board Involvement*

To test for Hypotheses 2, we use further variables that we will describe in this section. Following Cronqvist and Fahlenbrach (2009), we control for the ownership percentage stake of financial institutions (*FinOwn*) and other companies (*OtherCompany*), since they may also motivate management behavior on earnings management. We also control for board size (*ExBoSize, SupBoSize*), since it may affect earnings quality (García-Ramos and García-Olalla, 2011; Prencipe and Bar-Yosef, 2011). Finally, we include the relative involvement of family members on the executive (*ExBoFamRel*) or supervisory boards (*SupBoFamRel*). We assume that increased family involvement in a firm, as captured by board membership, will significantly impact its earnings management behavior.

## 3.4 Results

### 3.4.1 Descriptive Statistics

Table 3.2 presents descriptive information about the governance and firm-specific characteristics of our sample. Beginning with ownership, the descriptive statistics indicate a highly concentrated structure in family firms. Families hold on average 56.2 % of common shares, compared to 4.1 % in non-family firms. Interestingly, founding families tend to hold significant ownership stakes, 35.0 % on average within the pooled sample, compared to 1.8 % in non-family firms.

This observation is in line with the descriptive statistics in Achleitner et al. (2014). In contrast, however, we find a higher ownership concentration (*HHI*) in family firms than their counterparts in both median and mean values. Results indicate further that families in family firms are actively involved on the executive board, and to a lesser extent on the supervisory board. Thus, they have voting power due to large ownership stakes (common shares), as well as management influence due to executive or supervisory board positions.

Consistent with prior research, we find, with respect to the controlling variables, that family firms tend to be less leveraged and more profitable (Villalonga and Amit, 2006). They also exhibit higher growth (Achleitner et al., 2014). Moreover, they are significantly smaller in size, younger in firm age (Ampenberger, 2010; Achleitner et al., 2014), and are less likely to be audited by a Big 4 auditing company (Achleitner et al., 2014). Table 3.2 also indicates that family firms are more likely to pay higher dividend shares and less likely to face a loss situation.

**Table 3.2:** Summary Statistics

| | Mean | | Median | | Stand. Dev. | | Observ. | | Sig. of diff. | |
|---|---|---|---|---|---|---|---|---|---|---|
| **Variables** | **NF** | **FF** | **NF** | **FF** | **NF** | **FF** | **NF** | **FF** | **Mean** | **Med** |
| *Family Ownership* | | | | | | | | | | |
| FamOwn | 0.041 | 0.562 | 0.000 | 0.538 | 0.072 | 0.191 | 1273 | 1686 | *** | *** |
| FoundFamOwn | 0.018 | 0.350 | 0.000 | 0.389 | 0.059 | 0.278 | 1273 | 1686 | *** | **** |
| *Family Involvement* | | | | | | | | | | |
| ExBoFamRel | 0.066 | 0.258 | 0.000 | 0.200 | 0.185 | 0.320 | 1200 | 1598 | *** | *** |
| SupBoFamRel | 0.042 | 0.128 | 0.000 | 0.000 | 0.120 | 0.182 | 1186 | 1584 | *** | *** |
| *Control Variables* | | | | | | | | | | |
| LOSS | 0.192 | 0.134 | 0.000 | 0.000 | 0.394 | 0.341 | 1273 | 1686 | *** | - |
| SIZE | 12.44 | 11.83 | 12.10 | 11.49 | 2.413 | 2.107 | 1189 | 1624 | *** | *** |
| GROWTH | 0.089 | 0.106 | 0.051 | 0.052 | 0.467 | 0.574 | 1189 | 1613 | n.s. | n.s. |
| BIG4 | 0.677 | 0.533 | 1.000 | 1.000 | 0.467 | 0.499 | 1273 | 1686 | *** | - |
| PERF | 0.016 | 0.022 | 0.029 | 0.032 | 0.131 | 0.143 | 1193 | 1625 | n.s. | ** |
| HHI | 0.776 | 0.840 | 0.893 | 0.999 | 0.240 | 0.208 | 1149 | 1686 | *** | *** |
| EmplMgmt | 0.010 | 0.006 | 0.000 | 0.000 | 0.043 | 0.028 | 1273 | 1686 | *** | n.s. |
| INTACCTG | 0.835 | 0.836 | 1.000 | 1.000 | 0.370 | 0.369 | 1273 | 1686 | n.s. | - |
| LEVERAGE | 0.563 | 0.524 | 0.595 | 0.527 | 0.223 | 0.212 | 1193 | 1625 | *** | *** |
| LogAge | 3.575 | 3.467 | 3.496 | 3.367 | 1.110 | 1.029 | 1270 | 1685 | *** | ** |
| DivPayoutShs | 21.72 | 24.69 | 10.54 | 21.74 | 25.65 | 26.53 | 1098 | 1516 | *** | *** |
| ExBoSize | 3.565 | 3.142 | 3 | 3 | 1.987 | 1.454 | 1200 | 1598 | *** | *** |
| SupBoSize | 8.395 | 6.017 | 6 | 5 | 6.363 | 4.228 | 1191 | 1595 | *** | *** |
| FinOwn | 0.125 | 0.034 | 0.000 | 0.000 | 0.210 | 0.083 | 1273 | 1686 | *** | *** |
| OtherCompany | 0.228 | 0.018 | 0.000 | 0.000 | 0.341 | 0.072 | 1273 | 1686 | *** | *** |

This table reports the summary statistics for the variables employed; for definitions, see Appendix. FF (NF) denotes family (non-family) firms using FamOwn25 as a measure of family firms. Significance of differences is assessed based on t-test (mean) two tails and the Wilcoxon/Mann-Whitney test (median). N.s. denotes non-significance. Significance of differences in dummy variables is assessed using a chi-squared test.

### 3.4.2 Multivariate Results

Table 3.3 presents the regression results for our basic model estimating the influence of family ownership on earnings management. For our two ABEM models (Models 1 and 2), we find a negative coefficient estimate for family ownership (*FamOwn*), which is significant at the 0.05 level, as well as for founding family ownership (*FoundFamOwn*), which is significant at the 0.10 level. Both indicate more negative ABEM practices.

**Table 3.3:** Regression Results of Basic Model on Family Ownership

| | (1) | (2) | (3) | (4) | (5) | (6) | (7) | (8) |
|---|---|---|---|---|---|---|---|---|
| **Variables** | ABEM | | REM_CFO | | REM_DISC | | REM_PROD | |
| Crisis | 0.009** | 0.008* | -0.080*** | -0.082*** | -0.008 | -0.007 | -0.008 | -0.009 |
| | (1.972) | (1.897) | (-6.738) | (-6.875) | (-0.846) | (-0.802) | (-0.823) | (-0.886) |
| PostCrisis | 0.002 | 0.001 | -0.090*** | -0.092*** | -0.000 | -0.000 | -0.003 | -0.003 |
| | (0.448) | (0.264) | (-9.813) | (-9.885) | (-0.028) | (-0.009) | (-0.176) | (-0.239) |
| LOSS | 0.008 | 0.008 | 0.004 | 0.005 | -0.031 | -0.032 | -0.011 | -0.011 |
| | (0.982) | (1.035) | (0.352) | (0.451) | (-1.553) | (-1.589) | (-0.508) | (-0.491) |
| SIZE | -0.011*** | -0.011*** | -0.001 | -0.001 | 0.001 | 0.000 | 0.002 | 0.002 |
| | (-4.009) | (-3.899) | (-0.226) | (-0.186) | (0.066) | (0.049) | (0.527) | (0.517) |
| GROWTH | 0.008 | 0.009 | -0.152*** | -0.152*** | -0.072*** | -0.072*** | -0.046 | -0.046 |
| | (0.640) | (0.652) | (-2.914) | (-2.921) | (-4.965) | (-4.938) | (-1.541) | (-1.543) |
| PERF | 0.670*** | 0.670*** | -0.186*** | -0.186*** | -0.112* | -0.113* | -0.279*** | -0.280*** |
| | (19.73) | (19.71) | (-4.570) | (-4.639) | (-1.851) | (-1.864) | (-4.640) | (-4.649) |
| HHI | 0.008 | 0.008 | 0.008 | 0.011 | 0.020 | 0.022 | 0.067*** | 0.070*** |
| | (0.641) | (0.665) | (0.361) | (0.508) | (0.531) | (0.581) | (2.582) | (2.623) |
| EmplMgt | 0.157** | 0.150** | 0.113 | 0.096 | 0.145 | 0.149 | 0.087 | 0.079 |
| | (2.060) | (2.000) | (0.652) | (0.560) | (0.658) | (0.680) | (0.527) | (0.470) |
| BIG4 | -0.014 | -0.014 | | | | | | |
| | (-1.143) | (-1.116) | | | | | | |
| INTACCTG | -0.032*** | -0.031*** | 0.049* | 0.048* | -0.061** | -0.060** | -0.020 | -0.020 |
| | (-3.771) | (-3.793) | (1.930) | (1.899) | (-2.034) | (-1.979) | (-0.878) | (-0.889) |
| LEVERAGE | -0.048* | -0.047* | -0.058 | -0.057 | -0.063 | -0.064 | 0.001 | 0.001 |
| | (-1.753) | (-1.706) | (-1.483) | (-1.476) | (-1.399) | (-1.427) | (0.029) | (0.019) |
| DivPayoutShs | -0.000 | -0.000 | -0.000 | -0.000 | -0.000 | -0.000 | -0.000 | -0.000 |
| | (-1.501) | (-1.471) | (-1.549) | (-1.503) | (-0.439) | (-0.423) | (-1.01) | (-0.964) |
| LogAge | -0.021*** | -0.022*** | 0.025* | 0.024* | -0.009 | -0.008 | -0.003 | -0.003 |
| | (-3.057) | (-3.098) | (1.758) | (1.717) | (-0.419) | (-0.393) | (-0.312) | (-0.318) |
| FamOwn | -0.023** | | -0.054* | | 0.043 | | -0.008 | |
| | (-1.980) | | (-1.673) | | (1.213) | | (-0.335) | |
| FoundFamOwn | | -0.026* | | -0.078** | | 0.022 | | -0.024 |
| | | (-1.834) | | (-2.382) | | (0.497) | | (-0.879) |
| Constant | 0.273*** | 0.272*** | -0.007 | 0.001 | -0.327** | -0.314** | -0.071 | -0.064 |
| | (6.489) | (6.297) | (-0.085) | (0.014) | (-2.097) | (-2.109) | (-1.142) | (-1.074) |
| Observations | 1,901 | 1,901 | 2,375 | 2,375 | 2,198 | 2,198 | 2,334 | 2,334 |
| No. of Firms | 248 | 248 | 272 | 272 | 263 | 263 | 272 | 272 |
| Industry FE | Yes | Yes | Yes | Yes | Yes | Yes | Yes | Yes |
| RE-Mod | Yes | Yes | Yes | Yes | Yes | Yes | Yes | Yes |
| R-sq. overall | 0.600 | 0.598 | 0.340 | 0.338 | 0.455 | 0.455 | 0.122 | 0.122 |

Robust z-statistics in parentheses.

*** $p<0.01$, ** $p<0.05$, * $p<0.1$

Our REM estimation models show mixed results. Family ownership and founding family ownership have a significantly negative effect on the abnormal level of cash flow from operations. Increasing family (and founding family) ownership is therefore associated with lower levels of *REM_CFO*. Models 5–8 on the abnormal levels of discretionary expenses and production costs find no significant influence of family ownership.

Note that the control variables included in our estimation models reveal different results depending on the proxy for earnings management. Larger (*SIZE*), older (*LogAge*), and more leveraged (*LEVERAGE*) firms, as well as firms that have adopted international accounting standards (*INTACCTG*), tend to exhibit more negative discretionary accruals. We find the opposite result for firms with higher performance (*PERF*) and higher employee ownership (*EmplMgt*). During the financial crisis (2008 and 2009), firms were more inclined to report lower non-cash expenses within their discretion in order to improve reported net income (as indicated by the positive association of ABEM and the dummy variable Crisis). Coincidentally, we find that firms tended to engage less in REM activities as measured by the abnormal level of cash flow from operations, which continued during the post-crisis years.

In addition, more growth firms (coefficient significantly negative for *REM_CFO* and *REM_DISC*) and more profitable firms (coefficient significantly negative for all REM proxies) indicate lower REM activities. Older firms, as measured by the abnormal levels of cash flow from operations, and firms with higher ownership concentration (*HHI*), as measured by abnormal levels of production costs, are associated with higher REM involvement. Firms that adopted international accountings standards (*INTACCTG*) show lower abnormal levels of discretionary expenses, but higher abnormal levels of cash flow from operations. We find no significant effect on earnings management for our dummy variables *LOSS* and *BIG4* auditing or for the dividend payout ratio.

In Table 3.4, we present the regression results on family board influence, while controlling for the complete ownership structure of firms. Model 1 shows that our basic family ownership model holds after controlling for financial shareholders and other companies as shareholders. Model 2 reveals a negative coefficient estimate for the relative influence of the shareholding family on the executive board (*ExBoFamRel*). This is significant at the 0.05 level, suggesting that a higher percentage of shareholding family members on the executive board is associated with more negative discretionary accruals.

**Table 3.4a:** Regression Results of Advanced Model on Family Board Involvement

| | (1) | (2) | (3) | (4) | (5) | (6) | (7) | (8) | (9) | (10) | (11) | (12) |
|---|---|---|---|---|---|---|---|---|---|---|---|---|
| **Variables** | | | ABEM | | | | | | REM_CFO | | | |
| Crisis | 0.009** | 0.009* | 0.009** | 0.008* | 0.009* | 0.009** | -0.081*** | -0.083*** | -0.084*** | -0.082*** | -0.085*** | -0.085*** |
| | (1.992) | (1.951) | (2.002) | (1.905) | (1.907) | (1.962) | (-6.879) | (-6.871) | (-6.839) | (-7.032) | (-6.948) | (-6.923) |
| PostCrisis | 0.002 | 0.001 | 0.002 | 0.001 | 0.000 | 0.001 | -0.089*** | -0.091*** | -0.093*** | -0.092*** | -0.093*** | -0.095*** |
| | (0.461) | (0.222) | (0.414) | (0.265) | (0.077) | (0.280) | (-9.790) | (-9.742) | (-9.410) | (-9.826) | (-9.734) | (-9.396) |
| LOSS | 0.008 | 0.005 | 0.005 | 0.008 | 0.005 | 0.005 | 0.005 | 0.007 | 0.008 | 0.006 | 0.008 | 0.009 |
| | (0.976) | (0.632) | (0.593) | (1.031) | (0.663) | (0.621) | (0.386) | (0.580) | (0.635) | (0.468) | (0.653) | (0.708) |
| SIZE | -0.011*** | -0.011*** | -0.012*** | -0.011*** | -0.011*** | -0.012*** | -0.001 | -0.002 | 0.001 | -0.001 | -0.002 | 0.001 |
| | (-3.970) | (-3.795) | (-4.000) | (-3.878) | (-3.712) | (-3.937) | (-0.246) | (-0.322) | (0.0950) | (-0.201) | (-0.265) | (0.116) |
| GROWTH | 0.008 | 0.011 | 0.011 | 0.009 | 0.011 | 0.011 | -0.152*** | -0.157*** | -0.157*** | -0.152*** | -0.157*** | -0.158*** |
| | (0.626) | (0.808) | (0.825) | (0.658) | (0.839) | (0.856) | (-2.931) | (-2.913) | (-2.927) | (-2.934) | (-2.917) | (-2.931) |
| PERF | 0.671*** | 0.656*** | 0.658*** | 0.671*** | 0.656*** | 0.659*** | -0.186*** | -0.177*** | -0.181*** | -0.187*** | -0.177*** | -0.181*** |
| | (19.80) | (18.51) | (18.39) | (19.79) | (18.51) | (18.39) | (-4.591) | (-3.949) | (-4.034) | (-4.648) | (-3.999) | (-4.078) |
| HHI | 0.007 | 0.005 | 0.006 | 0.008 | 0.006 | 0.007 | 0.023 | 0.023 | 0.020 | 0.028 | 0.028 | 0.025 |
| | (0.538) | (0.345) | (0.431) | (0.643) | (0.426) | (0.515) | (1.020) | (0.984) | (0.854) | (1.197) | (1.164) | (1.056) |
| EmplMgt | 0.154** | 0.158** | 0.147* | 0.151** | 0.158** | 0.146* | 0.157 | 0.128 | 0.125 | 0.147 | 0.125 | 0.119 |
| | (1.969) | (2.101) | (1.854) | (1.978) | (2.144) | (1.872) | (0.818) | (0.677) | (0.668) | (0.775) | (0.667) | (0.645) |
| BIG4 | -0.014 | -0.013 | -0.013 | -0.014 | -0.012 | -0.013 | | | | | | |
| | (-1.139) | (-1.022) | (-1.102) | (-1.118) | (-0.991) | (-1.073) | | | | | | |
| INTACCTG | -0.032*** | -0.033*** | -0.033*** | -0.031*** | -0.032*** | -0.032*** | 0.048* | 0.047* | 0.047* | 0.047* | 0.046* | 0.046* |
| | (-3.813) | (-3.839) | (-3.780) | (-3.799) | (-3.811) | (-3.755) | (1.903) | (1.816) | (1.779) | (1.884) | (1.819) | (1.792) |
| LEVERAGE | -0.048* | -0.064** | -0.066*** | -0.047* | -0.062** | -0.064** | -0.060 | -0.077* | -0.073* | -0.058 | -0.075* | -0.071* |
| | (-1.756) | (-2.573) | (-2.651) | (-1.700) | (-2.488) | (-2.571) | (-1.520) | (-1.800) | (-1.683) | (-1.517) | (-1.794) | (-1.672) |
| LogAge | -0.021*** | -0.019*** | -0.020*** | -0.022*** | -0.020*** | -0.020*** | 0.025* | 0.029** | 0.032** | 0.024* | 0.028** | 0.031** |
| | (-3.081) | (-2.816) | (-2.879) | (-3.101) | (-2.847) | (-2.903) | (1.789) | (2.090) | (2.233) | (1.757) | (2.051) | (2.201) |
| DivPayoutShs | -0.000 | -0.000 | -0.000 | -0.000 | -0.000 | -0.000 | -0.000 | -0.000 | -0.000 | -0.000 | -0.000 | -0.000 |
| | (-1.537) | (-1.415) | (-1.383) | (-1.446) | (-1.343) | (-1.313) | (-1.382) | (-1.434) | (-1.496) | (-1.312) | (-1.364) | (-1.418) |

*(Continued)*

**Table 3.4a:** Continued

| | (1) | (2) | (3) | (4) | (5) | (6) | (7) | (8) | (9) | (10) | (11) | (12) |
|---|---|---|---|---|---|---|---|---|---|---|---|---|
| Variables | ABEM | | | | | | REM_CFO | | | | | |
| FinOwn | -0.007 | -0.003 | -0.003 | -0.000 | 0.003 | 0.004 | 0.084 | 0.064 | 0.062 | 0.091* | 0.076 | 0.075 |
| | (-0.302) | (-0.141) | (-0.119) | (-0.002) | (0.143) | (0.156) | (1.594) | (1.205) | (1.159) | (1.798) | (1.523) | (1.497) |
| OtherCompany | -0.004 | -0.003 | -0.001 | 0.005 | 0.006 | 0.007 | -0.020 | -0.031 | -0.037 | -0.010 | -0.018 | -0.023 |
| | (-0.223) | (-0.135) | (-0.034) | (0.320) | (0.297) | (0.391) | (-0.641) | (-0.925) | (-1.066) | (-0.441) | (-0.743) | (-0.920) |
| FamOwn | -0.026** | -0.023* | -0.023* | | | | -0.049 | -0.057 | -0.061* | | | |
| | (-2.026) | (-1.737) | (-1.669) | | | | (-1.328) | (-1.576) | (-1.679) | | | |
| FoundFamOwn | | | | -0.025* | -0.020 | -0.019 | | | | -0.070** | -0.075** | -0.080*** |
| | | | | (-1.737) | (-1.334) | (-1.321) | | | | (-2.134) | (-2.535) | (-2.743) |
| ExBoFamRel | | -0.028** | -0.027* | | -0.029** | -0.027* | | 0.015 | 0.013 | | 0.016 | 0.014 |
| | | (-1.966) | (-1.848) | | (-1.988) | (-1.857) | | (0.366) | (0.303) | | (0.398) | (0.343) |
| SupBoFamRel | | -0.022 | -0.015 | | -0.023 | -0.016 | | -0.044 | -0.055 | | -0.044 | -0.055 |
| | | (-1.092) | (-0.684) | | (-1.185) | (-0.751) | | (-0.856) | (-1.039) | | (-0.856) | (-1.024) |
| ExBoSize | | | 0.000 | | | 0.000 | | | 0.002 | | | 0.002 |
| | | | (0.136) | | | (0.219) | | | (0.294) | | | (0.434) |
| SupBoSize | | | 0.002* | | | 0.002** | | | -0.004*** | | | -0.004** |
| | | | (1.957) | | | (1.965) | | | (-2.652) | | | (-2.485) |
| Constant | 0.278*** | 0.288*** | 0.294*** | 0.271*** | 0.280*** | 0.286*** | -0.0256 | -0.010 | -0.031 | -0.022 | -0.010 | -0.032 |
| | (6.114) | (5.725) | (5.797) | (6.013) | (5.619) | (5.694) | (-0.322) | (-0.0935) | (-0.298) | (-0.291) | (-0.104) | (-0.332) |
| Observations | 1,901 | 1,830 | 1,830 | 1,901 | 1,830 | 1,830 | 2,375 | 2,271 | 2,271 | 2,375 | 2,271 | 2,271 |
| No. of firms | 248 | 239 | 239 | 248 | 239 | 239 | 272 | 261 | 261 | 272 | 261 | 261 |
| Industry FE | Yes | Yes | Yes | Yes | Yes | Yes | Yes | Yes | Yes | Yes | Yes | Yes |
| RE-Mod | Yes | Yes | Yes | Yes | Yes | Yes | Yes | Yes | Yes | Yes | Yes | Yes |
| R-sq. overall | 0.600 | 0.601 | 0.604 | 0.598 | 0.599 | 0.602 | 0.344 | 0.346 | 0.347 | 0.343 | 0.345 | 0.346 |

Robust z-statistics in parentheses.
*** $p<0.01$, ** $p<0.05$, * $p<0.1$

**Table 3.4b:** Regression Results of Advanced Model on Family Board Involvement (cont'd)

| | (13) | (14) | (15) | (16) | (17) | (18) | (19) | (20) | (21) | (22) | (23) | (24) |
|---|---|---|---|---|---|---|---|---|---|---|---|---|
| Variables | REM_DISC | | | | | | REM_PROD | | | | | |
| Crisis | -0.010 | -0.012 | -0.012 | -0.009 | -0.011 | -0.011 | -0.009 | -0.013 | -0.013 | -0.010 | -0.013 | -0.013 |
| | (-1.139) | (-1.277) | (-1.365) | (-0.936) | (-1.172) | (-1.246) | (-0.922) | (-1.222) | (-1.235) | (-0.959) | (-1.267) | (-1.273) |
| PostCrisis | -0.002 | -0.002 | -0.004 | -0.001 | -0.001 | -0.003 | -0.003 | -0.006 | -0.006 | -0.004 | -0.006 | -0.007 |
| | (-0.139) | (-0.154) | (-0.301) | (-0.038) | (-0.092) | (-0.230) | (-0.206) | (-0.387) | (-0.414) | (-0.245) | (-0.427) | (-0.448) |
| LOSS | -0.031 | -0.027 | -0.027 | -0.032 | -0.028 | -0.028 | -0.010 | -0.006 | -0.006 | -0.010 | -0.006 | -0.006 |
| | (-1.559) | (-1.336) | (-1.320) | (-1.617) | (-1.366) | (-1.349) | (-0.486) | (-0.268) | (-0.270) | (-0.483) | (-0.253) | (-0.257) |
| SIZE | 0.000 | 0.003 | 0.005 | 0.000 | 0.003 | 0.005 | 0.002 | 0.003 | 0.003 | 0.002 | 0.003 | 0.003 |
| | (0.011) | (0.380) | (0.589) | (0.012) | (0.381) | (0.596) | (0.624) | (0.595) | (0.526) | (0.550) | (0.593) | (0.523) |
| GROWTH | -0.071*** | -0.069*** | -0.069*** | -0.071*** | -0.069*** | -0.069*** | -0.047 | -0.045 | -0.045 | -0.047 | -0.045 | -0.045 |
| | (-5.302) | (-5.568) | (-5.590) | (-5.163) | (-5.437) | (-5.460) | (-1.554) | (-1.492) | (-1.487) | (-1.552) | (-1.493) | (-1.488) |
| PERF | -0.109* | -0.127** | -0.132** | -0.112* | -0.130** | -0.135** | -0.279*** | -0.291*** | -0.292*** | -0.279*** | -0.291*** | -0.292*** |
| | (-1.793) | (-2.083) | (-2.143) | (-1.838) | (-2.153) | (-2.213) | (-4.639) | (-4.451) | (-4.451) | (-4.658) | (-4.464) | (-4.460) |
| HHI | 0.044 | 0.044 | 0.044 | 0.041 | 0.041 | 0.041 | 0.078*** | 0.081*** | 0.081*** | 0.080*** | 0.083*** | 0.083*** |
| | (1.124) | (1.100) | (1.103) | (1.049) | (1.049) | (1.043) | (3.012) | (2.900) | (2.825) | (3.051) | (2.937) | (2.857) |
| EmplMgt | 0.220 | 0.187 | 0.210 | 0.207 | 0.172 | 0.195 | 0.132 | 0.102 | 0.112 | 0.116 | 0.092 | 0.102 |
| | (0.982) | (0.862) | (0.966) | (0.942) | (0.804) | (0.908) | (0.788) | (0.610) | (0.669) | (0.687) | (0.546) | (0.602) |
| BIG4 | | | | | | | | | | | | |
| INTACCTG | -0.056* | -0.056* | -0.057* | -0.057* | -0.058* | -0.058* | -0.019 | -0.017 | -0.017 | -0.019 | -0.017 | -0.017 |
| | (-1.908) | (-1.832) | (-1.838) | (-1.865) | (-1.819) | (-1.819) | (-0.834) | (-0.682) | (-0.675) | (-0.846) | (-0.699) | (-0.693) |
| LEVERAGE | -0.058 | -0.065 | -0.061 | -0.062 | -0.067 | -0.064 | 0.002 | -0.003 | -0.003 | 0.001 | -0.003 | -0.003 |
| | (-1.290) | (-1.390) | (-1.312) | (-1.383) | (-1.457) | (-1.377) | (0.050) | (-0.056) | (-0.066) | (0.016) | (-0.063) | (-0.071) |
| LogAge | -0.008 | -0.006 | -0.008 | -0.007 | -0.005 | -0.006 | -0.003 | -0.002 | -0.003 | -0.003 | -0.002 | -0.003 |
| | (-0.376) | (-0.315) | (-0.370) | (-0.342) | (-0.238) | (-0.293) | (-0.330) | (-0.225) | (-0.316) | (-0.297) | (-0.211) | (-0.297) |
| DivPayoutShs | -0.000 | -0.000 | -0.000 | -0.000 | -0.000 | -0.000 | -0.000 | -0.000 | -0.000 | -0.000 | -0.000 | -0.000 |
| | (-0.103) | (-0.219) | (-0.237) | (-0.183) | (-0.279) | (-0.297) | (-0.862) | (-0.935) | (-0.932) | (-0.825) | (-0.896) | (-0.897) |

*(Continued)*

**Table 3.4b:** Continued

| | (13) | (14) | (15) | (16) | (17) | (18) | (19) | (20) | (21) | (22) | (23) | (24) |
|---|---|---|---|---|---|---|---|---|---|---|---|---|
| **Variables** | REM_DISC | | | | | | REM_PROD | | | | | |
| FinOwn | 0.144*** | 0.155*** | 0.157*** | 0.104** | 0.125** | 0.126** | 0.070** | 0.076* | 0.077* | 0.062* | 0.072* | 0.073* |
| | (2.762) | (2.840) | (2.857) | (2.254) | (2.528) | (2.532) | (1.968) | (1.863) | (1.860) | (1.858) | (1.894) | (1.890) |
| OtherCompany | 0.106** | 0.104** | 0.103** | 0.060 | 0.069 | 0.068 | 0.019 | -0.004 | -0.002 | 0.011 | -0.009 | -0.007 |
| | (2.358) | (2.004) | (1.989) | (1.644) | (1.526) | (1.501) | (0.531) | (-0.087) | (-0.046) | (0.308) | (-0.200) | (-0.159) |
| FamOwn | 0.104** | 0.083* | 0.085** | | | | 0.009 | 0.001 | 0.002 | | | |
| | (2.210) | (1.908) | (1.971) | | | | (0.301) | (0.031) | (0.071) | | | |
| FoundFamOwn | | | | 0.049 | 0.041 | 0.045 | | | | -0.014 | -0.018 | -0.016 |
| | | | | (1.026) | (0.858) | (0.968) | | | | (-0.463) | (-0.577) | (-0.494) |
| ExBoFamRel | | 0.123** | 0.119** | | 0.128** | 0.124** | | 0.026 | 0.026 | | 0.029 | 0.028 |
| | | (2.408) | (2.328) | | (2.426) | (2.337) | | (0.953) | (0.925) | | (1.028) | (0.990) |
| SupBoFamRel | | 0.039 | 0.032 | | 0.049 | 0.041 | | 0.027 | 0.029 | | 0.031 | 0.032 |
| | | (0.448) | (0.340) | | (0.557) | (0.444) | | (0.525) | (0.535) | | (0.603) | (0.597) |
| ExBoSize | | | -0.005 | | | -0.005 | | | -0.003 | | | -0.003 |
| | | | (-0.900) | | | (-0.897) | | | (-0.694) | | | (-0.654) |
| SupBoSize | | | -0.001 | | | -0.001 | | | 0.001 | | | 0.001 |
| | | | (-0.447) | | | (-0.428) | | | (0.566) | | | (0.493) |
| Constant | -0.400** | -0.452*** | -0.441*** | -0.355** | -0.425*** | -0.416*** | -0.099 | -0.111 | -0.106 | -0.084 | -0.103 | -0.099 |
| | (-2.466) | (-2.810) | (-2.726) | (-2.374) | (-2.804) | (-2.732) | (-1.580) | (-1.474) | (-1.417) | (-1.423) | (-1.462) | (-1.415) |
| Observations | 2,198 | 2,109 | 2,109 | 2,198 | 2,109 | 2,109 | 2,334 | 2,226 | 2,226 | 2,334 | 2,226 | 2,226 |
| No. of firms | 263 | 252 | 252 | 263 | 252 | 252 | 272 | 261 | 261 | 272 | 261 | 261 |
| Industry FE | Yes | Yes | Yes | Yes | Yes | Yes | Yes | Yes | Yes | Yes | Yes | Yes |
| RE-Mod | Yes | Yes | Yes | Yes | Yes | Yes | Yes | Yes | Yes | Yes | Yes | Yes |
| R-sq. overall | 0.459 | 0.463 | 0.464 | 0.459 | 0.461 | 0.464 | 0.124 | 0.125 | 0.125 | 0.124 | 0.125 | 0.125 |

Robust z-statistics in parentheses.
*** p<0.01, ** p<0.05, * p<0.1

The regression results in Model 5 show that the negative influence of founding family ownership (*FoundFamOwn*) on discretionary accruals does not hold after controlling for the management influence of family on the boards. Family executive board influence remains negative at the 0.05 significance level. Model 6 further indicates that the level of family influence on the supervisory board does not pose a significant impact, but the size of the supervisory board is associated with more positive discretionary accruals.

Models 7 and 8 show that the significantly negative effect of family ownership on abnormal levels of cash flow from operations, as depicted in our basic model in Table 3.3, does not necessarily hold when we control for other shareholders and the influence of the family on the executive board[60]. Neither family ownership nor family management involvement significantly influences this REM measure. Founding family ownership (*FoundFamOwn*), in contrast, significantly lowers the magnitude of abnormal cash flow from operations (Models 10–12), as do larger supervisory boards (*SupBoSize*) (Model 12).

Family management influence, however, becomes visible for abnormal levels of discretionary expenses. Despite the influence of family ownership (*FamOwn*) (Models 13–15), the results reveal that a higher level of family involvement on the executive board (*ExBoFamRel*) is associated with a higher magnitude of abnormal discretionary expenses (Models 14–15). Founding family ownership is not significant (Models 16–18), while the coefficient estimate *ExBoFamRel* remains significant on a 0.05 level. For REM activities related to abnormal levels of production costs, we find no significant family influence - neither by ownership nor by family management.

Accounting for other shareholders and the family management influence, the coefficients of our control variables remain stable. The exception is *LEVERAGE*, which turns negative at a 0.1 significance level for REM as measured by abnormal levels of cash flow from operations. Ownership of financial institutions (*FinOwn*) is associated with higher REM activities, as measured by abnormal levels of discretionary expenses and production costs. And the significant effect of ownership by other companies (*OtherCompanies*) on abnormal levels of discretionary expenses disappears when accounting for founding family ownership.

Overall, our results confirm Hypothesis 1, that earnings management is significantly related to family ownership. After controlling for other blockholders

---

60 Except for Model 9 (p-value 0,084), family ownership is insignificant in all three REM_CFO models.

and family management influence, family ownership is significantly associated with more negative discretionary accruals and a higher magnitude of abnormal discretionary expenses. Furthermore, founding family ownership significantly lowers REM activities based on abnormal levels of cash flow from operations.

Thus, for the first time, we are able to provide a granular measurement model that suggests family management involvement matters. We can confirm Hypothesis 2a, that earnings management in family firms is significantly related to the level of involvement on the executive board for ABEM, and, with reservations, for REM. We find that a higher percentage of shareholding family members on the executive board is associated with more negative discretionary accruals, i.e. more earnings-decreasing ABEM practices. It also accounts for more REM activities related to discretionary expenses.

However, Hypothesis 2b, on family involvement on the supervisory board, is rejected. Nevertheless, we find that the size of the supervisory board affects ABEM-related activities (more positive discretionary accruals) and REM practices as measured by abnormal levels of cash flow from operations (negative association).

To summarize, after controlling for other large shareholders and management involvement of family members, our estimation models suggest that (1) family ownership is associated with more earnings-decreasing ABEM practices, which is at least partly linked to the degree of executive board family involvement; (2) lower levels of REM activities, as measured by abnormal level of cash flow from operations, appears to hold more for founding family ownership than for family ownership in general; (3) the magnitude of abnormal discretionary expenses increases with an increasing influence of family members on the executive board; (4) supervisory board family involvement has no significant effect on earnings management; and (5) larger supervisory boards are associated with more positive discretionary accruals and lower REM activities based on abnormal levels of cash flow from operations.

## 3.5 Discussion

Within the German setting of high ownership concentration (Faccio and Lang, 2002), high average levels of family voting rights (Becht and Boehmer, 2003), and a predominant agency conflict between large controlling and minority shareholders (Gugler and Yurtoglu, 2003), we expect the entrenchment effect of family ownership to be prevalent. Our regression models indeed show that family ownership is associated with more negative discretionary accruals and more earnings-decreasing ABEM practices, which is in line with the findings of Ali et al. (2007) and Achleitner et al. (2014) (Table 3.3).

Expanding on that literature, our models in Table 4 reveal that a precise measure of family management influence is crucial to observing and explaining earnings management behavior in family firms. This factor has thus far been disregarded in the literature. Our models suggest that the management influence of families is a significant driver of earnings management. The results indicate that family ownership, which is associated with more earnings-decreasing ABEM practices, is at least partly linked to the degree of executive board family involvement (Models 1–6 in Table 3.4). Our findings are in line with Acero and Alcalde (2016), who find a high degree of insider ownership in family firms is associated with an increased risk of expropriation.

The same observation also accounts for larger magnitudes in abnormal discretionary expenses (Models 13–15 in Table 3.4). Our observations suggest that families use their ownership voting power, management influence, and information advantage to expropriate other shareholders through lower reported earnings. We find they are motivated potentially by decreased dividend pressure (Gugler and Yurtoglu, 2003; García Lara et al., 2005), and to maintain the wealth in their family firms (for example, a long-term orientation).

We recognize that finding more REM activities based on abnormal discretionary expenses (*REM_DISC*) at first seems contradictory. Nevertheless, we see this result as in line with families avoiding future value-destroying REM activities (Achleitner et al., 2014). Managing discretionary expenses is a one-off activity (e.g. reducing SG&A or R&D expenses) that allows a rather simple earnings management practice to meet earning targets.

In contrast to managing cash flows by boosting sales (*REM_CFO*), it may endanger future cash flows to a lesser extent. This is because reducing prices or offering more lenient credit terms may be more difficult to readjust for in future periods. Especially for founding family shareholders (*FoundFamOwn*), this appears to be a major concern. Findings indicate that founding family ownership is associated with less *REM_CFO*, while no effect was found for family ownership.

In addition to founding family ownership, supervisory board size also tends to lower *REM_CFO* (Models 7–12 in Table 3.4). It is also associated with more positive discretionary accruals. This may be because larger supervisory boards have better monitoring ability for this specific case of earnings manipulation.

For robustness reasons, we recalculated our models on accrual-based earnings management and real earnings management to test for potential survivorship bias. We integrate a proxy for insolvency (dummy variable). The coefficient estimates, shown in Tables 3.3 and 3.4, remain unchanged in their significance levels.

## 3.6 Conclusion

This study investigates the influence of family control on earnings management in German-listed family firms. Against a framework of low investor protection, high ownership concentration, a high level of family ownership, and a two-tiered corporate board governance system, we expect the entrenchment effect of family ownership to be prevalent. Families in Germany tend to be present in the management of the firms they are invested in, so they possess both the ability and the motivation to expropriate minority shareholders and manage earnings according to their own interests. Since a high percentage of their wealth is usually invested in their firms, they are expected to avoid actions that might endanger future firm value.

To investigate earnings management in family firms, we extend prior literature that usually employs family ownership as well as dummies for CEO and board attributes. To this end, we account for the specific influence of family members on firms' boards. We introduce a unique and hand- collected sample of 278 firms listed in Germany from 2000 through 2013. We document that family ownership and family management involvement are positively associated with more earnings-decreasing accrual-based earnings management (ABEM) practices. The same construct is associated with higher levels of real earnings management (REM) based on abnormal discretionary expenses. Our study emphasizes the relevance of a more precise measurement of family board influence in order to account for the broad heterogeneity of family firms in future earnings-management research (Paiva et al., 2016).

Specifically, we find that families use their powerful positions as shareholders and executive board members to lower earnings through discretionary accruals and to manage earnings through discretionary expenses. Although these two activities appear contradictory, the latter can actually be explained by family firms preferring the one-time character of reducing discretionary expenses (e.g. SG&A and R&D expenses). This practice may be seen as less value-endangering than engaging in REM practices that are more difficult to reverse, such as boosted sales or overproduction. The finding that founding family ownership significantly lowers sales-related earnings management activities amplifies our view.

Because Germany features specific legal and corporate governance settings, our results are limited in their transferability to other countries. In order to further support our argumentation of minority shareholder expropriation, further research could estimate the predictability of future cash flows, earnings persistence, or the quality of corporate governance disclosure. This could negate the argument that family firms report better quality earnings by not increasing earnings (Ali et al., 2007).

On a practical level, we demonstrate that both the level of family ownership and that of family management involvement on the executive board influence earnings management activities. In order to avoid expropriation (such as reduced dividends), minority shareholders in Germany may thus wish to campaign for the permanent establishment of currently voluntary audit committees. These have been shown to mitigate at least accrual-based earnings management (Albersmann and Hohenfels, 2017).

With regard to German co-determination on the supervisory board, minority shareholders would be well advised to cooperate closely with workers' representatives on the board in order to appoint balanced and experienced board members (Ferramosca and Allegrini, 2018). This could effectively reduce the earnings-related outcomes of agency conflicts among shareholders.

This study has some limitations, which could provide opportunities for further research. First, we use data from listed firms from only one country and for a specific sample period, which is why the results may not apply to non-listed firms and are only valid for this period and its specific regulatory environment. Second, our analysis is based on a sample of CDAX firms between 2003 and 2013. We cannot rule out that results from a larger sample with more recent data might provide additional insights.

Third, future investigations should also include other corporate governance characteristics, if valid information is publicly available. In particular, the independence of executive and supervisory board or the CEO-Chairman duality could have a lasting impact on the effectiveness of management or the monitoring role of the supervisory board. In addition, the composition of the supervisory board and the election of its members is of crucial importance as one of the main functions of the supervisory board is to appoint and to dismiss the members of the executive board.

Fourth, although we control for a variety of variables that could be related to earnings management, we cannot completely exclude the possibility that some latent governance or firm- specific measures drive our results. In the same vein, the strategic use of both earnings management strategies in family firms requires a deeper analysis to capture the possible complementary or substitutive relationship between ABEM and REM metrics.

Fifth, Shleifer and Vishny (1997) argue that the entrenchment of family members, e.g. a founder remaining in the company although he might no longer be competent, is probably one of the largest costs a large shareholder can impose. It would be interesting to analyze the CEO tenure of founders in family firms to control for this effect in German listed family firms.

Finally, Gugler and Yurtoglu (2003) report an effect on accrual-based earnings management in family firms when there are larger holdings of the second largest owner. In further research, the impact and effects of other large shareholders should be investigated. Within this analysis, one may also prove for their identity. Mietzner and Schweizer (2014) and Mietzner and Schiereck (2016), for example, document that strategic investors and financial investors in particular can be assumed to have an intention to influence the corporate policy of German companies in the long term.

## 3.7 Appendix

**Table 3.5:** List of Variables

| Variable | Description |
|---|---|
| Variables used for ABEM and REM metrics estimations | |
| ACC | Total accruals, defined as income before extraordinary items (Worldscope Item: 04001) minus cash flow from operations |
| CFO | Cash flow from operations, measured as net cash flow – operating activities (Worldscope Item: 04860) minus extraordinary items (Worldscope Item: 04225) received from the statement of cash flows |
| A | Total assets (Worldscope Item: 02999) |
| DCFO | An indicator that equals 1 if cash flow from operations at time t is negative (i.e. $CFO_t - CFO_{t-1} < 0$), and 0 otherwise |
| DCFO* CFO | Proxy for economic losses |
| S | Net sales or revenues in year t (Worldscope Item: 01001) |
| PROD | Production costs at year t, defined as the sum of COGS (Worldscope Item: 01051) and $\Delta INV_t = INV_t - INV_{t-1}$ (Worldscope Item: 02101) |
| DISEXP | Discretionary expenses, defined as the sum of research and development expenses (Worldscope Item: 01201) and selling, general, and administrative (SG&A) expenses (Worldscope Item: 01101), as long as SG&A expenses are available. If these items are missing from Worldscope, R&D expenses are set to 0. |

**Table 3.5:** Continued

| | |
|---|---|
| ABEM metric | |
| ABEM | Value of abnormal accruals, calculated as industry-year-specific residuals, $\varepsilon_t$ , from the Ball and Shivakumar (2005) model |
| REM metrics | |
| REM_CFO | Discretionary cash flow from operations is the residuals from the Roychowdhury (2006) linear model that expresses actual cash flow from operations as a function of contemporaneous sales and changes in sales. The measure is multiplied by (-1) to allow for easier interpretation |
| REM_DISC | Discretionary expenses are the residuals from the Roychowdhury (2006) linear model that expresses actual discretionary expenses as a function of lagged sales. The measure is multiplied by (-1) to allow for easier interpretation |
| REM_PROD | Discretionary production costs are the residuals from the Roychowdhury (2006) linear model that expresses actual productions costs as a function of contemporaneous sales and of contemporaneous and lagged changes in sales |
| Family firm definitions | |
| FamOwn25 | Proxy for family firms; dummy variable that equals 1 if the cumulative percentage of common shares held by individuals or families (FamOwn) exceeds 25 % |
| Family influence | |
| FamOwn | Percentage of common shares held by family members individually, via holing entities, family foundations or family offices* |
| FoundFamOwn | Percentage of common shares held by founding family members |
| ExBoFamRel | Number of family members represented on the executive board scaled by total members of the executive board |
| SupBoFamRel | Number of family members represented on the supervisory board scaled by total members of the supervisory board |
| Control variables | Basic Model |
| LOSS | Dummy variable that equals 1 if net income is less than zero |
| SIZE | Natural logarithm of market value of firm i at the end of fiscal year t, winsorised at the 1 % and 99 % quantiles |
| GROWTH | Change in sales from t-1 to t, compared to previous year, winsorised at the 1 % and 99 % quantiles |

*(Continued)*

**Table 3.5:** Continued

| | |
|---|---|
| PERF | Net income at t divided by average total assets for firm i at time t, winsorised at the 1 % and 99 % quantiles |
| HHI | Herfindahl Index |
| EmplMgt | Cumulative percentage of voting rights held by management or employees |
| BIG4 | Dummy variable that equals 1 if the firm is audited by one of the Big4 auditors: PwC, KPMG, Deloitte, or Ernst & Young |
| INTACCG | Dummy variable that equals 1 if the firm uses US GAAP or IFRS |
| LEVERAGE | Leverage at time t, calculated as total liabilities scaled by total assets, winsorised at the 1 % and 99 % quantiles |
| DivPayoutShs | Dividend payout ratio of firm i at time t |
| LogAge | Natural logarithm of the year of observation minus the founding year |
| Crisis | Dummy variable accounting for the years of financial distress, i.e. 2008 and 2009, following Höwer (2016) |
| PostCrisis | Dummy variable accounting for the years beginning in 2010, following Höwer (2016) |
| Control variables | Advanced model |
| FinOwn | Cumulative percentage of voting rights held by financial institutions |
| OtherCompany | Cumulative percentage of voting rights held by other companies |
| ExBoSize | Total number of executive board members |
| SupBoSize | Total number of supervisory board members |

* further specification of family ownership added for clarification (not presented in published paper)

# 4 Family Affairs – Corporate Governance Involvement of Families and Stock Market Returns

**Abstract***: This study explores the association between family influence in firms and stock market returns in Germany, a country with a less investor-friendly corporate governance system where shareholders cannot directly influence top managers. The study forms portfolios of firms with and without the influence of families as shareholders or members of the firm's legal bodies. The models estimate portfolio returns from 2003 to 2013 using a four-factor model. Results suggest that corporate governance is highly correlated with stock returns in Germany. Specifically, they document a significant relationship between family influence and firm valuation. Firms with stronger family influence via voting rights and board-participation are found to have a higher firm value (annualized excess return: 0.48%–6.00 %). The study interprets this to mean that families may improve a firm's internal corporate governance, as their strong motivation and ability to become actively engaged in a firm's daily operations or to assume a monitoring role distinguishes them from other corporate blockholders. The results add to those of an increasing number of publications finding a positive association between strong family governance and performance. They contribute to a year-long scholarly exploration of performance differences among family and non-family businesses, mainly by defining the former by mere ownership. The study combines a large set of governance provisions into a novel, transparent, and replicable index of family involvement and then estimates the empirical relation with market performance. The index captures influence via shareholder voting rights, considers direct influence of owners on day-to-day operations, and controls for indirect influence via supervisory board.

## 4.1 Introduction

A country's shareholder structure is significantly impacted by its legal and constitutional setting (La Porta et al., 1998, 1999). Due to the relatively low level of shareholder protection, German firms tend to exhibit fairly concentrated structures (Faccio and Lang, 2002; Becht and Boehmer, 2003; Barontini and Caprio, 2006; Achleitner et al., 2009, 2019). Despite the fact that large

---

* This article is published in *Investment Management and Financial Innovations*, Vol. 18 No. 2, Franzoi, F. and Mietzner, M., Family Affairs – Corporate Governance Involvement of Families and Stock Market Returns, 350–364, Copyright: Franzoi, F. and Mietzner, M. (2021).

shareholders may be more effective at firm monitoring (Shleifer and Vishny, 1986), recent studies note these blockholders differ in their impact on corporate policies and corporate performance (Cronqvist and Fahlenbrach, 2009; Mietzner and Schweizer, 2014).

In contrast to prior studies on other regions, recent research documents blockholders' heterogeneity in Europe and Germany (Andres, 2008; Mietzner and Schiereck, 2016; Schüler et al., 2019). Capital markets, however, react differently to shareholders who actively handle agency problems. Consider, for example, private equity investors. They have been shown to create higher abnormal returns than hedge funds – presumably due to their long-term orientation and better adaptability to the given corporate governance framework (Mietzner and Schweizer, 2014).

Given their monitoring incentives and firm-specific knowledge (Klein, 2000; Anderson and Reeb, 2003a), the paper posits that families as blockholders represent a specific type of large shareholder that imposes a particular corporate governance setting on family firms. Unlike other investors, families are generally more long-term-oriented (Anderson and Reeb, 2003a), and have a high proportion of wealth invested in their companies (Anderson and Reeb, 2003b).

Germany has an unusual corporate governance framework, featuring (1) a two-tier board system that is mandatory for listed firms (i.e. executive and supervisory board), and (2) employees' codetermination on the supervisory board, which substantially limits shareholders' control over top executives at annual meetings (Gorton and Schmid, 2000). Families carry an inherent interest in monitoring and affecting management decisions (Anderson and Reeb, 2004). To effectively control their assets, a significant number of family members belong to the executive or supervisory board in listed family firms (Andres, 2008; Ampenberger, 2010)[61]. The corporate governance framework of Germany provides family shareholders with various options to either directly influence firm policies via representatives on the executive board or to control and influence the firms they are invested in via representatives on the supervisory board (Franzoi et al., 2021). Family involvement may therefore serve as a proxy for the specific corporate governance framework of family firms in Germany.

---

61 A significant share of a family' s capital is tied-up in the family business, which is why families often have poorly diversified portfolios (Anderson and Reeb, 2003a). For this reason, family shareholders have an inherent interest in affecting firm policies and control managers (Anderson and Reeb, 2004).

Differences in the performance of family firms and non-family firms, as well as the means of family influence on firm performance, are the prominent points of a year-long discussion in the literature (Mazzi, 2011; O'Boyle et al., 2012; Wagner et al., 2015; Taras et al., 2018; Azila-Gbettor et al., 2018). Various studies have explored differences in the market anticipation and performance of firms held by families/founders/CEOs and non-family firms. Most find equal or superior performance of family firms (Corstjens et al., 2006; Cella, 2009; Fahlenbrach, 2009; Miralles-Marcelo et al., 2013, 2014; von Lilienfeld and Ruenzi, 2014; Lipiec, 2014; Eugster and Isakov, 2019). Some studies on Germany have explored stock ownership variables (Corstjens et al., 2006), or the imprecise application of dummy-variables for the management participation of a family member (e.g. Cella, 2009).

None of the previously cited publications consider the degree of family-shareholder involvement in the company's legal bodies. Thus, the real influence of the family on the firms' corporate governance is under-researched. This research gap is particularly severe in states with a minor level of shareholder protection like in Germany, where minority shareholders' influence is mainly limited to the annual shareholders' meeting. Gompers et al. (2003); Bebchuk et al. (2009), and other authors have shown that the stock market performance of listed firms in general may be significantly influenced by corporate governance differences between firms. However, these publications focus on an outsider-controlled system in the United States (results are therefore not directly transferrable to the corporate governance system of Germany), and, most important, they do not at all focus on family investors. Due to their previously argued features, this paper posits that corporate governance systems characterized by family ownership and family board presence may explain these differences in corporate governance and subsequently stock market returns in Germany.

The sample employed for this study embodies a unique research opportunity as it identifies every family shareholder as well as the (family-) background of every single member of the executive and the supervisory board of every firm-year by hand. To the best of the authors' knowledge, no such fine-graded data set exists in Germany, since the build-up of this data is extremely time-consuming and costly. The paper argues that in the corporate governance framework of Germany (Becht and Boehmer, 2003), such a depth of information is inevitable to assess the influence of family investors throughout the shareholder structure and legal bodies of listed firms, while solely considering voting shares would be insufficient. The methodology of the study subsequently adapts the idea of Gompers et al. (2003) and forms annually adjusted family and non-family portfolios using a novel, transparent, and replicable index of family involvement in a firm. Next, the study estimates a four-factor model of monthly stock market data from 2003 to 2013 to identify potential abnormal returns between portfolios containing firms with a specific corporate governance shaped by families and portfolios with non-family firms.

## 4.2 Literature Review

### 4.2.1 Families as Blockholders

The legal and institutional framework of a country has major effects on its ownership structures (Becht and Boehmer, 2003; Djankov et al., 2008). Countries with low shareholder protection with a civil law origin like Germany (La Porta et al., 1998) give rise to relatively underdeveloped capital markets with more concentrated ownership structures (La Porta et al., 1999; Becht and Boehmer, 2003; Faccio and Lang, 2002; Djankov et al., 2008). As a consequence, large and actively engaged blockholders are expected to mitigate agency conflicts alongside shareholders and managers and thus increase firm value (Shleifer and Vishny, 1997).

Yet these blockholders differ from each other, as Cronqvist and Fahlenbrach (2009) find blockholder-fixed effects and that "different large shareholders have distinct investment and governance styles". They conclude that blockholders with higher monitoring abilities are found to have larger impacts on both firm policy and performance. Correspondingly, Mietzner and Schweizer (2014) find that German capital markets react differently on the engagement of different investors, depending on their monitoring abilities and incentive structure. Mietzner and Schiereck (2016) describe that the size of value creation in case of newly formed blocks of shareholders depends on the identity of the block acquirer and subsequent monitoring implications, as shown for strategic investors and activist sponsors.

Other studies find similar effects specifically for family investors as family-based acquisitions in Continental Europe have been analyzed to generate significant abnormal returns (Schüler et al., 2019). While controlling for different types of blockholders in firms, Andres (2008) concludes that families as shareholders appear to successfully balance agency problems associated with the existence of a large blockholder, especially in the case of families.

Families as large blockholders have a specific effect on the firms' corporate policies and on the agency relations within the firm and among other shareholders of the firm. Due to the legal preconditions in Germany, firms tend to exhibit rather concentrated ownership structures (Becht and Boehmer,

2003; Barontini and Caprio, 2006), and families are among the most prevalent blockholders (Faccio and Lang, 2002; Achleitner et al., 2009, 2019). Hence, due to their concentrated shareholding family, blockholders are highly incentivized to monitor their assets (Demsetz and Lehn, 1985). Furthermore, the corporate governance of a firm may profit from the family's superior knowledge of the firm (Klein, 2000; Anderson and Reeb 2003a), as for example in Germany in 55 % of firms held by families, a family member is also a CEO on the executive board (Ampenberger, 2010). Hence, the corporate governance system of firms may profit from family blockholders by reducing agency conflicts between managers and shareholders through advanced monitoring.

At the same time, the prominent influence of family members in the firm may hamper firm value due to costs arising from agency conflicts between the majority shareholder (e.g. the family blockholder) and other minority shareholders that may fear expropriation (Shleifer and Vishny, 1997; Anderson and Reeb, 2004; Villalonga and Amit, 2006). However, this risk may be offset by the fact that unlike other investors, families are basically perceived as long-term-oriented (Anderson and Reeb, 2003a) with an intrinsic incentive for the success and survival of their investment (Gottardo and Moisello, 2017), as they usually have a major proportion of their assets and wealth of the family invested in their firms (Anderson and Reeb, 2003b).

### 4.2.2 Corporate Governance and Stock Market Returns

Shareholders' direct influence on corporate decisions is limited in Germany. Unlike in Switzerland, the UK or US, the German stock corporation law prescribes a two-tier board corporate governance framework prescribing an executive and a supervisory board. The shareholders' meeting may not issue instructions to the executive board and can only appoint limited positions in the supervisory board, as due to the German concept of co-determination, some members of this board may be appointed by employees (Gorton and Schmid, 2000). The executive board is indirectly appointed by the supervisory board.

Hence, to safeguard their assets, family shareholders are commonly engaged in the legal bodies of their firms (Andres, 2008). Studies in Germany, for example, find that members of the shareholding founding families are present in more than two thirds of executive boards and more than one third of supervisory boards (Ampenberger, 2010; Achleitner et al., 2019). The means of engagement of shareholding family members may thus vary from voting as a shareholder during the annual stockholders'/general meeting to monitoring the firm as a supervisory board-member or to actively participating in the executive board of a company. With regard to these means, family involvement is expected to serve as a proxy for the particular corporate governance framework in German family firms.

Differences in accounting-, operational- and market[62] performance between family firms and non-family firms are found to be related to family management-involvement, although family involvement is often captured via the imprecise application of a dummy variable for the management participation of family members (i.a. Mazzi, 2011; Taras et al., 2018). The findings on the moderating role of family management presence have been similar in Western- and Continental-European countries (Maury, 2006; Barontini and Caprio, 2006) and Germany (Andres, 2008; Achleitner et al., 2019).

By contrast, the few existing studies on stock market returns of family businesses are primarily based on pure ownership definitions of family firms (i.a. Corstjens et al., 2006; Eugster and Isakov, 2019). Results of these studies show an equal or better performance of family firms: Family firms in Switzerland appear to generate significant abnormal returns (Eugster and Isakov, 2019). In Portugal and Spain, Miralles-Marcelo et al. (2014) find at least the same performance for family as for non-family businesses. The number of studies on stock returns of family firms in Germany is rather limited. In a cross-country study of Western-European countries, Cella (2009) finds that in Germany, family firms outperform their non-family counterparts. Corstjens et al. (2006) investigate the stock market development of family firms and non-family firms in France, Germany, the UK and the US. They conclude that the performance of family firms is at least as good as the performance of non-family firms across all states investigated.

Following this literature review, the pivotal research objective of this paper is the notion that with regards to differences in market performance of family and non-family firms, the real-world influence of family shareholders and members on the firms' corporate governance has generally been under-researched. This is particularly the case in a less investor-friendly corporate governance system (like in Germany) where shareholders cannot exercise direct control over top executives (like in the US). Especially blockholder-specific incentive structures and monitoring abilities are assumed to explain differences in stock market performances. This factor is disregarded in the few existing studies that access the stock market returns of family firms primarily via ownership definitions. In

62 Market performance differences are largely accessed via Tobin's Q by literature (Taras et al., 2018).

their influential publication, Gompers et al. (2003) showed that stock market performance in general may be explained by differences in corporate governance of firms over a longer span of time. Subsequent articles such as by Bebchuk et al. (2009) replicated the results on stock market returns for different sets of corporate governance proxy variables. While the methodological approach of these publications may serve as a blueprint for the assessment of corporate governance influences on equity prices, their results are not directly transferrable to Continental Europe: Firstly, the authors analyze firms in the United States in an outsider-controlled system of corporate governance. Approaching corporate governance influences in an insider-controlled system like in Germany may require information on the presence of blockholders in the institutions of the firm (Becht and Boehmer, 2003). Secondly, while Cronqvist and Fahlenbrach (2009) find ort heer-specific effects on corporate policies (without assessing stock market returns), the aforementioned publications of Gompers et al. (2003) and Bebchuk et al. (2009) do not at all consider the specific effects of families as investors on corporate governance. The literature review of this study concludes that family investors in Germany feature a variety of unique implications for both corporate governance and performance. Against the backdrop of the particular legal framework of German stock corporations, this paper hypothesizes, that the firm-specific influences of families on the corporate governance systems of the companies they are invested in may explain stock market return differences between family firms and non-family firms.

## 4.3 Methodology

### 4.3.1 Sample and Family Influence Index

The employed panel dataset includes 278 listed German companies (Composite Deutscher Aktienindex/CDAX) from 2003 to 2013. The sample further excludes banks and insurance companies and preferred shareholders without voting rights, and only covers common shareholdings. Financial data is retrieved from Datastream by Refinitiv. The start in 2003 avoids distortions due to the introduction of the German Corporate Governance Index that came into effect in August 2002. The paper argues that the observation period up to 2013 (including the financial crises) is particularly well suited for the research objective of this paper to examine the management and monitoring capabilities of family investors and connected capital market valuation. Caused by ongoing conventional and unconventional monetary policy interventions, the period since 2014 is increasingly shaped by a disconnection between financial markets developments and fundamentals of the real economy[63]– peaking in the latest financial market anomalies in 2020 (Financial Stability Committee, 2017; Sigl-Glöckner, 2018; Igan et al., 2020). As it would be increasingly difficult to differentiate the influence of corporate governance on capital market valuation in an environment with suspected market bubbles (Hudepohl et al., 2019), this study excludes the years after 2013 to ensure that the findings are generalizable to an economic steady state.

Research on family businesses has struggled somewhat to adequately define what constitutes a family firm, especially when studying performance (Mazzi, 2011). This paper builds on prior approaches of Astrachan et al. (2002), Klein (2000), and Achleitner et al. (2009, 2019) and introduces an advanced tool to measure family influence that was created particularly to assess the effect of corporate governance features.

The approach used in this study has two key elements: (1) It avoids dichotomous distinctions between non-family firms and family firms while allowing for a diverse assessment of family influence, and (2) it does not rely on companies' self-assessment of databases (e.g. the F-PEC scale), which may be imprecise or out of date. The dataset provides for uniquely fine-graded information on the corporate governance influence of families. While this paper considers such a depth of information inevitable against the backdrop of the German corporate governance system, to the best of the authors' knowledge, no such dataset on German listed firms exists, as the collection of this data is extremely time-consuming.

To begin, for each year in the observation period, company-specific information on each shareholder (with >5 % of voting rights), the background of each member of the board of directors ("Vorstand"), as well as the supervisory board ("Aufsichtsrat"), is hand-collected from the yearly financial statements, information provided by the firm (e.g. web site, press releases), and the data provider Dafne. The general methodology of the paper then follows Gompers et al. (2003) in their construction of a governance index (G-index) to investigate the empirical relationship with stock market performance[64]. For each firm, one point is added for a characteristic of the family governance influence (maximum

---

63 The leading German stock market index DAX surged by 37.4 % from 2014 to 2018 alone and the MSCI Europe increased by almost 50 % up to the beginning of 2020.

64 In their popular study, Gompers et al. (2003) built a "Governance Index/G-Index" to assess the level of shareholder rights. The G-index is the sum of one scalar for the presence of each out of 24 governance rules and used as a proxy for the correlation of corporate governance on the one hand and performance on the other hand.

index score of 12), which keeps the index transparent, straightforward, and effortlessly replicable. A detailed list of index components and definitions is in Table 4.1.

**Table 4.1:** Family Influence Index

| Index Component | Definition |
|---|---|
| Ownership | Family voting share >5 % |
| | Family voting share >25 % |
| | Family voting share >50 % |
| Executive Board | Family member holds CEO position |
| | Family members are present on executive board |
| | Family holds majority of executive board positions |
| Supervisory Board | Family member holds chairman position |
| | Family members are present on supervisory board |
| | Family holds majority of supervisory board positions |
| Founder Presence | Founder holds CEO or executive board position |
| | Founder holds supervisory board position |
| | Founder/founding family voting share > 25 % |

This table reports the construction of the family index used to identify the firms attributed to the family portfolios. Company-specific information on each shareholder (>5 % of voting rights), and the background of each representative in the executive board and supervisory board in each year is hand-collected from yearly financial statements, information provided by a firm (e.g. web site, press releases), and the data provider Dafne. One point is added for each characteristic of family governance influence that the firm meets (maximum index score of 12).

As the G-Index by Gompers et al. (2003), the family firm-index in this study consists of partial indices which are based on: (1) Ownership, (2) Management participation (via Executive Board), (3) Control (via the Supervisory Board), and (4) Founding Family Presence. These partial indices account for particularities of the German Corporate Governance System. The Ownership Index takes into account, for example, the fact that the German Stock Corporation Act (Aktiengesetz/AktG) stipulates that decisions such as the dismissal of a Supervisory Board member (Section 103 AktG) require a majority of more than 75 % at the company's Annual General Meeting. Majority shareholders with more than 25 % but less than 50 % of outstanding voting rights can therefore block important strategic corporate decisions (Achleitner et al., 2009). By adding one point to the ownership index if a family holds at minimum voting rights-stake of 25 %, the index accounts for this influence. Similarly, other partial indices increase with rising family representation on the executive and/or supervisory board, as well as the presence of the founder or the founding-family to account for their broadly recognized impact on performance (e.g. Mazzi et al., 2011).

## 4.3.2 Model

The empirical methodology uses the annual index scoring of the firms to model two separate portfolios[65]: The Family Portfolio contains companies with a score of ≥7; the Non-Family Portfolio contains companies with a score of 0. Portfolios are remodeled each year according to the firm's specific annual scoring (Gompers et al., 2003). To model the annual buy-and-hold returns, the total return index value $I_i$ of stock $i$ on the first trading day of the following month is divided by the index value of the first day of month $t$, before subtracting 1. Portfolios are equally value-weighted according to the market capitalization of the companies in relation to the total market capitalization of the corresponding portfolio.

$$(1) \qquad R_P = \alpha + \beta_1 \left(R_m - R_f\right) + \beta_2 SMB + \beta_3 HML + \beta_4 WML + \varepsilon_t$$

The study employs a four-factor model (Fama and French, 1993; Carhart, 1997) to estimate the potential influence of corporate governance regimes shaped by families on stock market returns. The dependent variable $R_P$ denotes either the portfolio excess return $\left(R_P - R_f\right)$, or the difference between the returns of the Family Portfolio less the return of the Non-Family Portfolio $\left(R_{FP} - R_{NFP}\right)$. This equals an investment strategy long on firms with family influence and short on firms with no family influence. Data on German-specific factors come from Richard Stehle's website[66]. The estimated intercept $\alpha$ is perceived as the abnormal return in excess of what could have been achieved by passive investments in the factors (Gompers et al., 2003; Bebchuk et al., 2009).

---

65 The use of portfolios to estimate differences among family/non-family firms and portfolio excess returns has been used before (e.g., Cella, 2009; Fahlenbrach, 2009; Miralles-Marcelo et al., 2013; Eugster & Isakov, 2019). However, to the best of the author' s knowledge, it has not been operationalized in this way with an index of family influence in ownership and management.

66 https://www.wiwi.hu-berlin.de/de/professuren/bwl/bb/daten/fama-french-factors-germany/fama-french -factors-for-germany.

## 4.4 Results and Discussion

### 4.4.1 Family Index and Portfolio Buy-and-hold Returns

The companies in the sample are sorted into three portfolios based on their year-specific value in the family influence index. Table 4.2 lists the quantity of firms in portfolios. Table 4.3 gives summary statistics for the family influence index and its four subindices (1) Ownership, (2) Management participation (via Executive Board), (3) Control (via the Supervisory Board), and (4) Founding Family Presence over time.

Summary statistics find that, on average, 75.3 % of firms in the sample exhibit a degree of family influence (index score ≥1, see Table 4.2). This finding confirms other research contributions that demonstrate that the share of family firms among publicly listed companies is relatively high compared to that in other European countries (Faccio and Lang, 2002; Barontini and Caprio, 2006; Andres, 2008; Achleitner et al., 2009). For firms that exhibit family influence, the median ownership share is at least 25 % (ownership index score of 2).

**Table 4.2:** Family and Non-family Portfolios

| | Number of Firms in each portfolio | | | | Percent of Firms in each portfolio | | |
|---|---|---|---|---|---|---|---|
| **Year** | **Non-family portfolio** | **Intermediate portfolio** | **Family portfolio** | **Total** | **Non-family portfolio** | **Intermediate portfolio** | **Family portfolio** |
| 2003 | 37 | 83 | 26 | 146 | 25.3 % | 56.8 % | 17.8 % |
| 2004 | 37 | 95 | 25 | 157 | 23.6 % | 60.5 % | 15.9 % |
| 2005 | 41 | 118 | 24 | 183 | 22.4 % | 64.5 % | 13.1 % |
| 2006 | 54 | 144 | 25 | 223 | 24.2 % | 64.6 % | 11.2 % |
| 2007 | 60 | 145 | 32 | 237 | 25.3 % | 61.2 % | 13.5 % |
| 2008 | 56 | 153 | 34 | 243 | 23.0 % | 63.0 % | 14.0 % |
| 2009 | 58 | 157 | 28 | 243 | 23.9 % | 64.6 % | 11.5 % |
| 2010 | 61 | 152 | 29 | 242 | 25.2 % | 62.8 % | 12.0 % |
| 2011 | 59 | 151 | 25 | 235 | 25.1 % | 64.3 % | 10.6 % |
| 2012 | 62 | 140 | 27 | 229 | 27.1 % | 61.1 % | 11.8 % |
| 2013 | 56 | 131 | 23 | 210 | 26.7 % | 62.4 % | 11.0 % |
| Mean | 52.82 | 133.55 | 27.09 | 213.45 | 24.7 % | 62.3 % | 12.9 % |

This table provides an overview of the portfolio sizes over the 2003–2013 period. Portfolios are formed according to the score of the family index, which, in turn, is calculated from the family variables as described in Table 4.1.

**Table 4.3:** Family Influence Index Statistics

| **Index Statistic** | **'03** | **'04** | **'05** | **'06** | **'07** | **'08** | **'09** | **'10** | **'11** | **'12** | **'13** |
|---|---|---|---|---|---|---|---|---|---|---|---|
| **Number of firms** | **146** | **157** | **183** | **223** | **237** | **243** | **243** | **242** | **235** | **229** | **210** |
| | **Max Score** | | | | | | | | | | |
| Index Total | 10 | 10 | 10 | 11 | 10 | 11 | 12 | 10 | 10 | 10 | 10 |
| Ownership Index | 3 | 3 | 3 | 3 | 3 | 3 | 3 | 3 | 3 | 3 | 3 |
| Executive Board Index | 3 | 3 | 3 | 3 | 3 | 3 | 3 | 3 | 3 | 3 | 3 |
| Supervisory Board Index | 3 | 3 | 3 | 3 | 3 | 3 | 3 | 3 | 3 | 3 | 3 |
| Founder Presence Index | 3 | 3 | 3 | 3 | 3 | 3 | 3 | 3 | 3 | 3 | 3 |
| | **Average Score (Mean)** | | | | | | | | | | |
| Index Total | 4.21 | 4.14 | 4.04 | 3.98 | 4.00 | 4.03 | 3.91 | 3.81 | 3.77 | 3.72 | 3.65 |
| Ownership Index | 1.67 | 1.68 | 1.69 | 1.57 | 1.58 | 1.64 | 1.63 | 1.60 | 1.58 | 1.57 | 1.56 |
| Executive Board Index | 0.92 | 0.88 | 0.84 | 0.85 | 0.85 | 0.83 | 0.76 | 0.74 | 0.71 | 0.73 | 0.71 |
| Supervisory Board Index | 0.60 | 0.58 | 0.56 | 0.55 | 0.59 | 0.57 | 0.58 | 0.57 | 0.55 | 0.54 | 0.51 |
| Founder Presence Index | 1.08 | 1.06 | 1.00 | 0.96 | 0.95 | 0.94 | 0.90 | 0.87 | 0.88 | 0.85 | 0.82 |

This table provides summary statistics on the family influence index and its four partial indices 1) Ownership, 2) Management participation (via Executive Board), 3) Control (via Supervisory Board), and 4) Founding Family Presence over time. Table 4.1 gives detailed information on the construction of each index.

The average level of family involvement overall (total index score) decreased from 4.2 in 2003 to 3.7 in 2013. Moreover, in 50 % of the sample firms that exhibit family influence, the founder or founding family still held more than a 25 % ownership stake, or held a position on the executive or supervisory board. These statistics support the assumption that corporate governance in these firms is shaped significantly by members of a shareholding family throughout all governance bodies covered under the German corporate law. The sample also confirms other studies that find that members of shareholder families in Germany are often engaged in executive or supervisory boards (Andres, 2008; Achleitner et al., 2009, 2019).

The study notes that some firms on the German CDAX are very large in size and constitute a significant fraction of market capitalization. Hence, applying equally-weighted portfolios and value-weighted portfolios may prevent results from being skewed due to these large-cap firms (Corstjens et al., 2006; Eugster and Isakov, 2019). Moreover, firms without family shareholders are significantly larger in terms of market capitalization than family firms (see Figure 4.3 in

Appendix). This finding affirms the value of using both equally and value-weighted approaches in modeling portfolios.

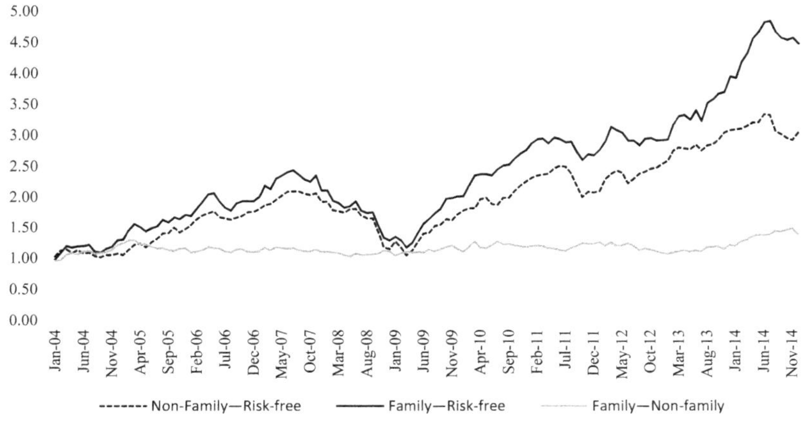


**Figure 4.1:** Equally-weighted Portfolios (Buy-and-Hold Returns)

The figure shows cumulative returns of the family form portfolio, the non-family firm portfolio and the return on a zero-investment portfolio that is long in the family firm portfolio and short in the non-family firm portfolio for equally weighted portfolios for 2004–2014. The portfolios are updated annually with the last update in 2013.

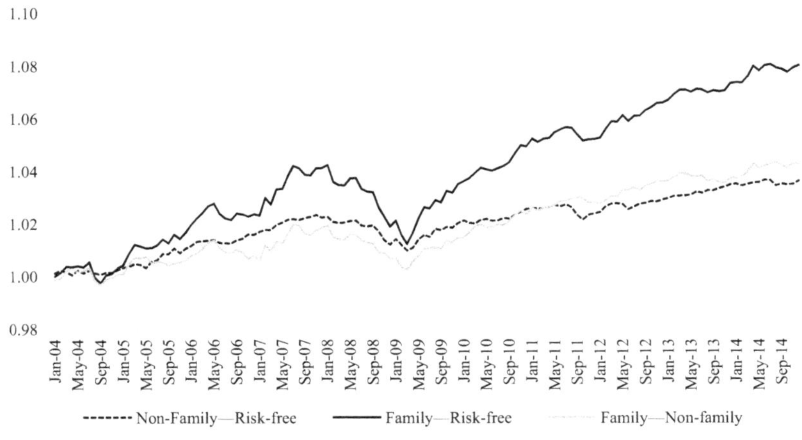


**Figure 4.2:** Value-weighted Portfolios (Buy-and-Hold Returns)

The figure shows cumulative returns of the family form portfolio, the non-family firm portfolio and the return on a zero-investment portfolio that is long in the family firm portfolio and short in the non-family firm portfolio for value-weighted portfolios in the period 2004–2014. The portfolios are updated annually with the last update in 2013.

Figures 4.1 and 4.2 plot the portfolio returns over time. The cumulative buy-and-hold return of family portfolios (less risk-free returns) is higher than that for non-family portfolios for equally-weighted, as well as for value-weighted portfolios and throughout the entire sample period. This result is comparable to studies of Achleitner et al. (2009, 2019) who find similar higher cumulative returns of family firms in Germany.

A comparison of operative performance variables such as Return on Assets (ROA) or Return on Equity (ROE) does not reveal a consistent and significant difference between family portfolios and non-family portfolios (see Table 4.5 in Appendix). Among other financial measures, significant differences can be primarily found in size (market capitalization and total assets). The four-factor model employed in this study controls for size effects via the momentum effect (WML) and the size factor (SMB). In addition, test statistics reveal that firms in family portfolios are found to be less leveraged than non-family firms, which confirms the findings of other authors on Germany (Schmid, 2013; Ampenberger et al., 2013; Motylska-Kuzma, 2017).

However, there are several reasons consistent with the above-cited literature suggesting that governance could matter for firm performance. Valuation effects arising from the acquisition of minority and majority stakes, for instance, show that share prices adjust quickly to relevant changes in corporate governance (e.g. Drees et al., 2013; Mietzner and Schiereck, 2016; Mietzner and Schweizer, 2014). Thus, "corporate governance matters for firm performance" (Gompers et al., 2003) and this association is reflected in equity prices.

This reasoning is also true for long-term performance differences between family and non-family firms, assuming that corporate governance in general, but the ability and motivation of specific shareholders to directly influence corporate policy, in particular, play a role but are not directly reflected in stock prices (Gompers et al., 2003; Bebchuk et al., 2009). As differences in long-term realized returns may be propelled by different risk factors or market sentiment, the study uses a four-factor model to examine the long-term cross section of stock returns on a risk-adjusted basis. Specifically, this model controls for different exposures to systematic risk (market risk premium), as well as company size (size factor), value characteristics (return on a book-to-market factor), and market sentiment (momentum factor). Analogous to Gompers et al. (2003), it is assumed that if the family firm portfolio differs significantly from the non-family firm-portfolio in these factors, long-lasting return drifts can be attributed, at least in part, to specific risk characteristics of family firms and non-family firms. Then again, once the study controls for specific risk and market characteristics, differences in long-term performance can to some extent be attributed to differences in governance characteristics.

### 4.4.2 Stock Return Regression

Table 4.4 presents the results on the four-factor model estimation. The returns are generally driven by the relative market portfolio performance, as well as by size. Regarding abnormal returns, the estimations for family portfolios and non-family portfolios exhibit significantly positive excess returns (columns (2)-(3)). A zero-investment strategy long on family firms and short on non-family firms continues to yield a 0.50 % positive abnormal return that is significant at the 10 % level (column (4)). This equals an annualized excess return of 6.00 %.

**Table 4.4:** Four-factor Model

| | Equally-weighted portfolios | | | Value-weighted portfolios | | |
|---|---|---|---|---|---|---|
| | **Non-family-Risk free** | **Family-Risk free** | **Family-Non-family** | **Non-family-Risk free** | **Family-Risk free** | **Family-Non-family** |
| *Alpha* | 0.009** | 0.014*** | 0.005* | -0.001*** | -0.001*** | 0.0004*** |
| | (2.042) | (3.16) | (1.752) | (-7.631) | (-3.057) | (2.776) |
| $R_m$-$R_f$ | 0.346*** | 0.295*** | -0.051 | 0.016*** | 0.019*** | 0.003 |
| | (3.368) | (2.732) | (-0.684) | (4.192) | (3.065) | (0.658) |
| *SMB* | 0.496*** | 0.485*** | -0.011 | 0.02*** | 0.022** | 0.002 |
| | (3.458) | (3.219) | (-0.106) | (3.644) | (2.589) | (0.453) |
| *HML* | 0.266 | 0.098 | -0.168 | 0.009 | 0.005 | -0.004 |
| | (1.652) | (0.578) | (-1.434) | (1.46) | (0.529) | (-0.619) |
| *WML* | -0.046 | -0.134 | -0.088 | 0.001 | -0.008 | -0.009** |
| | (-0.484) | (-1.352) | (-1.284) | (0.235) | (-1.486) | (-2.576) |
| *N* | 132 | 132 | 132 | 132 | 132 | 132 |
| $R^2$ | 14.20 % | 13.22 % | 2.76 % | 15.87 % | 13.40 % | 7.32 % |
| Adj. $R^2$ | 11.50 % | 10.49 % | -0.30 % | 13.22 % | 10.67 % | 4.40 % |

This table reports the regression results of the four-factor model for equally value-weighted non-family and family portfolios. Regressions cover the 2003 to 2013 period. Row 2 shows the specification of the dependent variable, i.e. returns on a zero investment strategy, in non-family and family portfolios, as well as going long in the family firm-portfolio and short in the non-family firm-portfolio. Portfolio returns are regressed on the market-portfolio return less the risk-free return rate ($R_m$ - $R_f$), zero-investment benchmark-factors for size (Small Minus Big/SMB) and book-to-market-value (High Minus Low/HML), and the momentum effect (Winners Minus Losers/WML). Factor-specific data on the German stock market come from the website of Prof. Richard Stehle. Significance at the 10 % level, 5 % level, and 1 % level is indicated by *, **, and ***, respectively. Test statistics are in parentheses.

To control for any impact of small-cap firms, the study next re-estimates the four-factor model with value-weighted portfolios (Eugster and Isakov, 2019). As column 7 (Table 4.4) shows, the results for alpha report a 0.04 % positive abnormal monthly return that is significant at the 1 % level going long the family firm-portfolio and short the non-family firm-portfolio. Hence, the four-factor models widely confirm the return performances suggested by the descriptive statistics. Portfolios with a significant corporate governance influence of families yield annualized excess returns between 0.48 % (value-weighted) and 6.00 % (equally-weighted).

## 4.5 Discussion

The model's results are consistent with those of other authors who find that (1) ownership structure and concentration influence stock market returns (Cella, 2009), and (2) family ownership is associated with higher stock returns (see Eugster and Isakov, 2019; Cella, 2009). The estimated annualized abnormal return (equally-weighted) is even higher than the excess return of 3.6 % found by Cella (2009) for the period of 1993–2006 in Germany. The findings are also compatible with those of Schüler et al. (2019), who discover higher abnormal returns for acquisitions of family firms than for private equity firms. This suggests that market participants regard family business investors as more capable of managing and controlling acquired firms.

The findings further suggest that stock market return differences between family firms and non-family firms are due to perceptions of the differences in corporate governance systems between the two portfolios. The construction of the family portfolio containing firms with a minimum index score of 7 implies a severe degree of family influence throughout the firm's corporate governance bodies, as proscribed by German law[67]. Hence, the paper assumes that the market will view this high level of influence as beneficial for corporate governance.

Shareholding families are often poorly diversified (Anderson and Reeb, 2003b), since they are long-term-oriented in their shareholder positions (Anderson and Reeb, 2003a), as well as reputation-sensitive (Anderson et al., 2003; Tong, 2008). They are thus strongly incentivized to monitor corporate

67 The study also ran four-factor models long on family portfolios with only a medium family influence on corporate governance (index value >1 and <7), and short on non-family portfolios. Neither the equally nor value-weighted model specifications revealed any significant excess returns (results available upon request).

policies and performance. Given families' superior firm knowledge (founding families or founders are found to be present in 50 % of the family firms), as well as their regulation-driven presence on executive and supervisory boards (in the case of Germany), the corporate governance system of these firms is assumed to be highly effective.

## 4.6 Conclusion

The purpose of this study is to explore the relationship between the influence of family shareholders on the corporate governance system of the firms they are invested in and stock market returns. In an environment of low shareholder protection, like in Germany, more concentrated ownership structures follow the increasing effectiveness of large shareholders in mitigating agency conflicts. However, blockholders vary in their effectiveness, and capital markets react differently depending on shareholder type. Employing listed German corporations and a replicable index of family influence on corporate governance in these firms, the results of the study show that portfolios with family firms generate significant abnormal returns in comparison to portfolios with non-family firms (annualized abnormal return: 0.48 %–6.00 %). In conclusion, the results show that, due to their monitoring incentives and long-term orientation, family blockholders are highly successful in reducing agency problems, while offering superior firm knowledge. Under German corporate law, corporate control must be carried out in various governance bodies. Families are often present in these bodies, thereby creating a significant family-shaped form of corporate governance. The paper suggests that the specific family-characterized governance systems of firms in family portfolios are beneficial for the monitoring and controlling of these firms. Regarding practical implications, these findings suggest that the engagement of family investors may serve as a signal to smaller investors, for whom the ex-ante analysis and ex-post monitoring of investments is relatively costly. Doing so, family blockholders may help to reduce information asymmetries for minority investors or single stockholders (e.g. for individual retirement provisions), since the wealth of family investors is largely tied up in the firm and they are strongly incentivized to exercise monitoring and control.

## 4.7 Appendix

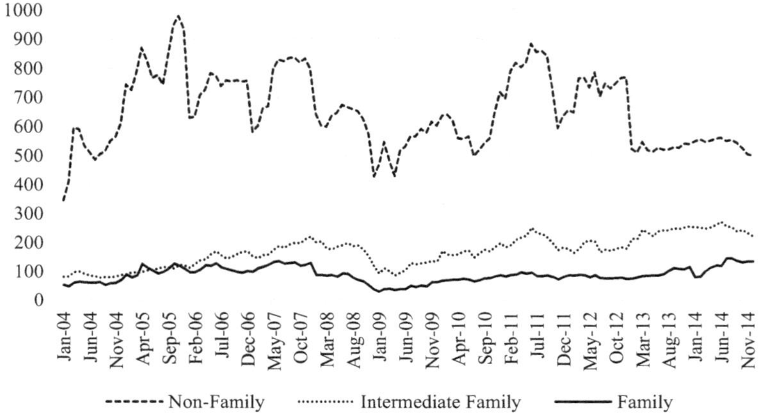


**Figure 4.3:** Market Capitalization by Portfolio (in mEUR)

**Table 4.5:** Comparison of Operating Performance per Year

| Variable | 2003 | 2004 | 2005 | 2006 | 2007 | 2008 | 2009 | 2010 | 2011 | 2012 | 2013 |
|---|---|---|---|---|---|---|---|---|---|---|---|
| | | | | No-family influence | | | | | | | |
| Total Assets (in mEUR) | 845.4 | 1,184.6 | 986.3 | 438.6 | 392.6 | 490.1 | 477.7 | 522.0 | 814.8 | 594.4 | 657.0 |
| Market Capitalization (in mEUR) | 324.7 | 539.1 | 558.7 | 497.1 | 455.6 | 355.7 | 444.0 | 761.2 | 586.6 | 386.6 | 1,020.2 |
| ROA (in %) | 1.24 | 3.48 | 4.86 | 4.87 | 5.29 | 4.74 | 2.31 | 4.97 | 5.17 | 5.23 | 5.30 |
| ROE (in %) | 2.22 | 7.74 | 9.57 | 10.75 | 11.67 | 11.07 | 5.93 | 10.32 | 10.81 | 11.41 | 9.96 |
| Equity in % of Total Assets | 31.66 | 33.62 | 38.03 | 38.91 | 38.02 | 34.34 | 36.42 | 37.89 | 38.08 | 37.12 | 39.03 |
| Current Ratio | 1.62 | 1.80 | 1.57 | 1.59 | 1.55 | 1.37 | 1.40 | 1.48 | 1.48 | 1.40 | 1.66 |
| Sales growth (in %) | 1.11 | 4.36 | 5.99 | 11.97 | 7.83 | 6.55 | -10.07 | 8.85 | 10.92 | 5.35 | 0.74 |
| Market-to-Book Ratio | 1.07 | 1.33 | 1.42 | 1.80 | 1.86 | 2.04 | 1.09 | 1.26 | 1.55 | 1.28 | 1.48 |
| Dividends per Share (in EUR) | 0.24 | 0.31 | 0.46 | 0.41 | 0.33 | 0.39 | 0.13 | 0.37 | 0.39 | 0.32 | 0.38 |
| | | | | Intermediate family influence | | | | | | | |
| Total Assets (in mEUR) | 142.7 | 139.5 | 149.4 | 163.0 | 174,.6 | 181.9 | 202.9 | 203.3 | 197.0 | 201.4 | 255.7 |
| Market Capitalization (in mEUR) | 65.3 | 71.1 | 131.0 | 119.3 | 149.6 | 100.8 | 113.9 | 141.7 | 152.4 | 167.8 | 217.6 |
| ROA (in %) | 3.21 | 4.07 | 4.28 | 6.54 | 6.29 | 5.00 | 3.82 | 4.78 | 5.62 | 5.37 | 5.34 |
| ROE (in %) | 6.05 | 9.37 | 9.40 | 13.89 | 12.24 | 10.79 | 6.27 | 10.74 | 10.90 | 10.18 | 11.53 |
| Equity in % of Total Assets | 38.79 | 40.30 | 45.48 | 46.51 | 42.46 | 42.17 | 42.03 | 45.95 | 48.69 | 47.37 | 45.89 |
| Current Ratio | 1.76 | 1.67 | 1.64 | 1.68 | 1.55 | 1.61 | 1.70 | 1.71 | 1.68 | 1.65 | 1.70 |
| Sales growth (in %) | -1.46 | 4.46 | 8.30 | 11.26 | 9.12 | 6.10 | -4.97 | 9.03 | 7.80 | 6.64 | 2.22 |
| Market-to-Book Ratio | 1.07 | 1.52 | 1.30 | 1.72 | 1.63 | 1.79 | 1.08 | 1.25 | 1.59 | 1.33 | 1.47 |
| Dividends per Share (in EUR) | 0.11 | 0.08 | 0.10 | 0.13 | 0.14 | 0.10 | 0.12 | 0.20 | 0.21 | 0.27 | 0.25 |

*(Continued)*

**Table 4.5:** Continued

| **Variable** | **2003** | **2004** | **2005** | **2006** | **2007** | **2008** | **2009** | **2010** | **2011** | **2012** | **2013** |
|---|---|---|---|---|---|---|---|---|---|---|---|
| High family influence | | | | | | | | | | | |
| Total Assets (in mEUR) | 125.6 | 118.0 | 128.4 | 118,.2 | 111.9 | 73,.0 | 60.0 | 86.3 | 110.2 | 147.2 | 120.1 |
| Market Capitalization (in mEUR) | 45.7 | 56.7 | 51.1 | 76.1 | 44.6 | 26.0 | 46.6 | 66.4 | 71.3 | 70.9 | 113.4 |
| ROA (in %) | 3.36 | 4.63 | 6.65 | 7.08 | 6.89 | 7.01 | 5.51 | 5.73 | 5.64 | 4.81 | 4.26 |
| ROE (in %) | 4.92 | 7.85 | 11.57 | 11.49 | 15.19 | 12.80 | 9.46 | 10.43 | 10.07 | 9.39 | 7.45 |
| Equity in % of Total Assets | 50.96 | 56.00 | 54.65 | 56.82 | 54.82 | 49.60 | 54.60 | 54.81 | 54.03 | 53.01 | 51.38 |
| Current Ratio | 1.66 | 1.85 | 1.98 | 1.92 | 2.06 | 1.69 | 2.17 | 2.06 | 1.87 | 2.17 | 1.55 |
| Sales growth (in %) | 3.97 | 8.69 | 6.29 | 9.56 | 8.15 | 6.00 | -2.42 | 11.76 | 10.66 | 4.53 | 5.69 |
| Market-to-Book Ratio | 0.90 | 1.46 | 1.42 | 1.38 | 1.61 | 1.86 | 1.18 | 1.40 | 2.41 | 1.73 | 1.47 |
| Dividends per Share (in EUR) | 0.00 | 0.00 | 0.00 | 0.12 | 0.10 | 0.15 | 0.13 | 0.27 | 0.23 | 0.17 | 0.20 |
| No-Family – Family: z-Score | | | | | | | | | | | |
| Total Assets | 2.81*** | 3.94*** | 3.45*** | 2.42** | 1.84* | 2.66*** | 2.26** | 2.99*** | 3.13*** | 3.00*** | 2.04** |
| Market Capitalization | 2.50** | 3.23*** | 3.0*** | 2.13** | 1.90* | 2.40** | 2.15** | 2.76*** | 2.91*** | 2.30** | 1.92* |
| ROA | -1.81* | 0.23 | -0.05 | -1.34 | -0.54 | -0.75 | -1.78* | -0.28 | -0.66 | 0.32 | -0.37 |
| ROE | -1.37 | 0.52 | 0.22 | -1.07 | 0.14 | 0.21 | -0.81 | 0.32 | -0.01 | 0.79 | -0.04 |
| Equity % Total Assets | -0.65 | -1.70* | -1.67* | -2.02** | -1.29 | -2.51** | -1.96** | -2.43** | -2.28** | -2.07** | -1.15 |
| Current Ratio | -0.18 | 0.51 | -0.40 | -0.70 | -0.42 | -0.99 | -1.29 | -1.76* | -1.72* | -1.38 | -0.63 |
| Sales growth | 0.27 | -0.41 | -1.13 | -0.58 | -1.24 | 0.30 | -1.96* | 0.52 | 1.73* | -1.08 | -1.20 |
| Market-to-Book Ratio | -0.27 | -0.65 | 0.02 | -0.07 | 0.98 | 0.77 | -0.21 | 0.53 | -0.29 | -0.53 | 0.53 |
| Dividends per Share | 0.52 | 1.53 | 2.82*** | 1.89* | 1.81* | 1.93* | 0.38 | 1.21 | 1.48 | 0.79 | 1.08 |

This table presents the median of selective financial figures of firms in the portfolios with no-family influence, intermediate- and high family influence, as well as the results of the test statistics on the medians of firms in the non-family vs. family portfolio (Wilcoxon rank test). ***, **, and * indicate statistical significance at the 1 %, 5 %, and 10 % levels, respectively.

# 5 Sunshine after the Rain? The Stock Market Performance of Family Firms in and after Financial Crises

**Abstract**[*]: This study applies financial crises as an exogenous shock to family and non-family firms to identify differences in stock market performance. We investigate 278 firms listed on the German Stock Exchange in the world financial crisis starting in 2007 as well as the Euro crisis starting in 2010. Based on the methodology of Gompers, Ishii, and Metrick (2003), we form portfolios with and without family blockholders and apply equally- as well as value-weighted four-factor models to identify differences in stock market performance. Results show that family firms do not necessarily perform better than non-family firms in years of economic downturn. But our models suggest that they outperform non-family firms three years after the beginning of the world financial crisis and in and after the Euro crisis. This implies that family firms recover faster than their non-family counterparts. We follow that the financial preconditions of family firms, differing financial strategies during recessions and the controlling incentives and capacities that are rooted in the long-term orientation and risk aversion of family blockholders, as well as the country-specific corporate governance framework of Germany, explain these differences. The paper contributes to the ongoing academic exploration on family firm performance as well as crisis resilience of family firms and suggests practical implications for policymakers in countries with high levels of family ownership among firms.

## 5.1 Introduction

Firms controlled by families are the most common firm-type in Continental Europe (Faccio and Lang, 2002; Barontini and Caprio, 2006). Due to less shareholder protection, the ownership structures of German firms are rather concentrated (Becht and Boehmer, 2003). Family firms are the backbone of the German economy (Gottschalk et al., 2019) and represent a significant share of thefirms listed on the national stock market (Achleitner et al., 2019). With regards to the two-tier corporate governance system in place, family shareholders are often present in the legal bodies of the firm to increase their influence and

---

* This article is published in *Risk Governance and Control: Financial Markets and Institutions*, Vol. 11 No. 3, Franzoi, F. and Mietzner, M., Sunshine after the Rain? The Stock Market Performance of Family Firms in and after Financial Crises, 41–54, Copyright: Franzoi, F. and Mietzner, M. (2021).

controlling abilities that would be otherwise limited primarily to the annual general meeting (Franzoi et al., 2021).

Theort hen of superior or inferior corporate performance is of great economic relevance in countries like Germany – besides a year-long academic discussion. Without final consensus, recent studies mostly find a better operative performance in case of family firms (Wagner et al., 2015; Hansen and Block, 2020), which also holds for Germany (Andres, 2008; Achleitner et al., 2019). While corporate finance suggests family firms could afford to profit from higher debt via leverage effect, they exhibit lower debt levels than non-family firms in Germany (Schmid, 2013). Among control considerations, this supports assumptions of higher risk aversion of family firms in literature (Mishra and McConaughy, 1999; Ampenberger et al., 2013).

We suggest that the combination of strong operative performance and low leverage may be beneficial particularly in times of economic crises. Family firms for example might afford to hold on to well-trained employees during recessions and benefit after economic recovery. If this is the case and family firms profit from their economic preconditions and corporate actions in/after crises, we suggest employing historical economic crises to test this assumption. We presume that capital markets anticipate such advantages and expect that family firms may recover faster in capital market performance than non-family firms. Before the recent impact of the COVID-19 pandemic on the economy, European economies have experienced two crisis – the world financial crisis and the subsequent Euro crisis. These events may serve as exogenous shocks to the liquidity, sales, supply chains and general financial and market performance of family firms (Lins et al., 2013; Minichilli et al., 2016; Aldamen et al., 2020).

Regarding market performance, most studies unveil a higher stock market performance of family firms in Europe (Sraer and Thesmar 2007, Cella, 2009; Eugster and Isakov, 2019). In Germany family firms perform at least as good (Corstjens et al., 2006) or better than non-family firms (Cella, 2009). Nevertheless, market performance-studies often cover phases of economic expansion when performance differences among firms may be masked by the general expansion of economies and record heights in stock performance.[68] Another concern with studies on firm performance is that variations in the

68 Managerial skills (Sun et al., 2019) and good governance (van Essen et al., 2013) may be more crucial in economic recessions that in times when general market growth may cover firm-specific weaknesses in governance.

financial behavior between family and non-family firms (e.g. such as financing policies) are unlikely to be exogenous questioning causality on firm performance and valuation (Lins et al., 2013).[69] The few publications already investigating time frames of economic recession, find mixed evidence (Lins et al., 2013) or a superior market performance of family firms (Amann and Jaussaud, 2012; Lipiec, 2014; Amore, 2021).

Using the same dataset as in this analysis, Franzoi and Mietzner (2021a) show that family firms record positive abnormal returns compared to non-family firms due to the corporate governance involvement of family blockholders. While their publication includes some years of recession, it does not focus on the crisis behavior of family firms at all. We argue that specifically in financial crises we can expect performance differences among family and non-family firms in Germany, as their behavior and economic preferences were shown to differ as well. Regarding the mentioned hold-on to firm-specific human capital during crisis, studies for example show that family firms indeed lay-off employees later during crises (Sraer and Thesmar, 2007; Mietzner and Tyrell, 2012). Utilization of federal short-term working programs supplement this notion: "We want to keep our well-trained people on board", the CEO of the large German machine manufacturer TRUMPF noted – know-how and personnel-capacity are regarded as key components in post-crises competitiveness and long-term success (Washington, 2010). Due to lower leverage, family firms have additional buffer to absorb financial crisis, afford crisis strategies beyond short-term-measures and potentially profit from a better starting position in times of economic recovery. As family-wealth is often largely concentrated in the company (Anderson et al., 2003), financial crises both endanger the family and the firm. Hence, in addition to the perceived differences in operative performance during recessions, family blockholders are highly incentivized for and committed to the long-term survival of the firm which may furthermore function as positive signal to the market (Amore et al., 2021).

We apply the two mentioned economic crises as natural experiments (Sun et al., 2019) and study performance differences from the perspective of an investor applying an investment strategy long in family firms and short in non-family firms right before the world financial crisis hit stock markets in Germany in 2007. We apply four-factor models to identify return differences between family portfolios and non-family portfolios in five-year windows from 2007

69 Giroud et al. (2012) argue similarly in investigating the debt overhang and performance of Austrian ski hotels.

(world financial crisis) and 2010 (Euro crisis). Despite the largely differing operative performance, regression results reveal that the stock market returns are higher for family firms than for non-family firms after the third year of the crises for the latest. We find family firms to earn an annualized excess return compared to non-family firms between 7.95–10.68 % (world financial crisis) and 7.92–13.59 % (Euro crisis). Additional long-term estimations show that the outperformance lasts over a ten-year period up to 2017 (excess return of 5.36 %).

We follow that family firms profit from their economic preconditions (e.g. lower leverage ratios), their long-term orientation and their monitoring incentives as well as perceived market reactions. Our results contribute to the ongoing exploration of scholars investigating the link between family influence in the firm and performance by showing that phases of the economic crisis may be differentiated from general time series estimations when investigating firm performance. Based on the findings, we discuss contributions for academia and implications for policymakers in Continental European countries with high levels of family ownership.

The remainder of this paper is organized as follows. Section 2 discusses literature and develops a hypothesis and Section 3 explains the empirical method. Subsequently, Section 4 presents the results that are discussed in Section 5, before Section 6 concludes.

## 5.2 Literature Review and Hypothesis

### 5.2.1 Family Firm Performance

Given the worldwide spread and presence of family- owned firms (La Porta et al., 1999; Faccio and Lang, 2002), scholars are increasingly exploring the influence of the presence of this ownership type on the financial behavior and corporate performance since the turn of the millennium. In pioneering publications, Anderson and Reeb (2003a), Villalonga and Amit (2006), Barontini and Caprio (2006) and others started a year-long debate on performance differences, suggesting that family firms were atleast as good or better in their corporate performance than non-family firms. The latest meta-studies on the operative performance of family firms either find no significant difference (O'Boyle et al., 2012) or a rather weak, but the superior performance of family firms, though depending on the assessment of family control as well as the observed performance-measure (Wagner et al., 2015; Taras et al., 2018; Gonzalez et al., 2019; Hansen and Block, 2020).

Regarding market-based performance measures most publications find family firms to outperform non-family firms (Taras et al., 2018). Specifically on European stock market returns, Miralles-Morello et al. (2014) show that family firms perform as least as good as non-family firms in Portugal and Spain, while Sraer and Thesmar (2007) and Eugster and Isakov (2019) find a better performance of family firms in France and Switzerland. Regarding the German stock market, Corstjens et al. (2006) exhibit no difference in stock market returns, while Cella (2009) and the study similar to our's by Franzoi and Mietzner (2021a) document a superior market performance for family firms.

Recent publications started putting a focus on performance differences during times of economic recession, however with mixed evidence (Calabrò et al., 2021). Minichilli et al. (2016) and Zhou at al. (2017) both find a higher operative performance for family firms during the world financial crisis (Return on Assets (ROA) or Return on Equity(ROE)). Regarding market performance, Lins et al. (2013) show in a cross-country analysis, that in cutting investments during times of crises, families are ready to accept an underperformance compared to the market to retain control of the family firm (no significant performance difference found for developed countries). Despite of this publication, there are only few more publications on the stock market performance of family firms specifically during financial crises: Lipiec (2014) discovers an outperformance of family firms in the construction sector on the Polish stock market and Amann and Jaussaud (2012) find a greater resilience for family firms during the Asian crisis of 1997. In a current working paper, Amore et al. (2021) show that family firms perform better than non-family firms on the Italian stock market during the recent COVID-19 recession. The only long-term study specifically on Germany by Franzoi and Mietzner (2021a) that documents positive abnormal returns for family firms also includes years of recession in its panel. But the fact that their publication does not discuss operating performance or focus on financial crises at all, connected with the evidence from other publications that document a structurally different financial behavior of family firms in general and in recession phases in particular, reinforces the need for a specific study for Germany.

### 5.2.2 Family Control, Financial Preconditions and Corporate Crisis Behavior

The determinants of market performance during recessions may be varied and are rooted in the different financial behavior of family firms in economic crises. Though they do not find significant results for developed countries, Lins et al. (2013) argue that the discovered overall-underperformance of family firms in the world financial crisis can be traced back to investment cuts[70] to preserve family funds as well as firms with higher agency problems with minority shareholders. Regarding operating expenditures by contrast, Sun et al. (2019) show that family firms invest more in research and development during recessions than non-family, if they are not financially constrained. Yet an additional factor for a market discount may be that family firms differ in their stakeholder management (Zellweger and Nason, 2008) as they for example are more restrained to layoff employees during economic shocks and more credible in their commitment towards their workforce (Sraer and Thesmar, 2007; Mueller and Philippon, 2011). Mietzner and Tyrell (2012) confirm this finding for Germany and show that family firms at the same time bear an increased risk valuation (higher beta) by the market.

While these aspects may cause discounts in market valuation, they may be reasonable strategies for families and their firms as for example. Not cutting R&D expenses or carrying unemployed human capital through economic recessions for example may increase the probability of long-term success[71]. Financial crises touch the core of the prosperity of family blockholders: As a large part of the family wealth is often tied up in the firm (Anderson et al., 2003), the family is suspect to increased risk during a financial crisis and as family firms tend to be less diversified, they may be susceptible to additional risk. Family firms are commonly perceived as having a longer investment horizon (Anderson and Reeb 2003a, Gómez-Mejía et al., 2007). As the natural interest of family firm owners is the desire to pass-on the business to the subsequent generation (Arrondo-Garcia et al., 2016), families have a high incentive for monitoring (Demsetz and Lehn, 1985) and good governance in crises. Furthermore, corporate governance profits from the involvement of family blockholders (Franzoi and Mietzner, 2021a) and the commitment of these shareholders may function as a positive signal to the market and external stakeholders (Amore et al., 2021).

In the German largely bank-financed economy (Gorton and Schmid, 2000; Breig and Elsas, 2009) family firms are found to be significantly less leveraged than non-family firms due to control considerations and/or risk aversion (Schmid, 2013; Ampenberger et al., 2013). A higher equity ratio may serve

70 Investments are assessed via capital expenditures (CAPEX)/total assets.

71 Various German family firms for example are located in non-metropolitan areas, employing highly skilled personnel (e.g. mechanical engineers) that is difficult to attract. Full personnel capacity in phases of economic recovery may be a significant competitive advantage compared to firms who must hire formerly laid-off staff.

as buffer in times of financial distress. With a lower leverage ratio in family firms, strategies of not extensively cutting R&D expenses or keeping employees in phases of general economic crises, might be more realistic with regards to headroom in debt covenants. In addition, family firms in Europe have higher cash holdings than non-family firms (Durán et al., 2016; Caprio et al., 2020). Following these remarks, we hypothesize for Germany that though family firms may suffer from worse market performance compared to non-family firms in the immediate impact of financial crises, family firms may exhibit a superior stock market performance in the aftermath due to their monitoring incentives, lower leverage, countercyclical personnel-policies, and long-term survival strategies aligned with aspired financial health (Aldamen et al., 2020).

## 5.3 Methodology

### 5.3.1 Sample and Period under Review

We use the same dataset as Franzoi and Mietzner (2021a) and investigate 278 firms listed on the Germany Stock Exchange (CDAX) at the year-end of 2006, the year before the world financial crisis hit stock exchanges worldwide. The ownership structure of these firms is hand-picked by investigating annual reports, company websites and Bureau van Dijk's Dafne database and identify every ownership stake larger than 5 %. Firms are classified as family held when a voting block larger than 25 % is held by a family. The definition refers to the blocking minority prescribed by German Stock Corporation Law as a shareholder (i.e. a family) with a voting share larger than 25 % can block important strategic decisions by the general meeting of the company (such as mergers or the dismissal of supervisory board members). This definition is in line with various other studies on the financial behavior of listed family firms in Germany (Franks et al., 2012; Ampenberger et al., 2013).

Data on the daily four-factors for Germany were retrieved from Richard Stehle's website[72] and on the daily three-factors for Europe from Kenneth R. French's website[73]. Daily returns and yearly financial data of the listed firms were obtained from Thomson Datastream.

The year 2007 marks the beginning of the first phase of the impact of the world financial crisis on the European economy (Swiss National Bank, 2008;

72 https://www.wiwi.hu-berlin.de/de/professuren/bwl/bb/daten/fama-french- factors-germany/fama-french-factors-for-germany

73 https://mba.tuck.dartmouth.edu/pages/faculty/ken.french/data_library.html

German Council of Economic Experts, 2011) and the start of our first five-year observation period. The starting year is in line with various other publications on the world financial crisis (e.g. Fahlenbrach and Stulz, 2010; Van Essen et al., 2013, 2015; Amato et al., 2020). The second five-year observation period on the Euro crisis starts in 2010 with the outbreak of the European debt crisis, the bailouts of Greece, Portugal and Ireland as well as the establishment of the Financial Stability Facility (EFSF) (Copelovitch et al., 2016).

### 5.3.2 Research Design

We employ a multivariate estimation method to assess the impact of family ownership on stock market returns during the two financial crises. We apply a method prominently introduced by Gompers et al. (2003) and subsequently used by different authors on estimating stock returns of different groups distinguished primarily through corporate governance or ownership means (Cella, 2009; Eugster and Isakov, 2019; Franzoi and Mietzner, 2021a) as well used for estimating asset prices during crisis periods (Lins et al., 2013).

All firms of the sample identified as family-held per year-end 2006 and all non-family firms are grouped into two different portfolios. We subsequently calculate daily buy-and-hold-returns of the family and non-family portfolios in the respective time periods by dividing the index value of stock *i* at the end of each trading day *t* by the index value of the previous trading day before subtracting 1.

(1) $$BHR = \left[ \prod_{t=\tau_i}^{T_i} (1 + R_{it}) - 1 \right] \times 100$$

We then apply the four-factor model by Carhart (1997) that has been tested for the German market by Hanauer et al. (2013) and is presented in equation (2):

(2) $$R_{pt} = \alpha_p + \beta_{1p} RMRF_t + \beta_{2p} SMB_t + \beta_{3p} HML_t + \beta_{4p} WML_t + e_{pt}$$

where $R_{pt}$ denotes the excess return of the portfolio over the risk-free rate or the excess return of the family portfolio over the non-family portfolio at time *t*, $RMRF_t$ is the market excess return over the risk-free rate, $SMB_t$ and $HML_t$ denote the zero investment benchmark factors for size and market-to-book value according to Fama and French (1993) and $WML_t$ captures prior performance of winners-minus-losers. $A_p$ captures the excess return over a passive investment into the factors with regards to the portfolios.

An alternative method to access the influence of family blockholders on stock market returns would be the estimation of a firm characteristics approach analogous to Gompers et al. (2003) and von Lilienfeld-Toal and Ruenzi (2014) that includes monthly Fama and MacBeth (1973) regressions as well as pooled panel regressions (with two-way-clustered standard errors over time and firms in the sample). Eugster and Iskakov (2019) apply a similar approach. Yet firstly, this approach is less efficient in Germany because, in contrast to the US (Gompers et al., 2003), significantly fewer companies are listed. Secondly, the chosen calculation of buy-and-hold returns and estimation of four-factor models also allows accessing the performance difference specifically between portfolios of family firms and non-family firms in time periods of economic crises.

## 5.4 Results

### 5.4.1 Operative Performance and Buy-and-hold Returns

Table 5.1 presents the summary statistics on the operative performance. Family firms are significantly smaller than non-family firms by total assets, revenue, and the number of employees. Unlike suggested by literature, family firms do not hold more cash, but as their current ratio is higher, they have more resources on balance to meet short term obligations. Accounting performance is superior in family firms, as their median in ROA and ROE ranges between 0.9 % and 1.0 % above the non-family portfolio (confirming findings of Minichilli et al., 2016; Zhou at al., 2017 for crisis periods). In terms of market valuation, firms in the family portfolio are valued with a lower market to book ratio. As described by Ampenberger et al. (2013) and Schmid (2013), family firms exhibit a more conservative financing structure as their median equity ratio is about 7.6 % higher. Over the period under review non-family firms invested less in CAPEX, but spend more in OPEX (operating expenditure) by R&D-expenses than family businesses. While ownership is far more concentrated, as more than 56 % of the shares are closely held, family firms also pay higher dividends per share than non-family firms.

Figures 5.1 and 5.2 plot the cumulated mean and median buy-and-hold returns of the family- and non-family portfolios less the risk-free rate in both crisis periods. During the world financial crisis (Figure 5.1) family firms mostly underperformed non-family firms up to mid-2010. Further on, both mean and median buy-and hold returns range above those of non-family firms. In the second observation period covering the Euro crisis (Figure 5.2), the family firm portfolio records buy-and-hold returns constantly above the respective returns of non-family firms (both mean and median). A comparison of buy-and hold returns based on value-weighted portfolios reveals similar results (not reported, figures available upon request). Correspondingly, Summary statistics on individual portfolio returns shows higher overall mean and median returns for the family firm portfolio in the two observation periods (Table 5.5 in Appendix).

**Table 5.1:** Operating Performance

| | Non-family | | | Family (Ownership) | | | Difference | | | |
|---|---|---|---|---|---|---|---|---|---|---|
| | **Mean** | **Median** | **N** | **Mean** | **Median** | **N** | **Mean** | **p** | **Median** | **z** |
| Total Assets *(in Mio.)* | 9,956.7 | 288.7 | 770 | 3,154.0 | 177.9 | 837 | -6,802.7 | *** | -110.8 | *** |
| Revenue *(in Mio.)* | 8,095.5 | 335.3 | 764 | 2,486.5 | 215.9 | 836 | -5,609.0 | *** | -119.4 | *** |
| Cash *(in % Total Assets)* | 12.72 | 9.28 | 693 | 12.58 | 9.12 | 699 | -0.13 | | -0.17 | |
| Current Ratio | 1.99 | 1.54 | 769 | 2.07 | 1.76 | 823 | 0.08 | | 0.22 | *** |
| Return on Assets *(in %)* | 2.22 | 4.44 | 769 | 4.79 | 5.37 | 834 | 2.57 | *** | 0.93 | *** |
| Retuirn on Equity *(in %)* | 48.38 | 9.61 | 748 | 4.56 | 10.62 | 829 | -43.82 | | 1.01 | *** |
| Price/Earnings Ratio | 35.62 | 16.4 | 635 | 26.35 | 15.80 | 757 | -9.27 | | -0.60 | |
| Market to Book Ratio | 2.43 | 1.67 | 903 | 1.90 | 1.57 | 939 | -0.52 | *** | -0.10 | *** |
| Equity Ratio | 40.36 | 38.68 | 770 | 46.32 | 46.24 | 837 | 5.96 | *** | 7.56 | *** |
| CAPEX *(in % NetPPE)* | 32.00 | 20.64 | 746 | 36.71 | 23.13 | 824 | 4.71 | * | 2.49 | ** |
| R&D *(in % Revenue)* | 6.86 | 3.46 | 462 | 6.16 | 2.50 | 388 | -0.70 | | -0.95 | ** |
| Dividend/Share | 39.98 | 36.35 | 384 | 42.91 | 38.91 | 531 | 2.93 | ** | 2.56 | * |
| Dividend Yield | 2.98 | 2.44 | 519 | 3.12 | 2.56 | 597 | 0.13 | | 0.12 | |
| Closely Held Shares (in %) | 38.18 | 30.76 | 593 | 55.83 | 56.05 | 638 | 17.65 | *** | 25.30 | *** |
| No. of Employees | 41,810 | 5,644 | 549 | 11,899 | 1,458 | 571 | -29,912 | *** | -4,186 | *** |

This table reports the mean and median of selective financial characteristics of firms in the portfolios with no-family ownership and >25 % family ownership as well as the results of the test statistics on the means (ttest) and medians (Wilcoxon rank test) of the firms in the non-family vs. family portfolio. ***, **, and * indicate statistical significance at the 1 %, 5 %, and 10 % levels, respectively.

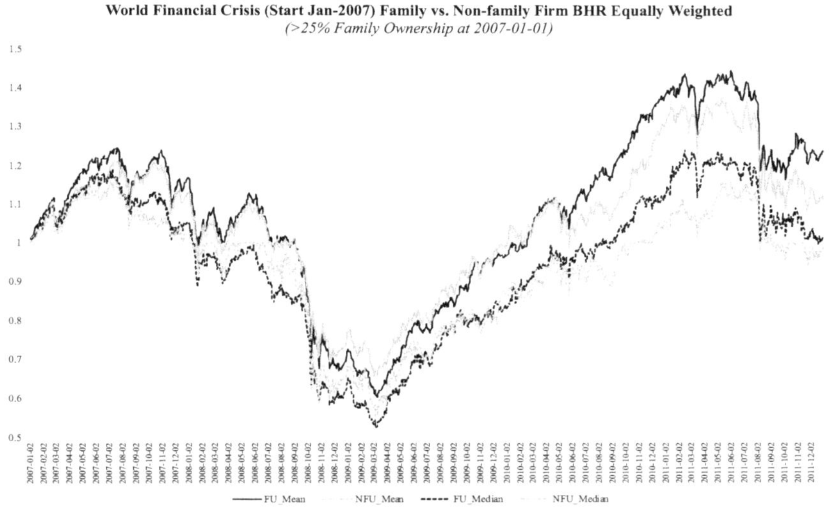


**Figure 5.1:** Buy-and-Hold Returns World Financial Crisis (2007–2011)

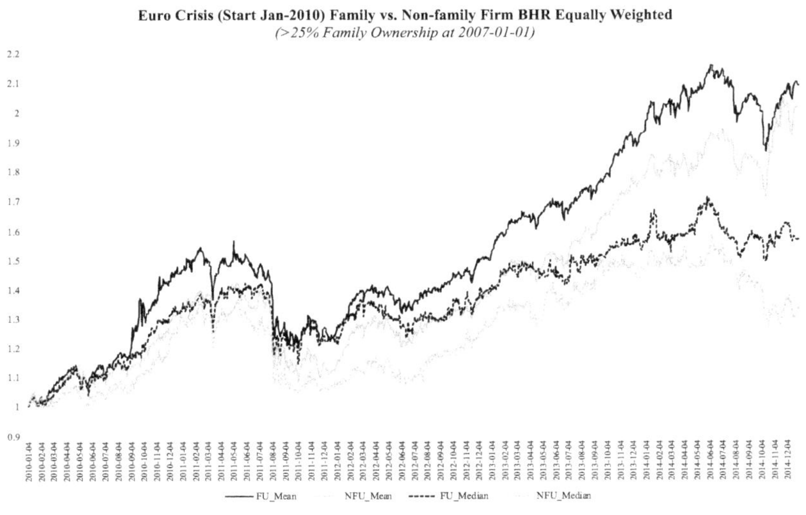


**Figure 5.2:** Buy-and-Hold Returns Euro Crisis (2010–2014)

### 5.4.2 Regression Results

Table 5.2 reports the results of the four-factor regression models on the world financial crisis in year-by-year expanding time frames from 2007 to 2008–2011 (equally-weighted). Columns 1–2 and 4–5 report the portfolio excess returns of the two portfolios. Both portfolios individually record a negative significant return during all time windows of the crisis. Column 3 and 6 report the excess returns on a strategy long in family firms vs. short in non-family firms. Excess returns are generally positively driven by size and negatively driven by momentum. We do not find a significant abnormal return for family firms in the two most severe years of the financial crisis. By contrast, the four-factor models reveal a significant excess return for family firms after the third year of the beginning of the financial crisis. Family firms outperform non-family firms by an annualized percentage between 7.95 % (2007–2010) and 10.69 % (2007–2011)[74].

Table 5.3 exhibits the regression results for the Euro crisis analogous to the previous table. Unlike in case of the first two years of the world financial crisis, the strategy long in the portfolio with family firms and short in the portfolio with non-family firms constantly reveals positive, significant alphas. These results suggest a five-year steady excess return of family firms over non-family firms. The excess return decreases over time and varies from 13.59 % (2010–2011, annualized) to 7.92 % (2010–2014, annualized).

As the regression models on Euro crisis reveal a decrease in the excess returns of family firms between 2010–2014 (compared to non-family firms), we estimate an additional long-term model covering a time frame of ten years since the outbreak of the world financial crisis. Results reveal, that a strategy long in the family firm portfolio and short in the non-family portfolio still records an annualized excess return of 5.36 %[75] (reported in Table 5.6 in the Appendix).

---

74 Calculated by average trading days per time window.

75 As data on the four-factors for Germany are only available up to 2016 by Prof. Richard Stehle, we applied a three-factor model with factors retrieved from the website of Prof. Kenneth R. French. The application of a three-factor model is also sufficient as publications on the German stock market have shown (Dirkx and Peter, 2020).

**Table 5.2:** World Financial Crisis 2007–2011: Four-factor Model (Equally-weighted)

| | **Non-family-Risk free** | **Family-Risk free** | **Family-Non-family** | **Non-family-Risk free** | **Family-Risk free** | **Family-Non-family** |
|---|---|---|---|---|---|---|
| | | 2007–2008 | | | 2007–2009 | |
| Alpha | -0.0156*** | -0.0153*** | 0.0003 | -0.0114*** | -0.0112*** | 0.0002 |
| | (-33.15) | (-31.56) | (1.14) | (-29.09) | (-27.64) | (1.11) |
| Rm-Rf | 0.009*** | 0.0091*** | 0.0000 | 0.01*** | 0.0097*** | -0.0003 |
| | (17.06) | (16.58) | (0.18) | (20.76) | (19.45) | (-1.38) |
| SMB | 0.0051*** | 0.0071*** | 0.002*** | 0.0064*** | 0.008*** | 0.0016*** |
| | (7.21) | (9.74) | (6.08) | (10.36) | (12.54) | (5.52) |
| HML | 0.0007 | 0.001 | 0.0003 | 0.0023*** | 0.0023*** | 0.0000 |
| | (0.8) | (1.13) | (0.77) | (3.71) | (3.65) | (0.13) |
| WML | -0.0018*** | -0.0021*** | -0.0003* | -0.002*** | -0.0022*** | -0.0002* |
| | (-5.42) | (-6.13) | (-1.94) | (-6.82) | (-7.44) | (-1.84) |
| N | 506 | 506 | 506 | 760 | 760 | 760 |
| $R^2$ | 54.73 % | 50.02 % | 17.79 % | 53.08 % | 46.76 % | 16.92 % |
| Adj. $R^2$ | 54.37 % | 49.63 % | 17.13 % | 52.84 % | 46.48 % | 16.48 % |
| | | 2007–2010 | | | 2007–2011 | |
| Alpha | -0.009*** | -0.0086*** | 0.0004** | -0.008*** | -0.0077*** | 0.0003** |
| | (-27.39) | (-24.87) | (2.21) | (-29.23) | (-26.64) | (2.28) |
| Rm-Rf | 0.0103*** | 0.01*** | -0.0003 | 0.0103*** | 0.01*** | -0.0003 |
| | (24.69) | (22.62) | (-1.56) | (29.49) | (27.29) | (-1.47) |
| SMB | 0.0066*** | 0.0081*** | 0.0015*** | 0.0064*** | 0.0081*** | 0.0017*** |
| | (11.98) | (13.99) | (5.58) | (13.98) | (16.73) | (6.86) |
| HML | 0.0027*** | 0.0027*** | 0.0000 | 0.0023*** | 0.0025*** | 0.0002 |
| | (5.29) | (4.95) | (-0.11) | (5.31) | (5.49) | (0.9) |
| WML | -0.0018*** | -0.002*** | -0.0002* | -0.0015*** | -0.0018*** | -0.0003** |
| | (-6.82) | (-7.36) | (-1.9) | (-6.39) | (-7.34) | (-2.51) |
| N | 1016 | 1016 | 1016 | 1273 | 1273 | 1273 |
| $R^2$ | 50.89 % | 43.23 % | 13.92 % | 53.45 % | 45.19 % | 15.99 % |
| Adj. $R^2$ | 50.70 % | 43.00 % | 13.58 % | 53.30 % | 45.02 % | 15.73 % |

This Table presents the regression results of the four-factor model (Fama and French 1993, Carhart 1997) for equally-weighted non-family and family portfolios. Regressions cover the period from 2007-01-02 to 2011-12-30 (daily). The specification of the dependent variable, i.e. returns on a zero investment strategy in non-family- and family-portfolios as well as on a strategy long on family firm-portfolios and short on non-family portfolios is denoted in row 3 of the table. Portfolio returns are regressed on the market portfolio-return less the risk free return rate (Rm-Rf), the zero-investment benchmark-facotors for size (SMB) and book-to-market-value (HML) as well as the momentum effect (WML). Factor-specific data for the German stock market has been retrieved from the website of Prof. Richard Stehle. Significance at the 10 %, 5 % and 1 % level is indicated by *, ** and ***, respectively. Test statistics are reported in parentheses.

**Table 5.3:** Euro Crisis 2010–2014: Four-factor Model (Equally-weighted)

| | **Non-family-Risk free** | **Family-Risk free** | **Family-Non-family** | **Non-family-Risk free** | **Family-Risk free** | **Family-Non-family** |
|---|---|---|---|---|---|---|
| | | 2010–2011 | | | 2010–2012 | |
| Alpha | -0.003*** | -0.0025*** | 0.0005** | -0.0023*** | -0.0019*** | 0.0004** |
| | (-16.4) | (-10.47) | (2.25) | (-15.42) | (-10.23) | (2.02) |
| Rm-Rf | 0.0087*** | 0.0086*** | 0 | 0.0083*** | 0.008*** | -0.0003 |
| | (30.64) | (23.53) | (-0.13) | (34.34) | (26.25) | (-1) |
| SMB | 0.0043*** | 0.0062*** | 0.002*** | 0.0038*** | 0.0054*** | 0.0016*** |
| | (11.72) | (13.19) | (4.23) | (12.1) | (13.73) | (4.17) |
| HML | 0.0008** | 0.0015*** | 0.0007 | 0.001*** | 0.0014*** | 0.0005 |
| | (2.48) | (3.42) | (1.54) | (3.36) | (3.91) | (1.26) |
| WML | 0.0011*** | 0.0003 | -0.0008** | 0.0007*** | 0.0002 | -0.0004* |
| | (3.89) | (0.72) | (-2.33) | (3.13) | (0.84) | (-1.66) |
| N | 513 | 513 | 513 | 767 | 767 | 767 |
| $R^2$ | 81.55 % | 64.14 % | 15.19 % | 78.07 % | 59.53 % | 12.86 % |
| Adj. $R^2$ | 81.40 % | 63.86 % | 14.52 % | 77.95 % | 59.32 % | 12.40 % |
| | | 2010–2013 | | | 2010–2014 | |
| Alpha | -0.0017*** | -0.0014*** | 0.0003* | -0.0015*** | -0.0012*** | 0.0003** |
| | (-12.85) | (-9.23) | (1.91) | (-12.64) | (-8.69) | (2.14) |
| Rm-Rf | 0.0082*** | 0.0078*** | -0.0005* | 0.008*** | 0.0074*** | -0.0006*** |
| | (35.68) | (29.27) | (-1.71) | (41.47) | (32.85) | (-2.78) |
| SMB | 0.0038*** | 0.0052*** | 0.0013*** | 0.0037*** | 0.0047*** | 0.001*** |
| | (13.02) | (15.27) | (3.9) | (14.86) | (16.36) | (3.46) |
| HML | 0.0011*** | 0.0015*** | 0.0004 | 0.0011*** | 0.0014*** | 0.0003 |
| | (4.07) | (4.89) | (1.34) | (4.81) | (5.43) | (1.26) |
| WML | 0.0006*** | 0.0002 | -0.0004* | 0.0006*** | 0.0005** | -0.0001 |
| | (2.97) | (0.79) | (-1.76) | (3.51) | (2.45) | (-0.55) |
| N | 1020 | 1020 | 1020 | 1272 | 1272 | 1272 |
| $R^2$ | 72.91 % | 57.08 % | 10.88 % | 72.72 % | 56.80 % | 9.10 % |
| Adj. $R^2$ | 72.80 % | 56.91 % | 10.53 % | 72.63 % | 56.67 % | 8.82 % |

This Table presents the regression results of the four-factor model (Fama and French 1993, Carhart 1997) for equally-weighted non-family and family portfolios. Regressions cover the period from 2010-01-04 to 2014-12-31 (daily). The specification of the dependent variable, i.e. returns on a zero investment strategy in non-family- and family-portfolios as well as on a strategy long on family firm-portfolios and short on non-family portfolios is denoted in row 3 of the table. Portfolio returns are regressed on the market portfolio-return less the risk free return rate (Rm-Rf), the zero-investment benchmark-facotors for size (SMB) and book-to-market-value (HML) as well as the momentum effect (WML). Factor-specific data for the German stock market has been retrieved from the website of Prof. Richard Stehle. Significance at the 10 %, 5 % and 1 % level is indicated by *, ** and ***, respectively. Test statistics are reported in parentheses.

As suggested by a comparison of the buy-and-hold returns of the two portfolios, the four-factor regression models confirm, that family firms did not reveal a significant difference in their stock market performance during the first phase of the financial crisis up to 2009. This finding largely corroborates findings by Lins et al. (2013) who were unable to identify find significant stock market performance differences between family and non-family firms in developed countries from 2008 to 2009. Nevertheless, the estimations reveal that since 2010 family firms record a significant excess return compared to non-family firms and keep up their outperformance during the Euro crisis.

## 5.5 Discussion

### 5.5.1 Explaining Performance Differences

Against the backdrop of the presented results, the question arises as to why family businesses, after being hit similarly to non-family firms by the world financial crisis in the first phase, were able to emerge with a superior stock market performance from 2010 onwards. Table 5.4 presents the year-by-year development of financial and performance figures for family and non-family firms: The time series of the accounting performance (ROA/ROE) of family firms decreased right from the first year of the financial crisis in 2007 onwards, while the decrease in performance of non-family firms started in 2008 and was more severe in terms of ROA. While furthermore the decrease in revenue due to the crisis was more severe in case of family firms, non-family firms recorded a sharper decrease in market-to-book ratio (i.e. market valuation). Sales and profitability variables confirm the notion suggested by buy-and-hold returns as well as the four-factor models, that family firms were heavily hit by the financial crisis up to 2009.

One explanation for the subsequent outperformance of family firms on the stock market might be the inherent reactions of family-owned firms to the impact of the financial crisis: Firstly, the earlier decrease in CAPEX for firms in the family-portfolio appears to confirm the arguments of Lins et al. (2013) and Zhou et al. (2017), that investment cuts are utilized to damper crisis impacts on liquidity. Hence, unlike non-family firms who suffered a decrease of 24.1 % in cash holdings in 2008, family firms did not record any decrease in cash up to 2011.

**Table 5.4:** Operating Performance by Year (Median)

| | 2006 | 2007 | 2008 | 2009 | 2010 | 2011 | 2012 | 2013 | 2014 |
|---|---|---|---|---|---|---|---|---|---|
| **Family Firms** | | | | | | | | | |
| Total Assets *(in Mio.)* | 127.4 | 147.7 | 164.4 | 161.4 | 167.2 | 177.8 | 186.0 | 232.4 | 249.5 |
| Revenue *(in Mio.)* | 166.1 | 168.3 | 217.3 | 181.3 | 207.3 | 211.8 | 208.7 | 266.3 | 308.5 |
| Cash *(in % Total Assets)* | 6.88 | 8.04 | 8.08 | 9.31 | 10.39 | 8.73 | 9.65 | 10.44 | 8.35 |
| Current Ratio | 1.67 | 1.76 | 1.65 | 1.89 | 1.88 | 1.78 | 1.77 | 1.74 | 1.64 |
| Return on Assets *(in %)* | 7.12 | 6.85 | 6.03 | 4.18 | 5.86 | 6.18 | 5.1 | 4.35 | 4.67 |
| Retuirn on Equity *(in %)* | 14.46 | 13.55 | 12.32 | 7.12 | 11.42 | 11.22 | 9.45 | 8.17 | 10.19 |
| Price/Earnings Ratio | 20.8 | 17.55 | 16.8 | 9.25 | 17.55 | 17.65 | 13.5 | 15.95 | 18.65 |
| Market to Book Ratio | 1.62 | 1.75 | 1.72 | 1.06 | 1.31 | 1.76 | 1.44 | 1.61 | 1.95 |
| Equity Ratio | 48.19 | 45.16 | 43.53 | 44.56 | 47.55 | 50.64 | 49.01 | 47.58 | 46.19 |
| CAPEX *(in % NetPPE)* | 25.26 | 27.74 | 26.81 | 22.27 | 21.14 | 22.35 | 24.97 | 24.76 | 21.01 |
| R&D *(in % Revenue)* | 2.3 | 2.42 | 2.39 | 2.53 | 2.22 | 2.55 | 2.74 | 2.71 | 2.67 |
| Dividend/Share | 35.21 | 35.71 | 34.21 | 42.66 | 41.2 | 40.67 | 39.21 | 38.49 | 38.79 |
| Dividend Yield | 1.76 | 1.89 | 2.29 | 4.35 | 3.28 | 1.92 | 3.05 | 2.77 | 2.29 |
| Closely Held Shares (in %) | 52.7 | 52.1 | 55.9 | 56.06 | 53.29 | 56.07 | 59.57 | 56.5 | 56.36 |
| No. of Employees | 1,168 | 1,189 | 1,513 | 2,420 | 1,492 | 1,337 | 1,382 | 1,455 | 1,909 |
| **Non-family Firms** | | | | | | | | | |
| Total Assets *(in Mio.)* | 224.7 | 222.0 | 243.5 | 254.8 | 243.8 | 257.6 | 318.3 | 425.8 | 424.7 |
| Revenue *(in Mio.)* | 257.4 | 268.0 | 309.1 | 302.9 | 291.7 | 377.2 | 396.7 | 424.6 | 466.8 |
| Cash *(in % Total Assets)* | 7.01 | 8.5 | 6.45 | 9.16 | 10 | 8.91 | 9.8 | 10.01 | 10.61 |
| Current Ratio | 1.6 | 1.53 | 1.39 | 1.42 | 1.59 | 1.54 | 1.63 | 1.6 | 1.56 |
| Return on Assets *(in %)* | 4.79 | 4.82 | 4.58 | 2.33 | 4.65 | 4.94 | 5.11 | 4.99 | 4.1 |
| Retuirn on Equity *(in %)* | 10.55 | 10.88 | 8.76 | 5.71 | 10.05 | 10.54 | 10.56 | 10.98 | 8.81 |
| Price/Earnings Ratio | 18.85 | 21.6 | 18.6 | 9.05 | 19.7 | 17.65 | 12.3 | 15.8 | 18.8 |
| Market to Book Ratio | 1.94 | 1.9 | 2.15 | 1.17 | 1.34 | 1.74 | 1.42 | 1.6 | 1.8 |
| Equity Ratio | 39.37 | 37.74 | 35.84 | 37.91 | 40.77 | 42.56 | 39.67 | 39.39 | 37.23 |
| CAPEX *(in % NetPPE)* | 21.61 | 22.07 | 23.67 | 18.37 | 17.71 | 20.83 | 19.77 | 20.62 | 21.58 |
| R&D *(in % Revenue)* | 3.7 | 3.49 | 3.37 | 3.65 | 3.49 | 3.45 | 3.16 | 2.87 | 2.93 |
| Dividend/Share | 34.73 | 34.38 | 34.85 | 37.73 | 36.63 | 32.31 | 36.09 | 37.6 | 40.24 |
| Dividend Yield | 1.98 | 1.82 | 1.9 | 3.56 | 2.93 | 2.08 | 2.9 | 2.5 | 2.28 |
| Closely Held Shares (in %) | 30.34 | 29.93 | 31.68 | 29.22 | 29.44 | 32.93 | 35.07 | 39.68 | 29.29 |
| No. of Employees | 4,327 | 5,791 | 5,480 | 6,679 | 4,916 | 2,456 | 6,075 | 6,530 | 4,421 |

This table reports the median of selective financial characteristics of firms with >25 % family ownership and non-family firms.

Secondly, the lower leverage ratio of family firms (Table 5.1) suggests that these firms are more solvent, which is specifically beneficial during phases of economic distress, as it allows these firms to easier access external funding. This argument is supported by scholars finding family firms as being less subject to credit restrictions compared to non-family firms during financial crises (Crespí and Martín-Oliver, 2015). Furthermore, government measures such as short-time working might support the liquidity of firms that are still solvent. Thirdly, summary statistics confirm findings of Sraer and Thesmar (2007) and Mietzner and Tyrell (2012) – family firms appear to execute layoffs rather as a reactive, than a proactive strategy to cope with surging financial crises. The same appears to be the case for R&D spending (as long as family firms are not financially constrained, see Sun et al., 2019). These observations are in line with family firms protecting their long-term success while accepting negative impacts on short-term performance in coping with negative economic consequences of the crises. Many family firms in Germany, for example, are located in rural areas where it is comparably difficult to attract skilled workers or engineers. Holding on to employees (or laying them off only as a subordinated reaction strategy to crises) may offer a significant competitive advantage when business activities increase again. This notion is supported by first findings in a working paper by Amore et al. (2021) who find firms with controlling family shareholders to outperform non-family firms during the recent COVID-19-crisis primarily in labour-intense industries.

Yet another reason for the outperformance after the rock bottom of the world financial crisis from 2010 onwards might be the inherent reaction of investors on the stock market: Eugster and Isakov (2019) record that the market may be positively surprised by good operative performances of family firms – specifically in terms of ROA. As Table 5.4 reveals, while non-family firms still record a decrease in revenues in from 2009 to 2010, family firms grow both by total assets and revenue. Doing so they also recover in their profitability (ROA, ROE, Price, and Earnings Ratio) – despite the fact that in 2010 the European economy recorded the first hits of the uprising Euro crisis.

Lastly, the corporate governance notion of family firms might support the comparably good performance of family firms: Stock market performance of both family- and non-family firms in the financial crisis is moderated by the corporate governance of these firms (Aldamen et al., 2020). Franzoi and Mietzner (2021a) show that the market generally regards the influence of family blockholders in firms as beneficial for corporate governance in Germany. Our results are in line with this finding. Minor differences in the observed returns and coefficients are due to the fact, that the research design of Franzoi and Mietzner (2021a) applies yearly rebalanced portfolios and additional governance data. This paper uses portfolios formed at year-end of 2006 as such a rebalancing is not applicable for the given research question. Furthermore, our family firm definition applies a stronger ownership threshold of 25 % (blocking minority) as with regards to the high share of family wealth that family blockholders invested in their firms (Anderson et al., 2003), the participation in management boards considered in the other study design is less relevant for our research question that covers financial crises threatening both the firm and family wealth. Our results extend the work of Franzoi and Mietzner (2021a) by suggesting that after controlling for other size and performance factors in our model, the beneficial influence attributed to the governance involvement of family shareholders holds true particularly during in and after financial crises. In addition, dividend policies as suggested by summary statistics do not call for caution of minority shareholders regarding a strong influence of family blockholders in corporate governance. Observed dividend trends do not support considerations of expropriation by controlling family blockholders as sometimes noted by literature. Unlike suggested by Attig et al., (2016), for example, family firms appear to have cut dividends to a lesser extent than firms in the non-family portfolio (Table 5.4).

### 5.5.2 Robustness and Contribution

Our results raise certain concerns regarding robustness: Despite of the fact that family firms are smaller than non-family firms by total assets, revenue and also market capitalization, listed firms in Germany also generally strongly vary in their capitalization (Achleitner et al., 2019). For robustness purposes we re-ran all regression models with portfolios weighted by the market capitalization of the comprised companies to account for potential distortions by small/large firms (Eugster and Isakov, 2019). The estimated value-weighted models reveal similar results, support our previous findings based on equally-weighted portfolios and are reported in Table 5.7 (world financial crisis) and Table 5.8 (Euro crisis) in the Appendix. Furthermore, for concerns regarding the employed four-factor model, we re-estimated all time frames with three- and five-factor models by applying Europe-specific factors retrieved from Kenneth. R. French's website. Both the equally- as well as the value-weighted variants confirm our findings derived from the Germany-specific four-factor model (results not reported and available upon request).

Robustness tests corroborate our empirical results that contribute both to academic and practical aspects. Our findings add to the year-long academic discussion on the performance of family and non-family firms by showing that phases of the economic recession may be analyzed separately when investigating performance differences. Furthermore, the results confirm literature on the resilience of family firms (Amann and Jaussaud, 2012; Minichilli et al., 2016) that appear to adapt to and absorb exogenous chocks with a combination of financial preconditions as well as intrinsic and long-term oriented features of family blockholders. Lastly, our study has important practical implications. For investors in family-controlled firms, our results suggest that even when these firms exhibit a financial behavior that may not appear as solely driven by economic decisions during financial crises, these firms and subsequently investors may profit from a superior performance after such periods. Most importantly, the findings support public policies of protecting current ownership structures of widespread family ownership in both listed and non-listed family firms (Minichilli et al., 2016). Family firms may damper macro-economic shocks through society, for example, because they are more cautious with layoffs while performing stronger than non-family firms in the mid- and long-run potentially benefitting thegeneral economic recovery of countries with high levels of family ownership.

## 5.6 Conclusion

Differences in the performance between family and non-family firms are widely noted by scholars. Only recently, publications also focus on differences in the financial behavior during financial crises. Studies on the stock market performance of family firms during and after economic shocks are rare. Observing German listed companies, we employ the world financial crisis and the Euro crisis as an exogenous shock to the earnings and performance of firms and document that family firms record excess stock market returns not later than three years after the outbreak of the first crisis. We find family firm portfolios outperforming non-family portfolios by 7.95–10.68 % (world financial crisis) and 7.92–13.59 % (Euro crisis) on an annualized level.

With regards to explanations for these findings, we follow that family firms react differently in the financial crisis than non-family firms, even though their reaction might hamper short-term performance. They appear to apply CAPEX-investment cuts to preserve liquidity while having better access to additional external funding due to their lower ex-ante leverage ratio. Furthermore, they appear to use personnel layoffs and cuts in R&D, which might endanger the long-term success of the firm, as a subordinated reaction strategy to crises and hence enable immediate productivity when markets recover. We find this behavior of family-owned firms aligned with families protecting their socioemotional wealth and the long-term survival of the family and thefirm. While minority shareholders might be worse off in the first place by short-term earnings being hurt by delayed cuts in the workforce or operative spending in a crisis, the smaller decrease in dividends per share compared to non-family firms does not support the notion of expropriation by family blockholders.

Due to the specific corporate governance framework and the fact that family members are frequently engaged in corporate boards as well as country-specific financial features such as the lower leverage ratio of family firms in Germany, our results are primarily limited to German listed firms. Hence, we highly encourage future studies to further explore the performance of family firms in periods of the economic downturn in other Continental European countries with a similar corporate governance system (e.g. Austria). Our study is particularly relevant for future research as it adds to the few existing publications investigating specifically the financial crises behavior of family firms and thereby broadens the range of available empirical literature in a research topic that is yet to be explored in more detail.

## 5.7 Appendix

**Table 5.5:** Market Performance

| | No. | Holding Period | | | Statistics | | | |
|---|---|---|---|---|---|---|---|---|
| **2007–2011** | **Firms** | **Start** | **End** | **N** | **Mean** | **t** | **Median** | **z** |
| Family Firms | 114 | 2007-01-02 | 2011-12-30 | 1304 | 0.079 | 182.37 | -0.011 | 31.28 |
| Non-family firms | 112 | 2007-01-02 | 2011-12-30 | 1304 | 0.055 | 218.44 | -0.019 | 31.28 |
| Diff. in Mean/ Median | | | | | 0.024 | 3.19 | 0.009 | 4.25 |
| 2010–2014 | | | | | | | | |
| Family Firms | 114 | 2010-01-04 | 2014-12-31 | 1303 | 0.550 | 176.20 | 0.365 | 31.27 |
| Non-family firms | 112 | 2010-01-04 | 2014-12-31 | 1303 | 0.425 | 185.33 | 0.273 | 31.27 |
| Diff. in Mean/ Median | | | | | 0.125 | 10.68 | 0.091 | 16.26 |

This table reports the mean and median return of firms in the portfolios with no-family ownership and >25 % family ownership as well as the results of the test statistics on the means (ttest) and medians (Wilcoxon rank test) of the firms in the non-family vs. family portfolio. ***, **, and * indicate statistical significance at the 1 %, 5 %, and 10 % levels, respectively. Frequency indicates the number of days within the holding period.

**Table 5.6:** Long-term Performance 2007–2017: Three-factor Model

| | **Equally-weighted portfolios** | | | **Value-weighted portfolios** | | |
|---|---|---|---|---|---|---|
| | **Non-family-Risk free** | **Family-Risk free** | **Family-Non-family** | **Non-family-Risk free** | **Family-Risk free** | **Family-Non-family** |
| | | 2007–2017 | | | 2007–2017 | |
| Alpha | -0.0018*** | -0.0016*** | 0.0002* | -0.0018*** | -0.0016*** | 0.0002* |
| | (-11.55) | (-10.84) | (1.76) | (-11.64) | (-10.84) | (1.79) |
| Rm-Rf | 0.0055*** | 0.0053*** | -0.0002* | 0.0055*** | 0.0053*** | -0.0002* |
| | (31) | (31.14) | (-1.84) | (31.07) | (31.14) | (-1.68) |
| SMB | 0.0024*** | 0.004*** | 0.0016*** | 0.0024*** | 0.004*** | 0.0016*** |
| | (5.91) | (10.16) | (5.57) | (5.81) | (10.16) | (5.79) |
| HML | -0.0005 | -0.0011*** | -0.0005** | -0.0006 | -0.0011*** | -0.0005** |
| | (-1.48) | (-3.13) | (-2.2) | (-1.56) | (-3.13) | (-2.12) |
| N | 2868 | 2868 | 2868 | 2868 | 2868 | 2868 |
| $R^2$ | 36.55 % | 31.97 % | 4.39 % | 36.74 % | 31.97 % | 4.42 % |
| Adj. $R^2$ | 36.48 % | 31.90 % | 4.29 % | 36.67 % | 31.90 % | 4.32 % |

This Table presents the regression results of the three-factor model (Fama and French, 1993; Carhart, 1997) for both equally- as well as value weighted non-family and family portfolios. Regressions cover the period from 2007-01-02 to 2017-12-27. The specification of the dependent variable, i.e. returns on a zero investment strategy in non-family- and family-portfolios as well as on a strategy long on family firm-portfolios and short on non-family portfolios is denoted in row 3 of the table. Portfolio returns are regressed on the market portfolio-return less the risk free return rate (Rm-Rf), the zero-investment benchmark-facotors for size (SMB) and the book-to-market-value (HML). Factor-specific data for the European stock market has been retrieved from the website of Prof. Kenneth R. French. Significance at the 10 %, 5 % and 1 % level is indicated by *, ** and ***, respectively. Test statistics are reported in parentheses.

**Table 5.7:** World Financial Crisis 2007–2011: Four-factor Model (Value-weighted)

| | Non-family-Risk free | Family-Risk free | Family-Non-family | Non-family-Risk free | Family-Risk free | Family-Non-family |
|---|---|---|---|---|---|---|
| | | 2007–2008 | | | 2007–2009 | |
| Alpha | -0.0156*** | -0.0153*** | 0.0002 | -0.0114*** | -0.0112*** | 0.0002 |
| | (-33.23) | (-31.56) | (1.1) | (-29.16) | (-27.64) | (1.11) |
| Rm-Rf | 0.0089*** | 0.0091*** | 0.0002 | 0.0099*** | 0.0097*** | -0.0002 |
| | (16.88) | (16.58) | (0.66) | (20.55) | (19.45) | (-0.84) |
| SMB | 0.0049*** | 0.0071*** | 0.0022*** | 0.0062*** | 0.008*** | 0.0018*** |
| | (7.01) | (9.74) | (6.56) | (10.12) | (12.54) | (6.09) |
| HML | 0.0006 | 0.001 | 0.0003 | 0.0022*** | 0.0023*** | 0.0001 |
| | (0.75) | (1.13) | (0.89) | (3.56) | (3.65) | (0.47) |
| WML | -0.0018*** | -0.0021*** | -0.0003* | -0.002*** | -0.0022*** | -0.0002* |
| | (-5.51) | (-6.13) | (-1.8) | (-6.89) | (-7.44) | (-1.75) |
| N | 506 | 506 | 506 | 760 | 760 | 760 |
| $R^2$ | 54.60 % | 50.02 % | 18.24 % | 52.95 % | 46.76 % | 17.31 % |
| Adj. $R^2$ | 54.23 % | 49.63 % | 17.58 % | 52.70 % | 46.48 % | 16.88 % |
| | | 2007–2010 | | | 2007–2011 | |
| Alpha | -0.009*** | -0.0086*** | 0.0004** | -0.008*** | -0.0077*** | 0.0003** |
| | (-27.41) | (-24.87) | (2.16) | (-29.28) | (-26.64) | (2.24) |
| Rm-Rf | 0.0102*** | 0.01*** | -0.0002 | 0.0101*** | 0.01*** | -0.0001 |
| | (24.45) | (22.62) | (-1) | (29.2) | (27.29) | (-0.79) |
| SMB | 0.0064*** | 0.0081*** | 0.0017*** | 0.0063*** | 0.0081*** | 0.0018*** |
| | (11.71) | (13.99) | (6.18) | (13.68) | (16.73) | (7.5) |
| HML | 0.0026*** | 0.0027*** | 0.0001 | 0.0022*** | 0.0025*** | 0.0003 |
| | (5.11) | (4.95) | (0.27) | (5.13) | (5.49) | (1.25) |
| WML | -0.0018*** | -0.002*** | -0.0002* | -0.0015*** | -0.0018*** | -0.0003** |
| | (-6.88) | (-7.36) | (-1.82) | (-6.48) | (-7.34) | (-2.38) |
| N | 1016 | 1016 | 1016 | 1273 | 1273 | 1273 |
| $R^2$ | 50.72 % | 43.23 % | 14.23 % | 53.25 % | 45.19 % | 16.12 % |
| Adj. $R^2$ | 50.53 % | 43.00 % | 13.89 % | 53.10 % | 45.02 % | 15.85 % |

This Table presents the regression results of the four-factor model (Fama and French, 1993; Carhart, 1997) for value-weighted non-family and family portfolios. Regressions cover the period from 2007-01-02 to 2011-12-30 (daily). The specification of the dependent variable, i.e. returns on a zero investment strategy in non-family- and family-portfolios as well as on a strategy long on family firm-portfolios and short on non-family portfolios is denoted in row 3 of the table. Portfolio returns are regressed on the market portfolio-return less the risk free return rate (Rm-Rf), the zero-investment benchmark-facotors for size (SMB) and book-to-market-value (HML) as well as the momentum effect (WML). Factor-specific data for the German stock market has been retrieved from the website of Prof. Richard Stehle. Significance at the 10 %, 5 % and 1 % level is indicated by *, ** and ***, respectively. Test statistics are reported in parentheses.

**Table 5.8:** Euro Crisis 2010–2014: Four-factor Model (Value-weighted)

| | **Non-family-Risk free** | **Family-Risk free** | **Family-Non-family** | **Non-family-Risk free** | **Family-Risk free** | **Family-Non-family** |
|---|---|---|---|---|---|---|
| | | 2010–2011 | | | 2010–2012 | |
| Alpha | -0.003*** | -0.0025*** | 0.0005** | 0.0005*** | 0.0009*** | 0.0003* |
| | (-16.47) | (-10.47) | (2.19) | (3.02) | (4.28) | (1.8) |
| Rm-Rf | 0.0086*** | 0.0086*** | 0.0001 | 0.005*** | 0.0045*** | -0.0005** |
| | (30.47) | (23.53) | (0.21) | (22.82) | (17.86) | (-2.13) |
| SMB | 0.0042*** | 0.0062*** | 0.0021*** | 0.0026*** | 0.0043*** | 0.0017*** |
| | (11.46) | (13.19) | (4.52) | (4.99) | (7.15) | (3.05) |
| HML | 0.0008** | 0.0015*** | 0.0007 | 0 | 0.0002 | 0.0002 |
| | (2.4) | (3.42) | (1.62) | (-0.08) | (0.25) | (0.34) |
| WML | 0.001*** | 0.0003 | -0.0008** | -0.0001 | 0.0008 | 0.0009 |
| | (3.81) | (0.72) | (-2.24) | (-0.18) | (0.79) | (1.02) |
| N | 513 | 513 | 513 | 781 | 781 | 781 |
| $R^2$ | 81.54 % | 64.14 % | 14.86 % | 64.34 % | 45.71 % | 9.31 % |
| Adj. $R^2$ | 81.39 % | 63.86 % | 14.19 % | 64.11 % | 45.36 % | 8.73 % |
| | | 2010–2013 | | | 2010–2014 | |
| Alpha | -0.0017*** | -0.0014*** | 0.0003* | -0.0015*** | -0.0012*** | 0.0003** |
| | (-12.99) | (-9.23) | (1.87) | (-12.95) | (-8.69) | (2.19) |
| Rm-Rf | 0.0081*** | 0.0078*** | -0.0004 | 0.0079*** | 0.0074*** | -0.0006** |
| | (35.76) | (29.27) | (-1.33) | (41.88) | (32.85) | (-2.43) |
| SMB | 0.0037*** | 0.0052*** | 0.0014*** | 0.0036*** | 0.0047*** | 0.0011*** |
| | (12.85) | (15.27) | (4.23) | (14.77) | (16.36) | (3.84) |
| HML | 0.0011*** | 0.0015*** | 0.0004 | 0.0011*** | 0.0014*** | 0.0003 |
| | (4.06) | (4.89) | (1.4) | (4.87) | (5.43) | (1.31) |
| WML | 0.0006*** | 0.0002 | -0.0004* | 0.0006*** | 0.0005** | -0.0001 |
| | (2.94) | (0.79) | (-1.71) | (3.67) | (2.45) | (-0.63) |
| N | 1020 | 1020 | 1020 | 1272 | 1272 | 1272 |
| $R^2$ | 73.19 % | 57.08 % | 10.72 % | 73.34 % | 56.80 % | 9.20 % |
| Adj. $R^2$ | 73.08 % | 56.91 % | 10.36 % | 73.26 % | 56.67 % | 8.92 % |

This Table presents the regression results of the four-factor model (Fama and French, 1993; Carhart, 1997) for value-weighted non-family and family portfolios. Regressions cover the period from 2010-01-04 to 2014-12-31 (daily). The specification of the dependent variable, i.e. returns on a zero investment strategy in non-family- and family-portfolios as well as on a strategy long on family firm-portfolios and short on non-family portfolios is denoted in row 3 of the table. Portfolio returns are regressed on the market portfolio-return less the risk free return rate (Rm-Rf), the zero-investment benchmark-facotors for size (SMB) and book-to-market-value (HML) as well as the momentum effect (WML). Factor-specific data for the German stock market has been retrieved from the website of Prof. Richard Stehle. Significance at the 10 %, 5 % and 1 % level is indicated by *, ** and ***, respectively. Test statistics are reported in parentheses.

# 6 Concluding Remarks

This doctoral thesis follows the research objective of improving the understanding of the influence of family shareholders on the financial behavior of family firms in the German corporate governance system that diverges from those of other countries. The core of this dissertation focusses on the assessment of the consequences of the corporate governance involvement of family blockholders in listed family firms, more specifically on current asset management, financial reporting practices, stock market performance as well as crisis behavior and performance recovery.

The study on working capital management of German family firms (Chapter 2) provides two important contributions to literature: First, against the backdrop of the general lack of research on this issue it can be shown that family firms exhibit a longer cash conversion cycle primarily due to slower inventory turnover. Second, the study underlines the research motivation of this thesis as not family ownership, but the degree of family involvement in management significantly increases the cash conversion cycle. For scholars this finding implies that the frequently applied control for family influence via dummy variables for plain management presence or even on the CEO position (which had no significant effect on the CCC) is insufficient. As the findings also suggest a lower level of professionalization in working capital handling, a further assessment of the drivers of slower turnover in family firms is demanded. Consequently, the results imply for practitioners and investors that especially in smaller family firms in Germany, even when they are listed on the stock exchange, there is headroom in financial management techniques and thus a more effective utilization of employed capital and shareholder value.

Due to the limitations in monitoring of the management by passively invested shareholders in the German corporate governance system for listed firms, incentives for skewed earnings reporting are increased. Family blockholders for example may be incentivized not to report high earnings to reduce the pressure to distribute to minority shareholders. The second study (Chapter 3) on earnings management shows that family blockholders use their powerful position to influence the financial reporting of family firms and that this influence is significantly driven by the degree of family management involvement in the executive board. Yet, the findings show that family influenced firms concentrate on earnings management techniques that achieve their "goal" from the perspective of a large family blockholder (such as lowering earnings by accruals management and mere accounting measures) but do not jeopardize the medium and long-term success of the business (such as for example lowering prices to boost sales in the current period).

These results underpin prior findings for example by Achleitner et al. (2014) in Germany but contribute to literature that the level of family involvement, specifically in the executive board, significantly affects earnings management practices. Hence, controlling for this influence is highly requested for future studies on reporting practices – at least in the German corporate governance system. Some practical recommendations for investors can also be derived from the results of the study. First, an appreciative understanding of the cooperation between representatives of smaller shareholder groups and employee representatives is essential for the effective exercise of a monitoring function in the supervisory board vis-à-vis the management board – especially when members of family blockholders are appointed to both boards. Second, results clearly recommend the establishment of audit committees. Only recently Germany introduced the Act to Strengthen Financial Market Integrity (FISG)[76] with increased supervision rights and mandatory audit committees. As this legal obligation to establish audit committees does not apply for supervisory boards with only three board positions (supervisory boards are significantly smaller in family firms than in non-family firms[77]) the study results suggest that investors urge family firms to set up an audit committee still voluntarily.

The first two papers demonstrate how necessary it is to differentiate the precise family influence via the management board and supervisory board respectively in the German corporate governance system. Active financial management and reporting decisions in family businesses are significantly driven by the extent of family influence. Small shareholders by contrast have only limited opportunities to exert direct influence on executive managers in this corporate governance environment.

Consistently, because of the concentration of family wealth and the perceived long-term orientation, family blockholders are expected to be particularly incentivized to actively engage in monitoring of the firm as the survival of the firm is closely tied to the welfare of the family. While capital markets are expected to react differently to blockholders who actively address agency problems in firms,

---

76 FISG (*Gesetz zur Stärkung der Finanzmarktintegrität*) came into force in June 2021 as a result of the Wirecard AG financial scandal.

77 The median supervisory board size in family-managed firms in the sample is three vs. six in non-family-managed firms (see Chapter 2).

the results of the third study (Chapter 4) support this notion. Portfolios of firms with a high degree of family involvement in corporate governance are found to realize annualized abnormal returns between 0.48 % and 6.00 %. While other market performance studies obtain similar results, the presented study shows that abnormal returns of family firms can be attributed to the engagement of family firms in the firms they are invested in. These results suggest that minority shareholders may rely on the incentive structure of family blockholders given that their own agency costs for monitoring are relatively more expensive.

The long-term orientation, financial behavior (such as a lower leverage ratio) and superior performance of family firms in Germany suggests that these firms may also differ in their performance during economic crises. While economic downturns are an exceptional situation for all corporations, the crises performance of family firms has been little explored in research so far. The fourth study (Chapter 5) finds significant differences in the operative performance that are in line with families protecting their socioemotional wealth (such as delayed layoffs of employees) but may hamper immanent financial performance during crises. Yet, findings reveal that family firms profit from their crisis behavior in their market performance at the latest three years after the beginning of the investigated economic crises. After controlling for size and growth family firms still record annualized excess returns in the world financial crisis of 7.75 %–10.68 % and 7.92 %–13.59 % in the Euro crisis. These findings are in line with those of the previous study that portfolios of family-influenced firms record excess returns. The results of this last study by contrast suggest and add to literature that the governance influence of family blockholders pays off especially in times of crisis and economic downturn. Finally, the finding that family firms record a smaller decrease in dividend payments during crisis contradicts the notion of entrenchment of minority shareholders und underlines the need for scholars to increasingly include a precise assessment of family involvement in corporate boards in future studies.

# List of Figures

# List of Tables

# References


Acero, I. and Alcalde, N. (2016). Controlling shareholders and the composition of the board: Special focus on family firms. *Review of Managerial Science*, 10 (1), 61–83.

Achleitner, A.-K., Günther, N., Kaserer, C. and Siciliano, G. (2014). Real earnings management and accrual-based earnings management in family firms. *European Accounting Review*, 23 (3), 431–461.

Achleitner, A.-K., Kaserer, C. and Kauf, T. (2012). The dynamics of voting ownership in lone-founder, family-founder, and heir firms. *Journal of Family Business Strategy*, 3 (2), 79–96.

Achleitner, A.-K., Kaserer, C., Kauf, T., Günther, N. and Ampenberger, M. (2009). Börsennotierte Familienunternehmen in Deutschland. Munich: Stiftung Familienunternehmen.

Achleitner, A.-K., Kaserer, C., Kauf, T., Günther, N. and Ampenberger, M. (2019). Börsennotierte Familienunternehmen in Deutschland. Munich: Stiftung Familienunternehmen.

Afrifa, G. A. (2016). Net working capital, cash flow and performance of UK SMEs. *Review of Accounting and Finance*, 15 (1), 21–45.

Afrifa, G. A. and Padachi, K. (2016). Working capital level influence on SME profitability. *Journal of Small Business and Enterprise Development*, 23 (1), 44–63.

Ahrens, J.-P., Istipliler, B., Keese, D., Kowalzick, M., Patzer, C. and Tänzler, J. K. (2019). Benchmark Familienunternehmen: eine vergleichende Analyse der Metropolregion Rhein-Neckar und der Region Stuttgart 2019. Mannheim: Institut für Mittelstandsforschung der Universität Mannheim.

Akerlof, G. A. (1970). The market for "Lemons": Quality uncertainty and the market mechanism. *The Quarterly Journal of Economics*, 84 (3), 488–500.

Akram, H. M. I., Shahzad, A. and Ahmad I. (2018). The impact of corporate governance on the working capital management efficiency of Pakistani manufacturing firms. *IUP Journal of Applied Finance*, 24 (4), 34–47.

Albersmann, B. T. and Hohenfels, D. (2017). Audit committees and earnings management – Evidence from the German two-tier board system. *Schmalenbach Business Review*, 2 (3), 147–178.

Aldamen, H., Duncan, K, Kelly, S. and McNamara, R. (2020). Corporate governance and family firm performance during the Global Financial Crisis. *Accounting and Finance*, 60 (2), 1673–1701.

Ali, A., Chen, T.-Y. and Radhakrishnan, S. (2007). Corporate disclosures by family firms. *Journal of Accounting and Economics*, 44 (1–2), 238–286.

Amann, B. and Jaussaud, J. (2012). Family and non-family business resilience in an economic downturn. *Asia Pacific Business Review*, 18 (2), 203–223.

Amato, S., Basco, R. Ansón, S. G. and Lattanzi, N. (2020). Family-managed firms and employment growth during an economic downturn: does their location matter? *Baltic Journal of Management*, 15 (4), 607–630.

Amihud, Y. and Lev, B. (1981). Risk reduction as a managerial motive for Conglomerate Mergers. *The Bell Journal of Economics*, 12 (2), 605–617.

Aminadav, G. and Papaioannou, E. (2020). Corporate control around the world. *Journal of Finance*, 75 (3), 1191–1246.

Amore, M. D., Quarato, F. and Pelucco, V. (2021). Family ownership during the Covid-19 Pandemic. *Bocconi University Management Research*, January 25, 2021.

Ampenberger, M. (2010). Unternehmenspolitik in börsennotierten Familienunternehmen – Eine Analyse von Investitions-, Diversifikations- und Kapitalstrukturentscheidungen. Dissertation, Technical University Munich

Ampenberger, M., Schmid T., Achleitner, A.-K. and Kaserer, C. (2013). Capital structure decisions in family firms: Evidence from a bank-based economy. *Review of Managerial Science*, 7, 247–275.

Anderson, R., Dur, A. and Reeb, D. (2012). Investment policy in family controlled firms, *Journal of Banking & Finance*, 36, 1744–1758.

Anderson, R. and Reeb, D. (2003a). Founding-Family ownership and firm performance: Evidence from the SandP 500. *The Journal of Finance*, 28 (3), 1301–1327.

Anderson, R. and Reeb, D. (2003b). Founding-Family ownership, corporate diversification and firm leverage. *The Journal of Law and Economics*, 46 (2), 653–684.

Anderson, R. C. and Reeb, D. M. (2004). Board composition: Balancing family influence in S&P 500 Firms. *Administrative Science Quarterly*, 49 (2), 209–237

Anderson, R. C., Mansi, S. A. and Reeb, D. M. (2003). Founding-family ownership and the agency cost of debt. *Journal of Financial Economics*, 68 (2), 263–285.

Andres, C. (2008). Large shareholders and firm performance – An empirical examination of founding-family ownership. *Journal of Corporate Finance*, 14 (4), 431–445.

Arrondo-García, R. A., Fernández-Méndez, C. and Menéndez-Requejo S. (2016). The growth and performance of family businesses during the global financial crisis: The role of the generation in control. *Journal of Family Business Strategy*, 7 (4), 227–237.

Astrachan, J. H., Klein, S. B. and Smyrnios, K. X. (2002). The F-PEC scale of family influence: A proposal for solving the family business definition problem. *Family Business Research*, 15 (1), 45–58.

Attig, N., Boubakri, N., El Ghoul, S., and Guedhami, O. (2016). The global financial crisis, family control, and dividend policy. *Financial Management*, 45 (2), 291–313.

Autukaite, R. and Molay, E. (2013). Cash holdings, working capital and firm value: Evidence from France. Conference Paper, International Conference of the French Finance Association (AFFI), May 11–13, 2011, Version July 2013.

Azila-Gbettor, E., Honyenuga, B. Q., Berent-Braun, M. M. and Kil, A. (2018). Structural aspects of corporate governance and family firm performance: A systematic review. *Journal of Family Business Management,* 8 (3), 306–330.

Baber, W. R., Fairfield, P. M. and Haggard, J. A. (1991). The effect of concern about reported income on discretionary spending decisions: The case of research and development. *The Accounting Review*, 66 (4), 818–829.

Ball, R. and Shivakumar, L. (2005). Earnings quality in UK private firms: Comparative loss recognition timeliness. *Journal of Accounting and Economics*, 39 (1), 83–128.

Baños-Caballero, S., Garcia-Teruel, P. J. and Martinez-Solano, P. (2010). Working capital management in SMEs. *Accounting and Finance*, 50, 511–527.

Baños-Caballero, S., Garcia-Teruel, P. J. and Martinez-Solano, P. (2012). How does working capital management affect the profitability of Spanish SMEs? *Small Business Economics*, 39, 517–529.

Baños-Caballero, S., Garcia-Teruel, P. J. and Martinez-Solano, P. (2014). Working capital management, corporate performance, and financial constraints. *Journal of Business Research*, 67, 332–338.

Barontini, R. and Caprio, L. (2006). The effect of family control on firm value and performance: Evidence from Continental Europe. *European Financial Management*, 12 (5), 689–723.

Basu, S. (1997). The conservatism principle and asymmetric timeliness of earnings. *Journal of Accounting and Economics*, 24 (1), 3–37.

Bebchuk, L., Cohen, A. and Ferrell, A. (2009). What matters in corporate governance? *Review of Financial Studies*, 22 (2), 783–827.

Becht, M. and Boehmer, E. (2003). Voting control in German corporations. International *Review of Law and Economics*, 23 (1), 1–29.

Becker, C. L., DeFond, M. L., Jiambalvo, J. and Subramanyam, K. R. (1998). The effect of audit quality on earnings management. *Contemporary Accounting Review*, 15 (1), 1–24.

Bennedsen, M., Nielson K. M., Perez-Gonzalez, F. and Wolfenzon, D. (2007). Inside the family firm: The role of families in succession decisions and performance. *The Quarterly Journal of Economics*, 122 (2), 647–691.

Berle, A. and Means, G. (1932). The Modern Corporation and Private Property. Harcourt, Brace, and World, New York, NY.

Berrone, P., Cruz, C., Gomez-Mejia, L. R. (2010). Socioemotional wealth and corporate responses to institutional pressures – Do family-controlled firms pollute less? *Administrative Science Quarterly*, 55 (1), 82–113.

Berrone, P., Cruz, C. and Gomez-Mejia, L. R. (2012). Socioemotional Wealth in Family Firms: Theoretical Dimensions, Assessment Approaches, and Agenda for Future Research. *Family Business Review*, 25 (3), 258–279.

Bhaumik, S. K. and Gregoriou, A. (2010). 'Family' ownership, tunneling and earnings management: A review of the literature. *Journal of Economic Surveys*, 24 (4), 705–730.

Block, J. (2009). Long-term Orientation of Family Firms. Dissertation Technical University Munich, Gabler Research, 1st edition, Wiesbaden.

Boisjoly, R. P., Conine Jr., T. E. and McDonald IV, M. B. (2020). Working capital management: Financial and valuation impacts. *Journal of Business Res*earch, 108, 1–8.

Bona-Sánchez, C., Pérez-Alemán, J. and Santana-Martin, D. J. (2007). Family control and earnings quality. *Revista de Contabilidad – Spanish Accounting Review*, 10 (1), 11–32.

Breig, C. M. and Elsas, R. (2009). Default risk and equity returns: A comparison of the bank-based German and the U.S. Financial System. *Discussion Papers in Business Administration*, 10978, University of Munich, Munich School of Management.

Burkart, M., Panunzi, F. and Shleifer, A. (2003). Family firms. *The Journal of Finance*, 58 (5), 2167–2201.

Calabrò, A., Frank, H., Minichilli, A. and Suess-Reyes, J. (2021). Business families in times of crises: The backbone of family firm resilience and continuity. *Journal of Family Business Strategy*, 12 (2), 1–8.

Caprio, L., Del Guidice, A. and Signori, A. (2020). Cash holdings in family firms: CEO identity and implications for firm value. *European Financial Management*, 26, 386–415.

Carhart, M. (1997). On persistence in mutual fund performance. *Journal of Financial Economics*, 52 (1), 57–82.

Cascino, S., Pugliese, A., Mussolini, D. and Sansone, C. (2010). The influence of family ownership on the quality of accounting information. *Family Business Review*, 23 (3), 246–265.

Cella, C. (2009). Ownership structures and stock market returns. Working Paper, SSRN. Retrieved from: https://dx.doi.org/10.2139/ssrn.1267268

Cennamo, C., Berrone, P., Cruz, C. and Gómez-Mejía, L. R. (2012). Socioemotional wealth and proactive stakeholder engagement: Why family-controlled firms Care More About Their Stakeholders, 36 (6), 1153–1173.

Chen, C. L., Huang, S.-H. and Fan, H.-S. (2012). Complementary association between real activities and accrual- based manipulation in earnings reporting. *Journal of Economic Political Reform*, 15 (2), 93–108.

Chen, S., Chen, X. and Cheng, Q. (2014). Conservatism and equity ownership of the founding family. *European Accounting Review*, 23 (3), 403–430.

Chrisman, J. J., Chua J. H. and Litz, R. A. (2004). Comparing the agency costs of family and non-family firms: Conceptual issues and exploratory evidence, *Entrepreneurship Theory and Practice*, 28 (4), 335–354.

Chrisman, J. J., Chua, J. H. and Sharma, P. (2005). Trends and directions in the development of a strategic management theory of the family firm. *Entrepreneurship Theory and Practice*, 29 (5), 555–576.

Chu, W. (2011). Family ownership and firm performance: Influence of family management, family control, and firm size. *Asia Pacific Journal of Management*, 28, 833–852.

Chua, J. H., Chrisman, J. J., Sharma, P. (1999). Defining the family business by behavior. *Entrepreneurship Theory and Practice*, 23 (4), 19–39.

Chua, J. H., Chrisman, J. J., Kellermanns, F. and Wu, Z. (2011). Family involvement and new venture debt financing. *Journal of Business Venturing*, 26 (4), 472–488.

Claessens, S., Djankov, S. and Lang, L. H. P. (2000) The separation of ownership and control in East Asian Corporations. *Journal of Financial Economics*, 58 (1–2), 81–112.

Claessens, S., Djankov, S., Fan, J. P. H. and Lang, L. H. P. (2002). Disentangling the incentive and entrenchment effects of large shareholdings. *The Journal of Finance*, 57 (6), 2741–2771.

Cohen, D. A. and Zarowin, P. (2010). Accrual-based and real earnings management activities around seasoned equity offerings. *Journal of Accounting Economics*, 50 (1), 2–19.

Cohen, D. A., Dey, A. and Lys, T. Z. (2008). Real and accrual-based earnings management in the pre- and post-Sarbanes-Oxley periods. *The Accounting Review*, 83 (2), 757–787.

Copelovitch, M., Frieden, J. and Walter., S. (2016). The political economy of the Euro crisis. *Comparative Political Studies*, 49 (7), 811–840.

Cornell, B. and Shapiro A. C. (1987). Corporate stakeholders and corporate finance. *Financial Management*, 16 (1), 5–14.

Corstjens, M., Peyer, U. and Van der Heyden, L. (2006). Performance of Family Firms: Evidence from US and European firms and investors. Working Paper, INSEAD, retrieved from https://www.insead.edu/sites/default/files/assets/faculty-personal-site/urs-peyer/ documents/jibs_mcuplvdh_final.pdf

Crespí, R. and Martín-Oliver, A. (2015). Do family firms have better access to external finance during crises? *Corporate Governance: An International Review*, 23 (3), 249–265.

Cronqvist, H. and Fahlenbrach, R. (2009). Large shareholders and corporate policies. *Review of Financial Studies,* 22 (10), 3941–3976.

Dechow, P. M. (1994). Accounting earnings and cash flows as measures of firm performance: The role of accounting accruals. *Journal of Accounting Economics*, 18 (1), 3–42.

Dechow, P. M. and Dichev, I. D. (2002). The quality of accruals and earnings: The role of accrual estimation errors. *The Accounting Review*, 77, 35–59.

Dechow, P. M. and Skinner, D. J. (2000). Earnings management: Reconciling the views of accounting academics, practitioners and regulators. *Accounting Horizons*, 14 (2), 235–250.

Dechow, P. M. and Sloan, R. G. (1991). Executive incentives and the horizon problem: An empirical investigation. *Journal of Accounting Economics*, 14 (1), 51–89.

Dechow, P. M., Sloan, R. G. and Sweeney, A. P. (1996). Detecting earnings management. *The Accounting Review*, 70 (2), 193–225.

DeFond, M. L. and Jiambalvo, J. (1994). Debt covenant violations and manipulation of accruals. *Journal of Accounting and Economics*, 17 (1–2), 145–176.

Deloof, M. (2003). Does working capital management affect profitability of Belgian firms? *Journal of Business, Finance and Accounting*, 30 (3), 573–587.

Demsetz, H. and Lehn, K. (1985). The structure of corporate ownership: Causes and consequences. *Journal of Political Economy*, 93 (6), 1155–1177.

Dirkx, P. and Peter, F. J. (2020). The Fama-French five-factor model plus momentum: Evidence for the German market. *Schmalenbach Business Review*, 72, 661–684.

Djankov, S., La Porta, R., Lopez-de-Silanes, F. and Shleifer, A. (2008). The law and economics of self-dealing. *Journal of Financial Economics*, 88 (3), 430–465.

Du Plessis, J. J. (2004). The German two-tier board and the German Corporate Governance Code. *European Business Law Review*, 15 (5), 1139–1164.

Duran, P., van Essen, M., Heugens, P. P. M. A. R., Kostova, T. and Peng, M. W. (2018). The impact of institutions on the competitive advantage of publicly listed family firms in emerging markets. *Global Strategy Journal*, 9 (2), 243–274.

Durán, R. F., Lonzano, M. B. and Yaman, S. (2016). Is family control relevant for corporate cash holding policy? *Journal of Business Finance & Accounting*, 43 (9), 1325–1360.

Drees, F, Mietzner, M. and Schiereck, D. (2013). Effects of corporate equity ownership on firm value. *Review of Managerial Science*, 7 (3), 277–308.

Dyreng, S. D., Hanlon, M. and Maydew, E. L. (2012). Where do firms manage earnings? *Review of Accounting Studies*, 17 (3), 649–687.

Eiben, Jan. and Redlefsen, M. (2006). Finanzierung von Familienunternehmen. INTES Institut für Familienunternehmen, WHU Otto Beisheim School of Management, Vallendar.

Eisenhardt, K. M. (1989). Agency theory: An assessment and review. *Academy of Management Review*, 14 (1), 57–74.

Elbadry, A. (2018). The determinants of working capital management in the Egyptian SMEs. *Accounting and Finance Research*, 7 (2), 155–165.

Eugster, N. and Isakov, D. (2019). Founding family ownership, stock market returns, and agency problems. *Journal of Banking and Finance*, 107, 1–20.

Ewert, R. and Wagenhofer, A. (2005). Economic effects of tightening accounting standards to restrict earnings management. *The Accounting Review*, 80 (4), 1101–1124.

Faccio, M. and Lang, L. H. P. (2002). The ultimate ownership of Western European corporations. *Journal of Financial Economics*, 65 (3), 365–395.

Faccio, M., Lang, L. H. P. and Young, L. (2001). Dividends and expropriation. *American Economic Review*, 91 (1), 54–78.

Fahlenbrach, F. (2009). Founder-CEOs, investment decisions, and stock market performance. *Journal of Financial and Quantitative Analysis*, 44 (2), 439–466.

Fahlenbrach, R. and Stulz, R. M. (2010). Bank CEO incentives and the credit crisis. *Journal of Financial Economics*, 99, 11–26.

Fama, E. F. and French, K. R. (1993). Common risk-factors in the returns on stocks and bonds. *Journal of Financial Economics*, 22 (1), 3–56.

Fama, E. F. and Jensen, M. (1983). Separation of ownership and control. *Journal of Law and Economics*, 26 (2), 301–325.

Fan, J. P. H. and Wong, T. J. (2002). Corporate ownership structure and the informativeness of accounting earnings in East Asia. *Journal of Accounting and Economics*, 33 (3), 401–425.

Fazzari, S. M. and Petersen, B. C. (1993). Working capital and fixed investment: new evidence on financing constraints. *RAND Journal of Economics*, 14 (3), 328–342.

Ferramosca, S. and Allegrini, M. (2018). The complex role of family involvement in earnings management. *Journal of Family Business Strategy*, 9 (2), 128–141.

Fiador, V. (2016). Does corporate governance influence the efficiency of working capital management of listed firms – Evidence from Ghana. *African Journal of Economic and Management Studies*, 7 (4), 482–496.

Fidrmuc, J., Schreiber, P. and Siddiqui, M. (2015). The transmission of Bank Funding to corporate loans: Deleveraging in Germany. *Open Economies Review*, 26 (3), 581–597.

Filbeck, G. and Lee, S. (2000). Financial management techniques in family businesses. *Family Business Review*, 13 (3), 201–216.

Financial Stability Committee. (2017). Vierter Bericht an den Deutschen Bundestag zur Finanzstabilität in Deutschland, June 17. Retrieved form https://www.bundesbank.de/resource/blob/600018/e9cedf31b59e4d341c6af2b0c46b362c/mL/2017-06-27-afs-bericht-data.pdf

Financial Times. (2020a). BMW mounts to robust defense of dividend payout, accessed August 20th, 2021. Retrieved from: https://www.ft.com/content/d1424c67-3879-4425-8509-95607bddf954

Financial Times. (2020b). Henkel's chief on guarding family spirit in global group, accessed August 20th, 2021. Retrieved from: https://www.ft.com/content/2c9503c8-c021-4796-b98f-6cc79f225475

Francis, J., Schipper, K. and Vincent, L. (2005). Earnings and dividend informativeness when cash flow rights are separated from voting rights. *Journal of Accounting and Economics*, 39 (2), 329–360.

Franks, J., Mayer, C., Volpin, P. and Wagner, H. F. (2012). The life cycle of family ownership: International evidence. *The Review of Financial Studies*, 25 (6), 1675–1712.

Franzoi, F. (2021). The influence of family board involvement on working capital management. *Corporate Board: Roles, Duties and Composition*, 17 (3), 42–60.

Franzoi, F. and Mietzner, M. (2021a). Family affairs – Corporate governance involvement of families and stock market returns. *Investment Management and Financial Innovations*, 18 (2), 350–364.

Franzoi, F. and Mietzner, M. (2021b). Sunshine after the rain? The stock market performance of family firms in and after financial crises. *Risk, Governance and Control*, 11 (3), 41–54.

Franzoi, F., Mietzner, M. and Thelemann, F. (2021). The influence of family board involvement on earnings management. *Corporate Ownership & Control*, 18 (2), 106–123.

Freeman, R. E. (1984). Strategic Management: A Stakeholder Approach. Cambridge University Press, Cambridge.

Fudenberg, D. and Tirole, J. (1995). A theory of income and dividend smoothing based on incumbency rates. *Journal of Political Economy*, 103 (1), 75–93.

García Lara, J. M., García Osma, B. and Mora, A. (2005). The effect of earnings management on the asymmetric timeliness of earnings. *Journal of Business, Finance and Accounting*, 32 (3–4), 691–726.

García-Meca, E. and Sánchez-Ballesta, J. (2009). Corporate governance and earnings management: A meta-analysis. *Corporate Governance: An International Review*, 17 (5), 594–610.

García-Ramos, R. and García-Olalla, M. (2011). Board characteristics and firm performance in public founder- and non-founder-led family businesses. *Journal of Family Business Strategy*, 2 (4), 220–231.

García-Sánchez, I.-M., Martínez-Ferrero, J. and García-Meca, E. (2020). Does family involvement monitor external CEOs' investment decisions? *Review of Managerial Science*, 14 (1), 159–192.

Garcia-Teruel, P. J. and Martinez-Solano, P. M. (2007). Effects of working capital management on SME profitability. *International Journal of Managerial Finance*, 3 (2), 164–177.

German Council of Economic Experts. (2011). Assuming Responsibility for Europe – Annual Report 2011/2012. Statistisches Bundesamt, November 2011, Wiesbaden. Retrieved from: https://rb.gy/h6i1ux

Ghosh, A., Marra, A. and Moon, D. (2010). Corporate boards, audit committees, and earnings management: Pre- and post-SOX evidence. *Journal of Business, Finance and Accounting*, 37 (9–10), 1145–1176.

Gill, A., Biger, N. and Mathur, N. (2010). The relationship between working capital management and profitability: Evidence from the United States. *Business and Economics Journal*, 2010, 1 (1), 1–9.

Gill, A. (2013). Financial policy and the value of family businesses in Canada. *International Journal of Entrepreneurship and Small Business*, 20 (3), 310–325.

Gill, A. and Biger, N. (2013). The impact of corporate governance on working capital management efficiency of American manufacturing firms. *Managerial Finance*, 39 (2), 116–132.

Gill, A., Flaschner, A. B., Mann, S. and Dana, L.-P. (2014). Types of governance, financial policy and the financial performance of micro-family-owned businesses in Canada. *International Journal of Business and Globalisation*, 13 (4), 542–558.

Giroud, X., Mueller H. M., Stomper, A. and Westerkamp, A. (2012). Snow and leverage. *The Review of Financial Studies*, 25 (3), 680–719.

Gitman, L. (1974). Estimating corporate liquidity requirements: A simplified approach. *The Financial Review*, 9 (3), 79–88.

Gomez-Mejia, L. R., Cruz, C., Berrone, P. and De Castro, J. (2011). The bind that ties: Socioemotional wealth preservation in family firms. *The Academy of Management Annals*, 5 (1), 653–707.

Gomez-Mejia, L., Cruz, C. and Imperatore, C. (2014). Financial reporting and the protection of socioemotional wealth in family-controlled firms. *European Accounting Review*, 23 (3), 387–402.

Gomez-Mejia, L., Makri, M. and Kintana, M. L. (2010). Diversification decisions in family-controlled firms. *Journal of Management Studies*, 47 (2), 223–252.

Gomez-Mejia, L. R., Haynes, K. T., Nuñez-Nickel, M., Jacobson, K. J. L. and Moyano-Fuentes, J. (2007). Socioemotional wealth and business risks in family-controlled firms: Evidence from Spanish Olive Oil Mills. *Administrative Science Quarterly*, 52 (1), 106–137.

Gompers, P., Ishii, J. and Metrick, A. (2003). Corporate governance and equity prices. *Quarterly Journal of Economics*, 118 (1), 107–155.

Gonzalez, M., Idrobo, J. D. and Taborda, R. (2019). Family firms and financial performance: A meta-regression analysis. *Academia Revista Latinoamericana de Administration*, 32 (3), 345–372.

Gorton, G. and Schmid, F. A. (2000). Universal banking and the performance of German firms. *Journal of Financial Economics*, 58 (1–2), 29–80.

Gottardo, P., & Moisello, A. M. (2014). The capital structure choices of family firms: Evidence from Italian medium-large unlisted firms. *Managerial Finance*, 40 (3), 254–275.

Gottardo, P. and Moisello, A. M. (2017). Family firms, risk-taking and financial distress. *Problems and Perspectives in Management,* 15 (2), 168–177.

Gottardo, P. and Moisello, A. M. (2019). Capital Structure, Earnings Management and Risk of Financial Distress. A Comparative Analysis of Family and Non-family Firms. SpringerBriefs in Business, Springer, Cham.

Gottschalk, S., Lubczyk, M., Hauer, A. and Keese, D. (2019). Die volkswirtschaftliche Bedeutung von Familienunternehmen. Stiftung Familienunternehmen, 5th Edition, Munich.

Gugler, K. and Yurtoglu, B. B. (2003). Corporate governance and dividend pay-out in Germany. *European Economic Review*, 47 (4), 731–758.

Guidry, F., Leone, A. and Rock, S. (1999). Earnings-based bonus plans and earnings management by business unit managers. *Journal of Accounting and Economics*, 26 (1–3), 113–142.

Habbershon, T. G. and Williams, M. L. (1999). A resource-based framework for assessing the strategic advantages of family firms. *Family Business Review*, 12 (1), 1–25.

Hanauer, M, Kaserer, C. and Rapp, M. S. (2013). Risikofaktoren und Multifaktormodelle für den Deutschen Aktienmarkt (Risk Factors and Multi-Factor Models ort he German Stock Market). *Betriebswirtschaftliche Forschung & Praxis*, CEFS Working Paper 01–2011, 65 (5), 469–492.

Hand, J. R. M. (1989). Did firms undertake debt-equity swaps for an accounting paper profit or true financial gain? *The Accounting Review*, 64 (4), 587–623.

Handelsblatt (2020). Fielmann sieht sich dank voller Kassen gut für Coronakrise gerüstet. Accessed August 20th, 2021. Retrieved from: https://www.handelsblatt.com/unternehmen/handel-konsumgueter/optiker-fielmann-sieht-sich-dank-voller-kassen-gut-fuer-coronakrise-geruestet/25787428.html

Hansen, C. and Block, J. (2020). Exploring the relation between family involvement and firms' financial performance: A replication and extension meta-analysis. *Journal of Business Venturing Insights*, 13, e00158, 1–21.

Harms, H. (2014). Review of family business definitions: Cluster approach and implications of heterogeneous application of family business research. *International Journal of Financial Studies*, 2, 280–314.

Harris, M. and Raviv, A. (1991). The theory of capital structure. *The Journal of Finance*, 46 (1), 297–355.

Hauck, J. and Prügl, R. (2015). Innovation activities during intra-family leadership succession in family firms: An empirical study from a socioemotional wealth perspective. *Journal of Family Business Strategy*, 6 (2), 104–118.

Hauck, J., Suess-Reyes, J., Beck, S., Prügl, R. and Frank, H. (2016). Measuring socioemotional wealth in family-owned and -managed firms: A validation and short form of the FIBER Scale. *Journal of Family Business Strategy*, 7 (3), 133–148.

Haunschild, L. and Wolter, H.-J. (2010). Volkswirtschaftliche Bedeutung von Familien- und Frauenunternehmen. Working Paper, IfM-Materialien 199, September 2010, Bonn. Retrieved from: http://hdl.handle.net/10419/51545

Hawawini, G., Viallet, C. and Vora, A. (1986). Industry influence on corporate working capital decisions. *Sloan Management Review*, 27 (4), 15–24.

Healy, P. M. (1985). The effect of bonus schemes on accounting decisions. *Journal of Accounting and Economics*, 7 (1–3), 85–107.

Healy, P. M. and Wahlen, J. M. (1999). A review of the earnings management literature and its implications for standard setting. *Accounting Horizons*, 13(4), 365–383.

Hernández-Linarez, R., Sarkar, S. and Cobo, M. J. (2018). Inspecting the Achilles heel: A quantitative analysis of 50 years of family business definitions. *Scientometrics*, 115, 020–051.

Hill, C. W. L. and Jones, T. M. (1992). Stakeholder-agency theory. *Journal of Management Studies*, 29 (2), 131–154.

Hofmann, E. and Wetzel, P. (2020). Working Capital Management Studie 2020 – Supply Chain Management. Supply Chain Finance-Lab University of St. Gallen and PostFinance, Bern. Retrieved from https://rb.gy/my5xs4

Holthausen, R. W., Larcker, D. F. and Sloan, R. G. (1995). Annual bonus schemes and the manipulation of earnings. *Journal of Accounting and Economics*, 19 (1), 29–74.

Holzamer, M. and Wendt, M. (2018). Finanzierung von Familienunternehmen in Deutschland. Roland Berger and Euler Hermes. Retrieved from https://rb.gy/0htiqx

Höwer, D. (2016). The role of bank relationships when firms are financially distressed. *Journal of Banking and Finance*, 65, 59–75.

Hudepohl, T., van Lamoen, R. and de Vette, N. (2019). Quantitative Easing and Exuberance in Stock Markets: Evidence from the euro area (DNB Working Paper, 660). Netherlands Central Bank.

Hutton, A. P. (2007). A discussion of 'corporate disclosure by family firms'. *Journal of Accounting and Economics*, 44 (1–2), 287–297.

Igan, D., Kirti, D. and Peria, S. M. (2020). The disconnect between financial markets and the real economy. International Monetary Fund Research, Special Notes Series on COVID-19, August 26. Retrieved from https://rb.gy/d9jwhz

Jaggi, B. and Lee, P. (2002). Earnings management response to debt covenant violations and debt restructuring. *Journal of Accounting, Auditing and Finance*, 17 (4), 295–324.

Jaggi, B., Leung, S. and Gul, F. (2009). Family control, board independence and earnings management: Evidence based on Hong Kong firms. *Journal of Accounting and Public Policy*, 28(4), 281–300.

Jensen, M. C. (1986). Agency costs of free cash flow, corporate finance, and takeovers. *The American Economic Review*, 76 (2), 323–329.

Jensen, M. C. and Meckling, W. H. (1976). Theory of the firms: Managerial behavior, agency costs and ownership structure. *Journal of Financial Economics*, 3 (4), 305–360.

Jiraporn, P. and Dadalt, P. J. (2009). Does founding family control affect earnings management? *Applied Economic Letters*, 16 (2), 113–119.

Kaserer, C. and Moldenhauer, B. (2008). Insider ownership and corporate performance: evidence from Germany. *Review of Managerial Science*, 2 (1), 1–35.

Kauf, T. (2014). The Heterogeneity of Founding Family Firms: Governance, Firm Policy, Economics, and Ownership Dynamics in Lone Founder, Family Founder, and Heir Firms. Dissertation, Technical University Munich.

Klein, A. B. (2000). Family businesses in Germany: Significance and structure. *Family Business Review*, 13 (3), 157–181.

Klein, A. B.; Astrachan, J. H. and Smyrnios, K. X. (2005). The F-PEC scale of family influence: Construction, validation, and further implication for theory. *Entrepreneurship Theory and Practice*, 29 (3), 321–339.

Knauer, T. and Wöhrmann, T. (2013). Working capital management and firm profitability. *Journal of Management Control*, 24, 77–87.

Kormann, H. (2017). Governance des Familienunternehmens. Habilitationsschrift, Zeppelin University Friedrichshafen, Springer Gabler, Wiesbaden.

Kortmann, R., Siemes, D., Rutz, B., Leidig, S., Gerding, C. and Zwinkels, M. (2021). Working capital report 2021 – GSA and Benelux regions. PwC, Frankfurt. Retrieved from https://rb.gy/k7tn5h

La Porta, R., Lopez-de-Silanes, F. and Shleifer, A. (1999). Corporate ownership around the world. *The Journal of Finance*, 54 (2), 471–517.

La Porta, R., Lopez-de-Silanes, F., Shleifer, A. and Vishny, R. (1997). Legal determinants of external finance. *The Journal of Finance*, 52 (3), 1131–1150.

La Porta, R., Lopez-de-Silanes, F., Shleifer, A. and Vishny, R. (1998). Law and finance. *Journal of Political Economy*, 106 (6), 1113–1155.

Laeven, L. and Levine, R. (2008). Complex ownership structures and corporate valuations. *The Review of Financial Studies*, 21 (2), 579–604.

Lafond, R. and Roychowdhury,S. (2008). Managerial ownership and accounting conservatism. *Journal of Accounting Research*, 46 (1), 101–135.

Lappalainen, J. and Niskanen, M. (2013). Behavior and attitudes of small family firms towards different funding sources. *Journal of Small Business and Entrepreneurship*, 26 (6), 579–599.

Le Breton-Miller, I., Miller, D. and Lester, R.H. (2011). Stewardship or agency? Social embeddedness reconciliation of conduct and performance in public family business. *Organization Science*, 22 (3), 704–721.

Lee, C.-W. J., Li, L. Y. and Yue, H. (2006). Performance, growth and earnings management. *Review of Accounting Studies*, 11 (2–3), 305–334.

Lee, M.-S. and Rogoff, E. G. (1996). Research note: Comparison of small businesses with family participation versus small businesses without family participation: An investigation of differences in goals, attitudes, and family business conflict. *Family Business Review*, 9 (4), 423–437.

Leuz, C., Nanda, D. and Wysocki, P. D. (2003). Earnings management and investor protection: An international comparison. *Journal Financial Economics*, 69 (3), 505–527.

von Lilienfeld, U. V. and Ruenzi, S. (2014). CEO ownership, stock market performance, and managerial discretion. *The Journal of Finance*, 69 (3). 1013–1050.

Lins, K., Volpin, P. and Wagner H. (2013). Does family control matter? International evidence from the 2008-2009 financial crisis, *The Review of Financial Studies*, 26 (10), 2583–2619.

Lipiec, J. (2014). Capital asset pricing model testing at Warsaw Stock Exchange: Are family businesses the remedy for economic recessions? *International Journal of Financial Studies*, 2 (3), 266–279.

Liu, M., Shi, Y., Wilson, C. and Wu, Z. (2017). Does family involvement explain why corporate social responsibility affects earnings management? *Journal of Business Research*, 75, 8–16.

Lubatkin, M., Schulze, W., Ling, Y. and Dino, R. (2005). The effects of paternal altruism on the governance of family-managed firms. *Journal of Organizational Behavior*, 26 (3), 313–330.

Lumpkin, G. T. and Brigham, K. H. (2011). Long-term orientation and intertemporal choice in family firms. *Entrepreneurship Theory and Practice*, 35 (6), 1149–1169.

Maijoor, S. J. and Vanstraelen, A. (2006). Earnings management within Europe: The effects of member state audit environment, audit firm quality and international capital markets. *Accounting and Business Research*, 36 (1), 33–52.

Martin, G., Campbell, J. T. and Gomez-Mejia, L. (2016). Family control, socioemotional wealth and earnings. *Journal of Business Ethics*, 133, 453–469.

Maury, B. (2006). Family ownership and firm performance: Empirical evidence from Western European corporations. *Journal of Corporate Finance*, 12 (2), 321–341.

Mazzi, C. (2011). Family business and financial performance: Current state of knowledge and future research challenges. *Journal of Family Business Strategy*, 2, 166–181.

Menon, K. and Williams, D. D. (2004). Former audit partners and abnormal accruals. *The Accounting Review*, 79 (4), 1095–1118.

Meyer, S; Lüdtke, J.-P. (2006). Der Einfluss von Working Capital auf die Profitabilität und Kreditwürdigkeit von Unternehmen. *Finanz Betrieb*, 10, 609–614.

Michiels, A. and Molly, V. (2017). Financing decisions in family businesses: A review and suggestions for developing the field. *Family Business Review*, 30 (4), 369–399.

Mietzner, M. and Schiereck, D. (2016). Value creation by block acquisitions and the importance of block owner identity. *Finance Research Letters*, 17, 118–124.

Mietzner, M. and Schweizer, D. (2014). Hedge funds versus private equity funds as shareholder activists in Germany – Differences in value creation. *Journal of Economics and Finance*, 38 (2), 181–208.

Mietzner, M. and Tyrell, M. (2012). Das Verhalten von Familienunternehmen gegenüber ihren Stakeholdern: Erste Ergebnisse aus der Forschung einer auf den deutschen Kapitalmarkt bezogenen Untersuchung. *Zeitschrift für Familienunternehmen und Stiftungen*, 3, 108–113.

Miller, D., Le Breton-Miller, I., Lester, R. H. and Cannella A. A. Jr. (2007). Are family firms really superior performers? *Journal of Corporate Finance*, 13 (5), 829–858.

Miller, D., Le Breton-Miller, I. and Scholnick, B. (2008). Stewardship vs. stagnation: An empirical comparison of small family and non-family-businesses. *Journal of Management Studies*, 45 (1) 51–78.

Minichilli, A., Brogi, M. and Calabrò, A. (2016). Weathering the storm: Family ownership, governance, and performance through the financial and economic crisis. *Corporate Governance: An International Review*, 24 (6), 552–568.

Miralles-Marcelo, J. L., Miralles-Quirós, M. d. M. and Lisboa, I. (2013). The stock performance of family firms in the Portuguese market. *Applied Financial Economics, 23* (22), 1721–1732.

Miralles-Marcelo, J. L., Miralles-Quirós, M. d. M. and Lisboa, I. (2014). The impact of family control on firm performance: Evidence from Portugal and Spain. *Journal of Family Business Strategy*, 5 (2), 156–168.

Mishra, C. S. and McConaughy, D. L. (1999). Founding family control and capital structure: The risk of loss of control and the aversion to debt. *Entrepreneurship Theory and Practice*, 23 (4), 53–64.

Morck, R., Shleifer, A. and Vishny, R. W. (1988). Management ownership and corporate valuation an empirical evaluation. *Journal of Financial Economics*, 20, 293–315.

Motylska-Kuzma, A. (2017). The financial decisions of family businesses. *Journal of Family Business Management*, 7, 351–373.

Mueller, H. and Philippon, T. (2011). Family firms and labor relations. *American Economic Journal: Macroeconomics*, 3 (2), 218–245.

Myers, J., Myers, L. and Skinner, D. J. (2007). Earnings momentum and earnings management. *Journal of Accounting, Auditing and Finance*, 22 (2), 249–284.

Niskanen, J. and Niskanen, M. (2006). The determinants of corporate trade credit policies in a bank-dominated financial environment: The case of Finnish Small Firms. *European Financial Management*, 12 (1), 81–102.

O'Boyle, E. H., Pollack, J. M. and Rutherford, M. W. (2012). Exploring the relation between family involvement and firms'financial performance: A meta-analysis of main and moderator effects. *Journal of Business Venturing*, 27, 1–18.

Paiva, I. S., Lourenço, I. C. and Branco, M. C. (2016). Earnings management in family firms: Current state of knowledge and opportunities for future research. *Review of Accounting and Finance*, 15 (1), 85–100.

Petersen, M. A. and Rajan, R. G. (1997). Trade credit: Theories and evidence. *Review of Financial Studies*, 10 (3), 661–691.

Prencipe, A. and Bar-Yosef, S. (2011). Corporate governance and earnings management in family-controlled companies. *Journal of Accounting, Auditing and Finance*, 26 (2), 199–227.

Prencipe, A., Bar-Yosef, S. and Dekker, H. C. (2014). Accounting research in family firms: Theoretical and empirical challenges. *European Accounting Review*, 23 (3), 361–385.

Richards, V. D. and Laughlin, E. J. (1980). A cash conversion cycle approach to liquidity analysis. *Financial Management*, 9 (1), 32–38.

Rieckers, O. and Spindler, G. (2004). Corporate governance: Legal aspects. In J. P. Krahnen and R. H. Schmidt (Eds.), The German financial system.

Roychowdhury, S. (2006). Earnings management through real activities manipulation. *Journal of Accounting and Economics*, 42 (3), 335–370.

Salvato, C. and Moores, K. (2010). Research on accounting in family firms: Past accomplishments and future challenges. *Family Business Review*, 23 (3), 193–215.

Schipper, K. (1989). Commentary on earnings management. *Accounting Horizons*, 3 (4), 91–102.

Schmid, T. (2013). Control considerations, creditor monitoring, and the capital structure of family firms. *Journal of Banking and Finance*, 37, 257–272.

Schüler, P., Mietzner, M. and Schiereck, D. (2019). Acquisitions by family businesses in continental Europe and their differences compared to private equity investors. *International Journal of Entrepreneurial Venturing*, 11 (2), 142–163.

Schraml, S. C. (2010). Finanzierung von Familienunternehmen. Dissertation, Technical University Munich, 2009, Achleitner, A.-K- and Kaserer, Springer Gabler, Wiesbaden.

Setia-Atmaja, L., Tanewski, G. A. and Skully, M. (2009). The role of dividends, debt and board structure in the governance of family controlled firms. *Journal of Business, Finance and Accounting*, 36 (7–8), 863–898.

Shin, H. H. and Soenen, L. (1998). Efficiency of working capital and corporate profitability. *Financial Practice and Education*, 8 (2), 37–45.

Shleifer, A. and Vishny, R. W. (1986). Large shareholders and corporate control. *Journal of Political Economy*, 94 (3), 461–488.

Shleifer, A. and Vishny, R. W. (1997). A survey of corporate governance. *The Journal of Finance*, 52 (2), 737–783.

Sigl-Glöckner, P. (2018). Ein Blick ins Innere des europäischen Finanzgetriebes, Visualization of ECB-Statistics. Retrieved from https://rb.gy/lxphnd

Smith, B. F. and Amoako-Adu, B. (1999). Management succession and financial performance of family-controlled firms. *Journal of Corporate Finance*, 5 (4), 341–368.

Spamann, H. (2010). The "Antidirector Rights Index" Revisited. *The Review of Financial Studies*, 23 (2), 467–486.

Sraer, D. and Thesmar, D. (2007). Performance and behavior of family firms: Evidence from the French Stock Market. *Journal of the European Economic Association*, 5 (4), 709–751.

Stankiewicz, J. (2016). Socioemotional wealth and the performance of family firms: the role of identification and transgenerational control. Dissertation, University of St. Gallen.

Stockmans, A., Lybaert, N. and Voordeckers, W. (2010). Socioemotional wealth and earnings management in private family firms. *Family Business Review*, 23 (3), 280–294.

Sun, X., Lee, S.-H. and Phan, P. H. (2019). Family firm R&D investments in the 2007–2009 great recession. *Journal of Family Business Strategy*, 10 (4), 100244.

Sure, M. (2014). Working Capital Management – Empirische Analyse der Gestaltungsfaktoren des Working Capitals und seiner Komponenten. Dissertation Technical University Dortmund, Springer Gabler, Wiesbaden.

Sweeney, A. P. (1994). Debt covenant violations and managers' accounting response. *Journal of Accounting and Economics*, 17 (3), 281–308.

Swiss National Bank. (2008). Financial Stability Report. Swiss National Bank, June 2008, Zurich. Retrieved from: https://rb.gy/xxf1sy

Taras, V., Memili, E., Wang, Z. and Harms, H. (2018). Family involvement in publicly traded firms and firm performance: A meta-analysis. *Management Research Review*, 41 (2), 225–251.

Tong, Y. H. (2008). Financial reporting practices of family firms. *Advances in Accounting*, 23, 231–261.

Troilo, M., Walkup, B. R., Abe, M. and Lee, S. (2019). Legal systems and the financing of working capital. *International Review of Economics and Finance*, 64, 641–656.

Trueman, B. and Titman, S. (1988). An explanation for accounting income smoothing. *Journal of Accounting Research*, 26, 127–139.

Van Essen, M., Engelen, P.-J. and Carney, M. (2013). Does "Good" corporate governance help in a crisis? The impact of country- and firm-level governance mechanisms in the European Financial Crisis. *Corporate Governance: An International Review*, 21(3), 201–224.

Van Essen, M., Strike, V. M., Carney, M. and Sapp, S. (2015). The resilient family firm: Stakeholder outcomes and institutional effects. *Corporate Governance: An International Review*, 23 (3), 167–183.

Villalonga, B. and Amit, R. (2006). How do family ownership, control and management affect firm value? *Journal of Financial Economics*, 80 (2), 385–417.

Villalonga, B. and Amit, R. (2009). How are U. S. family firms controlled? *The Review of Financial Studies*, 22 (8), 3047–3091.

Villalonga, B. and Amit, R. (2020). Family ownership, *Oxford Review of Economic Policy*, 36 (2), 241–257.

Villalonga, B., Amit, R., Trujillo, M.-A. and Guzmán, A. (2015). Governance of family firms. *Annual Review of Financial Economics*, 7, 635–654.

Volk, S. K. (2013). Einfluss der Eigentümerstruktur auf Finanzierungs- und Investitionsentscheidungen in privaten und börsennotierten Unternehmen. Dissertation, Technical University Munich.

Wagner, D. (2016). A meta-analysis about the relationship between family firms and firm performance. Dissertation, University Trier.

Wagner, D., Block, J. H., Miller, D., Schwens, C. and Xi, G. (2015). A meta-analysis of the financial performance of family firms: Another attempt. *Journal of Family Business Strategy*, 6 (1), 3–13.

Wang, D. (2006). Founding family ownership and earnings quality. *Journal of Accounting Research*, 44 (3), 619–656.

Wang, K. T. and Shailer, G. (2017). Family ownership and financial performance relations in emerging markets. *International Review of Economics and Finance*, 51, 82–98.

Wang, Y.-J. (2002). Liquidity management, operating performance, and corporate value: evidence from Japan and Taiwan, *Journal of Multinational Financial Management*, 12, 159–169.

Warfield, T. D., Wild, J. J. and Wild, K. L. (1995). Managerial ownership, accounting choices, and informativeness of earnings. *Journal of Accounting and Economics*, 20 (1), 61–91.

Warner, A., Montanus, D. and Stolte, F. (2019). Working Capital Studie: Flüssige Mittel und gebundenes Kapital. Deloitte. Retrieved from: https://rb.gy/frr8fs

Washington (2010). Making short work of things – How important was Germany's kurzarbeit program? *The Economist,* August 4. Retrieved from: https://www.economist.com/free-exchange/2010/08/04/making-short-work-of-things

Westhead, P. and Howorth, C. (2007). 'Types'of private family firms: An exploratory conceptual and empirical analysis. *Entrepreneurship and Regional Development: An International Journal*, 19 (5), 405–431.

Williamson, O. E. (1975a). Markets and Hierarchies: Analysis and Antitrust Implications. Free Press, New York.

Williamson, O. E. (1975b). Markets and hierarchies: Some elementary considerations. *American Economic Review*, 63 (2), 316–325.

Windhaus, D., Extra, W., Wicks, D., Ojeda, A. Tebbett, S. Boehme, S., Sentence, A. and Kupelian, B. (2018). Navigating uncertainty: PwC's annual global Working Capital Study. PwC, London. Retrieved from: https://rb.gy/k698l0

Wirsching, K. T. (2017). Familieneinfluss und Unternehmenserfolg. Dissertation, University Augsburg, Springer Gabler, 1st edition, Wiesbaden.

Wöhrmann, T., Knauer, T. and Gefken, J. (2012). Kostenmanagement in Krisenzeiten: Rentabilitätssteigerung durch Working Capital Management? *Zeitschrift für Controlling & Management*, Sonderheft, 3, 83–88.

Zang, A. Y. (2012). Evidence on the trade-off between real activities manipulation and accrual-based earnings management. *The Accounting Review*, 87 (2), 675–703.

Zellweger, T. M. (2006). Risk, Return and Value in the Family Firm. Dissertation, 3188, University of St. Gallen, Difo-Druck GmbH, Bamberg.

Zellweger, T. M. and Nason, R. S. (2008). A stakeholder perspective on family firm performance. *Family Business Review*, 21 (3), 203–216.

Zellweger, T. M., Kellermanns, F. W., Chrisman, J. J. and Chua, J. H. (2012). Family control and family firm valuation by family CEOs – The importance of intentions for transgenerational control. *Organization Science*, 23 (3), 851–868.

Zhou, H., He, F. and Wang, Y. (2017). Did family firms perform better during the financial crisis? New insights form the S&P 500 firm. *Global Finance Journal*, 33, 88–103.

Zimon, G. and Tarighi, H. (2021). Effects of the COVID-19 global crisis on the working capital management policy: Evidence from Poland. *Journal of Risk and Financial Management*, 14 (4), 169.

www.ingramcontent.com/pod-product-compliance
Ingram Content Group UK Ltd.
Pitfield, Milton Keynes, MK11 3LW, UK
UKHW020836290926
15470UKWH00004B/1379

9 783631 901274